The Dangers of
Christian Practice

The Dangers of Christian Practice

On Wayward Gifts,
Characteristic Damage, and Sin

LAUREN F. WINNER

Yale UNIVERSITY PRESS

New Haven and London

Published with assistance from the foundation established in memory of Henry Weldon Barnes of the Class of 1882, Yale College.

Excerpts from the poem "Lineage Maker," by Robyn Covelli-Hunt, from *Lines and Circles, A Celebration of Santa Fe Families,* edited by Valerie Martínez, appear courtesy of Sunstone Press, Santa Fe, New Mexico.

Quotations from *A Plantation Mistress on the Eve of the Civil War: The Diary of Keziah Goodwyn Hopkins Brevard, 1860–1861,* edited by John Hammond Moore, appear courtesy of the University of South Carolina Press, Columbia, South Carolina.

All biblical citations are to the New Revised Standard Version unless otherwise specified.

Yale University Press books may be purchased in quantity for educational, business, or promotional use. For information, please e-mail sales.press@yale.edu (U.S. office) or sales@yaleup.co.uk (U.K. office).

Set in Minion type by IDS Infotech Ltd., Chandigarh, India.
Printed in the United States of America.

Library of Congress Control Number: 2018930926
ISBN 978-0-300-21582-3 (hardcover: alk. paper)

A catalogue record for this book is available from the British Library.
This paper meets the requirements of ANSI/NISO Z39.48-1992 (Permanence of Paper).

10 9 8 7 6 5 4 3 2 1

This book is, in part, a quarrel with Stanley Hauerwas. It is dedicated to him, with gratitude in equal measure for his friendship, and for his having given the world ideas worth quarreling with.

With what pencil shall I be able to draw the deformed face of sin?

—THOMAS WATSON

Contents

The Dangers of
Christian Practice

Characteristic Damage

In this book I consider some of the ways beloved Christian practices deform. I examine how Christian practices, like the Eucharist and prayer, are damaged and extend damage, and I argue that when a Christian practice goes wrong, often it does so not incidentally but rather in ways that have to do with the practice itself. Although twenty-first-century Anglophone Christians often speak of practices like Eucharist and prayer only to commend them and laud the benefits they bestow upon practitioners, Christians need also to give accounts of, rather than evade, the damages Christian practice sustains by sin; in *The Dangers of Christian Practice* I attempt some of that accounting.

Nothing, not even the good practices of the church, is untouched by the Fall. The principal effect of the Fall is damage, though that damage operates differently in and on human beings than it does in and on, say, rocks. Human beings, creatures with agency, sustain damage and immediately intensify the damage by doing things that cause further harm (and, of course, being creatures with agency that is being rehabilitated by God, we also sometimes do things that can make things better, more beautiful, healed). Rocks, by contrast, are creatures without agency, so they do not—cannot—intensify the damage they have sustained. Once they have sustained damage, they just do what damaged rocks do: sit mutely; sometimes roll down a hill and kill someone; sometimes provide a picnic spot for a hiker; sometimes sparkle in a necklace; and eventually get eroded.

Sin is what's ushered in by the Fall and produces all this damage. That is, the word "sin" denotes habits, actions, and proclivities of human beings (and other creatures with agency, such as angels and perhaps certain other nonhuman primates)[1] that draw what God created away from God and that unleash damage into the world. The state of the damage is, by contrast, not a state of sin, although one often hears Christians colloquially speaking as though it were; no state like that exists, because sin is an absence (of the good), not a thing in itself. The state of damage is just that—a state of damage, one that creatures with agency perpetuate. Sometimes, the damage done by creatures with agency is causally related to the structural damage of creatures without agency. For example, the planet does not have agency. Rather, the planet simply reflects the damage unleashed by agents' sin. In sometimes alarmingly specific ways, some human actions that intensify damage not only harm us but also damage and intensify damage done to other creatures, such as the planet. We can melt ice caps, strip mountains, destroy species, and change temperatures, for example.

The Bible is full of testimony to the damage that even inanimate objects have sustained and express. The Bible likes to speak of this in terms of soundscape: Creation's groaning happens only because of our sin; were Creation not damaged, it would not groan. Similarly, our sin has brought about silences where there should be sound. The silence of the psalmist's mountains—mountains that should, and will, be singing—is also caused by (our) sin. If the mountains were not damaged, they would sing, and when God has consummated God's program of healing and redemption, they will.

Creatures are damaged, and creatures with agency perpetuate damage, in many different ways. The damage sometimes is arbitrary, or at least seems to be (human beings, in our damage, cannot confidently distinguish between being and seeming). By "arbitrary," I mean incidental to (rather than properly related to, or properly about) whatever is damaged or is perpetuating damage. But sometimes—often—things are damaged (or perpetuate damage) in ways that are *about* whatever is damaged or damaging. That is, the damage is often expressed in a way that is proper to that which expresses the damage.

Therefore, because nothing created is untouched by the Fall, Christians should not be surprised when lovely and good, potentially gracious Christian gestures are damaged, or when human beings deploy those Christian gestures in the perpetuation of damage. Because often damage is expressed in a way that is not arbitrary, but is proper to what is expressing it, Christians ought to be able to predict some of the characteristic damages that might be found in those potentially gracious gestures, and Christians ought to be able to predict some of the ways in which human beings put those gestures to work in perpetuating damage.[2]

In this book I read Christian practices—practices of the church, like the Eucharist and prayer—under the pressure of the foregoing understanding of sin and damage, with the aim of encouraging the church to be on the lookout for the ways good Christian practices may, and inevitably sometimes will, do the very opposite of what those practices were made, in their goodness (in God's goodness, and in God's good hopes for the church), to do. I read Christian practices with the aim of encouraging the church to anticipate the ways good Christian practices sometimes will not foster intimacy with God and growth in Christlikeness, but will rather perpetuate damage. (*Nota bene:* The practices themselves do not, of course, have agency, but practices necessarily involve agents. For this reason, one can speak of practices sometimes perpetuating damage, with the understanding that this is shorthand for the agents of those practices perpetuating damage, and the practices' expressing that damage.)

God created all things with forms. When created, formed by God, these creatures were perfect—the shape of every creature, whether an ocean or a lion or a human being, was all good, all Godward, all lovely. But in the present era, after the Fall and before the consummation of God's redemption, none of the things God formed is wholly good. We have lost some of our goodness; it has vanished into absence and curvature. We are all still formed as God formed us, but now our forms are distorted and our actions sometimes perverse.[3]

A thing's shape tells you something about what goodnesses it contains. A narrow, rectangular book is good for being held and carried. It is good for being laid open, and good for sitting closed. It is good for remembering wisdom and secrets, and sharing them, when asked; that is what it is good for, what it is shaped to do. The shape also tells you something about what ills will befall a thing. The spine of the rectangle will be broken and the white margins of the pages foxed. We can predict that those things will happen to books—they are, in part, internally generated (machine-made paper high in acid has a tendency to fox), though there are external causes, too (humidity can prompt foxing). Because foxing is predictable, we can, if we wish, be on the lookout for it, and try to prevent its happening (if we wish to guard against deterioration, we can be sure to use acid-free paper instead of untreated wood-pulp paper). In some cases, we can develop some strategies for repair when, despite our vigilance, things go wrong anyway. The repairs, of course, will be only partial; this side of eternity, that is all they can be.

In other words: Not all damage, but some damage, belongs to the form of the thing damaged, and is characteristic of it. Another way of naming a thing's characteristic damage is to say that the thing has been "deformed": Deformities, after all, are exactly that—related to (or, more pointedly, away from) a particular form. Most writers of literature understand that things are *characteristically* damaged, which is to say deformed, and writers often illustrate the principle of characteristic damage in the characters they create, in *dramatis personae* full of human beings whose foibles reveal their character (think of Lear; think of Miss Havisham and Estella in *Great Expectations*). But the concentrated deformations of literary characters are not the only illustrations available of characteristic damage. Indeed, we can see deformations, characteristic damage, in any of our institutions. It is characteristic of large-scale tobacco farming in eighteenth-century Virginia to require debt. The indebtedness of the planters tells us something about the deep structure of the farming they undertook (and it tells us something about the planters' love of luxury, and about the compression of the boom-and-bust cycle after 1750). It is characteristic of capitalist democracies that have commodified most things to commodify elections, that is, to feature electoral systems that are corrupted by unregulated campaign finance; commodified elections constitute a corruption that tells us something about what capitalist democracy is. It is characteristic of modern academia that its participants get corrupted by pride; pride is a corruption that tells us something about what academia is.

Sometimes, of course, things are damaged in ways that seem to be arbitrary—incidental to and not revealing about the thing that is damaged. Sometimes, a capitalist democracy's electoral system is corrupted by the lassitude of the candidates; sometimes, an academic becomes corrupted by overzealous self-abnegation. Those deformations are not obviously about democracy or academia, and are perhaps extrinsic to them. But still, some instances of damage are about the thing itself, proper to it, characteristic of the thing.

There are different kinds of particulars, and they express their characteristic deformations in different ways. Those with agency, for example—say, people—are damaged by sin, and, in their expression of that damage, sometimes creatively extend it. Those without agency are damaged by sin but do not, in their expressions of that damage, extend it with creativity, or with the kind of culpability agency entails. A leopard stalking her prey is expressing the damage unleashed by the Fall, but the leopard is not the agent of the damage, and she has no choice about going after gazelles and wildebeests—stalking prey is simply what postlapsarian leopards do (and, as Isaiah tells us, it is what eschatological leopards will not do). Similarly, a deteriorating building doesn't decide to do something that will, in turn, promote more damage.[4] Deterioration—and, indeed, entropy—have been caused by sin. Once begun, the entropy will simply continue, sometimes given assistance, not by the building, which has no capacity for agency, but by human beings. Entropy is abetted by the cavalier capitalists who built hemlock-extract camps in late-nineteenth-century Maine, and then, once the hemlock trees were exhausted, abandoned the camps; all their buildings, as one state official said straightforwardly, were "left to decay."[5] Entropy is abetted by the ecclesial jockeying of English Reformers, who allowed religious houses to crumble after the Dissolution. It is not the abbeys and the hemlock camps but sin itself, and the people who act as sin's accomplices as often as they act as sin's antagonists, that underwrite the ever-extending damage.

Sometimes damage is so obviously intrinsic to the damaged thing—so clearly proper to it—that it seems impossible to imagine the thing itself without the damage. Consider *kintsugi*—the Japanese art form wherein broken pottery is put back together with powdered gold and lacquer, highlighting, rather than trying to disguise, the fact that the bowl was broken, on the theory that the golden veins, and the history of brokenness, make the bowl more beautiful than it was before. Here the damage is definitional. Devotees of *kintsugi* are appreciative of something whose damage is intrinsic to the object of devotion; as, of course, are devotees of saints' relics, which bespeak the deepest evidence of damage there is, death.

What are we to say about damages—those now-golden cracks and fissures—that are delightful to us? When you look outside your window and see an owl nesting in a cavity of a tree, you are likely seeing something lovely that depends on decay—the tree cavity was likely produced by rot, and many birds wouldn't have homes without such rot-induced cavities. When tourists visit the ruins at Ayutthaya or the Jesuit ruins in Paraguay or the ruins of Desmond Castle in Ireland and are bowled over by the landscape, they are having a Romantic and numinous experience that depends on breakdown and decline. If you sip a glass of ice wine at dessert, you are enjoying a libation that was concocted on a lark by German vintners after their grapes were (the vintners thought) ruined in the freezing winter of 1829. But the grapes weren't ruined; in their damaged state, they yielded ice wine. When we look at (or sip) damage and experience pleasure, are we like the dreaming Dante in canto 19 of the *Purgatorio,* turning, through our own disordered desires and distorted perception, a hag into a beauty? Or is it a gift from God that even something definitionally damaged can delight us?

This question—what is really lovely, and what merely appears so because our capacity to perceive loveliness and its opposites is no less marred by sin than the objects of our perception—threads throughout Christian thought, revealing a good deal of worry about human beings' propensity to perceive loveliness where it is not. This worry sometimes betokens a general suspicion of the world, and a fear that the world's seeming loveliness will deter human beings from keeping our gaze heavenward—as in Christina Rossetti's "The World":

> By day she woos me, soft, exceeding fair:
> But all night as the moon so changeth she;
> Loathsome and foul with hideous leprosy
> And subtle serpents gliding in her hair.

> By day she woos me to the outer air,
> Ripe fruits, sweet flowers, and full satiety:
> But through the night, a beast she grins at me,
> A very monster void of love and prayer.

> By day she stands a lie: by night she stands
> In all the naked horror of the truth
> With pushing horns and clawed and clutching hands.
> Is this a friend indeed; that I should sell
> My soul to her, give her my life and youth,
> Till my feet, cloven too, take hold on hell?[6]

On Rossetti's account, the seeming beauties of the world are deceptions that mask the reality that the world is monstrously devoid "of love and prayer." These deceptions have consequences, eternal ones. So too Dante's hag-qua-siren has consequences, or would if the *donna santa e presta* hadn't interrupted Dante's gaze (as something interrupted Rossetti's gaze, or she couldn't have written the poem).

Dante's self-delusion in *Purgatorio* makes clear that it is not just that the world deceives us. Human beings are themselves complicit in this practice of seeing (perhaps compulsion to see) loveliness where it is absent. We needn't fall under a witch's spell to do so; rather, we need only garishly adorn that which should not be adorned, things whose deformations should be allowed to stand straightforwardly before us, offering a small reminder of the truth of things. As the sixteenth-century poet Torquato Tasso wrote, "If it is true that decoration makes things that are not beautiful appear to be so, the result will not be beautiful, but a travesty of it. Beauty makes things beautiful, whereas decoration only makes them appear to be so."[7]

Is the repaired Japanese bowl beautiful or decorative? When we find it beautiful are we deceived, or are we receiving a gift? *O felix culpa:* A doctrine of sin requires us to acknowledge that our perceptions are faulty—and a doctrine of providence requires us to acknowledge that in the face of sin, God will bring about goods that otherwise would never have existed. Both the faultiness of our perceptions and the surpassing beauty sometimes wrested from destruction are true. So with humility and reserve we may distinguish between and among the lovelinesses we perceive. For example: An aging woman's silvering hair (a silvering that would not have occurred without sin and death) is beautiful, sometimes more beautiful than the brown hair it has replaced, and I am right to find it so; in contrast, the pleasure a soldier takes in attacking a silver-haired townswoman is purely a product of the soldier's distorted perception. I will claim *kintsugi* as true beauty; as almost a paradigm of God's creating from brokenness particular beauties that could not have existed had there never been a Fall—but my judgment could be mistaken.

Emotions usefully illustrate characteristic damage: That is, emotions are good illustrations of deformations that are *about* the thing deformed. Consider the ways maternal love might become deformed. If I were to tell you that my friend Simone spent twenty years loving her son too much—focusing all her attentions and affections on him, giving him all her ardor and all her energy, and leaving her marriage to wither from inattention—you would not be surprised. This is a common story, and it is a story that makes sense. We can say it is a story of family love gone wrong, of marital and maternal loves misdirected, not ideal at all—but that is precisely the point: Simone's love was *family love gone wrong*. It is a going wrong that makes so much sense that it barely requires explanation. Or if I told you that Simone spent twenty years not wanting her son to be the truest, finest, most well-equipped-for-the-world version of himself that he could be, but rather she tried to turn Peter into an improved version of herself (she wanted him to excel at the tennis lessons she now regretted dropping when she was eleven, and to develop the study habits she had failed to learn when she was in high school), and that all of this interfered with Peter's becoming *Peter* (because in fact he didn't want to take tennis lessons either; he wanted to practice the harp), if I were to tell you that, you would nod knowingly and think of seven other parents who had done the same thing, and you would think it was less than ideal, a distortion of mother-love, but a very familiar one.

But if I told you that my friend Simone spent twenty years trying to turn her friend Amy into an improved version of

Simone, that would seem odd. It's a familiar distortion of maternal love to try to turn your kid into a better version of yourself; but it's not a familiar distortion of friend-love. There are, of course, familiar distortions of friend-love—drawing on the data of my own life, I'd say that the way close women friends sometimes want to consume each other, to eat each other, to find their own as-yet-inchoate identity in the identity of the other is a distortion that is arguably characteristic of, proper to, and expectable from friend-love; it is a distortion of friendship that is *about* friendship. But trying to turn your best friend into an improved version of yourself is not a familiar distortion of friendship. That isn't to say that it never happens—it well might; it is only to say that when it does happen, it warrants an elaborate explanation, because it doesn't seem to be an obvious way that friend-love can easily go off-course. The friendship in which somebody tries to make her friend into an improved image of herself is arguably not best understood as a deformation of friendship per se. The deformation is extrinsic to the friendship; the deformation is not *about* friendship—it's about something else. By contrast, Simone's wanting to turn her son into an improved version of herself is arguably a distortion that is *about* mother-love.

All things are like mother-love and friend-love—all things can sometimes go wrong in uncharacteristic ways, and all things can and do go wrong in characteristic ways. Let us return to the spine-cracked and page-foxed (which is to say, the characteristically damaged) book. Consider not the materiality of the book but the tale it tells, the story it holds. This particular foxed book was published in 1906. You picked the book up at a used bookstore, and it has sat unread on your shelf for three years.

To further imagine: The book is a novel. What, then, is its *form?* Literary theorists do not agree among themselves about how to answer that question. We could say that a novel is fictional; that it derives its plot from something other than a classical tale or a fable (this is why the genre, when it emerged in the eighteenth century, was called "novel"); that reading it requires a particular kind of attention. One of the most straightforward statements of the form of a novel comes from my favorite novelist, Jane Smiley. A novel, she writes, is a lengthy, written prose narrative with a protagonist.

> Every novel has all of these elements. If any of them is missing, the literary form in question is not a novel. All additional characteristics—characters, plot, themes, setting, style, point of view, tone, historical accuracy, philosophical profundity, revolutionary or revelatory effect, pleasure, enlightenment, transcendence, and truth—grow out of the ironclad relationships among these five elements. A novel is an experience, but the experience takes place within the boundaries of writing, prose, length, narrative, and protagonist.[8]

In her statement, Smiley stipulates the form of a novel (written, prose, long, narrative, protagonist) and she suggests what the goods of a novel might be. They might be pleasure, plot, profundity. Alan Jacobs articulates another possible good: a richly rendered ethical world. (And this is a good, to be found only—tautologically?—in good fiction. "Badly written fiction is another matter," Jacobs tartly notes.) There are, writes Jacobs, no "schemes or categories adequate to the ethical world of well-written fiction." If there were, "fiction would be unnecessary. . . . The moral philosopher who sought to produce 'examples' with the richness and depth necessary to an adequate account of the moral life would find himself or herself writing novels" (which is, Jacobs reminds us, just what Iris Murdoch did).[9]

All these proposed goods might inspire you to pick up the foxed novel and read it. But beware: Not just the material object but the novel itself is damaged; the novel is damaged by *sentimentality*, by which I mean (following the poet Mark Doty's definition) the condition that obtains when the writer feels more than the reader does about the subject of (or the characters who animate) the book.[10] Novels are not the only things that turn sentimental, and not all novels do. But the lapse into sentimentality is a familiar way for novels to be damaged, and the damage is about the thing a novel is: It is a kind of damage that is intimate with the form novels take and the goods they offer. It is a deformation that is about the novel and about the novelist. The novelist wouldn't have set out to write a novel about alienation from the land in the postbellum American South if he hadn't felt deeply about it, and now it turns out he feels more deeply than you do, and in fact he wants to force your feelings into the shape of his own. Because the novel, per Smiley, is long, the author has many opportunities to express his deep feelings and to try to manipulate yours. This is an intelligible, predictable, sensical way for novels to be damaged. It is not a sensical way for rose bushes to be damaged, or antilock brakes, or a nap; but it makes good sense for a novel to go wrong in just this way.

Another of a novel's potential goods, as suggested by the poststructuralists, is excess of meaning. There is, proper to a novel, more meaning than the text can contain, more meaning than we could ever get on top of; the text thus always exceeds not only its author's intention but the meaning any one reader or community of readers finds in it. Indeed, the meaning surpasses the text itself. This good, too, can become deformed in a way that is about what a novel is: Novels are the kind of thing that get damaged by being misread. Excess of meaning does not mean just any meaning (some meanings can be ruled out), and we can imagine the circumstances in which a novel is misinterpreted, damaged by its own excess. This, too, is an example of characteristic damage, damage that is about, and can expose something of, the form and goods of a novel.

The point here is not to argue something about friendship or maternal feeling or novels, but to show the mode of inquiry that animates this book. Throughout, I will focus on deformations of Christian practices that are characteristic of the practices themselves; deformations that are somehow *about* the practices. For this is really a book about the kind of accounts Christians give for the practices with which we order our lives before God and with neighbor. I aim to consider not primarily a practice's propensity for fostering holiness (there are plenty such accounts) but rather a practice's propensity for violence, for curvature, for being exploited for the perpetuation of damage rather than received for its redress.

Let us consider a final example of deformation, an example that edges closer to Christian practice than do the examples of mother-love or overly emotive fiction.

Things people do together, like meals, can become deformed. What is a meal? We might say that a meal is a ritualized and regulated social act in which the actors consume food. It is easy to see what good things might attend a practice with that form. As one French woman put it (in the course of an interview with ethnographer Annick Sjögren), "the meal is an institution. There is a menu, one sits, one talks, and one is together."[11] Or more grim: "At the table, family members have no choice but to face and focus on each other."[12] Assumed by both the foregoing accounts of "meal" is commensality, which in turn yields group (possibly familial) identity: The people you eat with are the people you belong to. (In North America, the commensality leads to one more potential, albeit secondary, good: Meals are a place where parents socialize, and exercise authority over, children.)

We could make a very long list of meals' potential goods, but for illustrative purposes, this short list will do, because even this short list suggests many ways in which a meal can characteristically express damage. A meal can be deformed by its exclusions—by excluding from the table, for example, the people who cooked the food. When that deformation occurs, it tells us something about a meal: One of the things meals do is define and bind communities—but that binding and defining can slip easily toward exclusion, the reification of boundaries, of exploitation.[13] The list of characteristic possible deformations goes on: Instead of enjoyment, meals can devolve into greed; instead of binding community together, meals can fracture community with envy (Christian prescriptive writers of the eighteenth century worried that meals would become sites of covetousness, with diners envying their friends' more fashionable cuisine). Parents socialize children at meals, but meals often dissolve into tense conflict about etiquette and nutrition.[14] Parents exercise authority over children at meals, but that authority can lead to a child's being forced to sit for seventeen hours until she cleans her plate, and ten years later her therapist will trace her eating disorder back to that parental exercise (misuse) of prandial authority. These are all characteristic ways meals can be deformed; they are deformations that are intimate with the form and goods of a meal.

A meal could also be damaged by the arrival of an armed robber who kidnaps the guest of honor; that would be a kind of damage extrinsic to the meal. The damage of excluding the person who cooked the meal, by contrast, or the damage of the child forced to sit all night in front of her Brussels sprouts is damage that is *about* the meal.

Of course, this aboutness can extend in many different directions at once. To say the damage of the child in front of her sprouts is a deformation of the meal is not to rule out the likelihood that it's also "about"—a deformation of—say, the parent-child relationship, or hierarchy. This is sin's wiliness—it can deform many things at once. But if one were writing about the characteristic goods and deformations of meals, it would be acceptable to focus primarily on that question, and leave the treatise on deformations proper to parent-child relationships for another day.

Form, expected goods, characteristic deformations: We can sketch those things as they obtain in novels, or in meals, or in friendships, or in sacraments. What I am after in this book are the damages, done to, via, and by the agents of Christian practice, that are *about* the practices. All things are tarnished by sin; that is a Christian commonplace, a given. In this book I propose something more specific: Things become deformed by sin in ways that are proper to the thing being deformed, and when those deformations have consequences, you cannot separate the consequences from the deformed thing itself, because it belongs to the thing potentially to have those very consequences. It is the aim of this book to suggest that deformations of Christian practices are part of the practices themselves, because nothing apart from God (not church, not sacraments, not saints) is exempt from the damage produced by the Fall.

The point of my inquiry into Christian practices' deformations is not despair about Christian practices. Indeed, the inquiry is a (soberly) hopeful one. Identification, rather than obfuscation, of the damage characteristic of indispensable (and sometimes dominically given) Christian practices helps us describe the practices more truthfully, and helps us be on the alert for deformations. To risk being a writer who feels more than her reader feels: I write about these three practices—Eucharist, prayer, and baptism—because I love them, and a lover wishes, in her rare mature moments, to know the truth of the object of her love, rather than to know only her wished-for, projected fantasy. In this interregnum between Fall and consummation, damage is inevitable. But—unlike the foxing of a book or the collapse of a castle—we can identify in some Christian practices a certain salutary recursivity. Some Christian practices (Christians can rightly hope) can generate from within themselves an awareness of the damages for which they have a propensity; and Christians may (we can, again, rightly hope) learn to notice and fitly respond to the damage.

Eucharist

The Klosterneuberg Abbey, in Lower Austria, is known for its altarpiece. Completed by Nicholas of Verdun in 1181, the altarpiece comprises enamel plates depicting forty-five biblical scenes: the binding of Isaac, the crossing of the Red Sea (one of the men walks with a bag slung over his shoulder, and out of the bag pokes the face of a small dog). About a third of the enamel plates depict scenes from the life of Jesus, including a striking representation of the Last Supper. In that plate, Jesus is shown giving bread to Judas and wine to Peter. "See, in two forms" says the inscription, "Christ holds himself in his hands."[1]

With this Communion scene, the Klosterneuberg altarpiece enters a tradition of visually depicting the Communion of Judas. It offers an unambiguous reading of a set of biblical texts (the accounts of the Last Supper) that seem, on their face, ambiguously to leave open the question of whether Judas in fact received (thereby the altarpiece takes a stand with readers, including Augustine and Aquinas, who said Judas did receive, against readers like Hilary of Poitiers, who said he did not). Thus the altarpiece—like other visual depictions of Judas's Communion, and like textual exegeses of the biblical Last

Supper accounts that argue for Judas's reception—is making a theological suggestion that, it seems to me, is crucial for an account of the Eucharist (and of Christian practice more generally): Judas received the Eucharist and then he immediately betrayed the Lord; written into the rite from its dominical inception, then, was the certainty of its going wrong.

In this chapter we shall read one instance of the Eucharist's going wrong, an instance located more than a millennium after the first Eucharist: the "host desecration" charges and attendant violence that raged across Europe in the Middle Ages. My reading of host desecration violence suggests that the violence against Jews undertaken in the name of supposed host desecration was not incidentally Eucharistic but intrinsically Eucharistic, and that the phenomenon of host desecration violence (or, to put it more pointedly, the phenomenon of Eucharistically funded violence against Jews) illustrates the characteristics of the Eucharist and of its deformations.

First, then, the history: What were host desecration narratives, how did they emerge, and of what larger violent choreography were they a part? My account of host desecration draws principally on the work of four historians: Miri Rubin, Anna Sapir Abulafia, Magda Teter, and Mitchell Merback. Following (especially) Rubin and Abulafia, I read host desecration narratives as inseparable from the theological debates about the Eucharist and the Incarnation that plagued the medieval church.

The phrase "host desecration narrative" can be taken to summarize an accusation, and the violence the accusation subtended (or, in some cases, justified post facto). Beginning in the late thirteenth century, Christians told stories in which Jews had procured a consecrated Eucharistic wafer and attempted to destroy it ("attempted," but did not succeed, because the wafer miraculously resisted destruction). These accusations functioned a bit like charges of rape leveled against African-American men in the late-nineteenth- and twentieth-century South: The charges were false, but they were used to justify killing the ones accused. In the case of medieval Christian violence against Jews, Christians usually killed (burned, often) the individual Jew accused of procuring and trying to destroy a host; often, Christians killed a handful of other neighboring Jews; and sometimes, they massacred whole Jewish communities.

The murderous Christians might raze the accused Jew's house and sometimes the local synagogue; then the Christian community would erect a chapel—sometimes chillingly called a *Hostienfrevelkirche*[2]—in the Jewish building's stead, or on another site central to that community's host desecration episode. This *Hostienfrevelkirche* was dedicated to the miraculous survival of the host; pilgrims came to give thanks for the miracle of the supposedly violated host's survival, and to pray in the presence of associated implements (like the knife the Jew supposedly used to try to destroy the host), and sometimes in the presence of the host itself. That choreography, from accusation to killing to subsequent devotion, is a "host desecration narrative"; "Gentile tales," Rubin has termed them, an appellation that stresses that although these tales present themselves as being about Jews, they were produced by, and served the interests of, (Gentile) Christian communities.

The narrative's etiology can be found in two intersecting places, intersections that begin in the twelfth century: first, the emergence of the Eucharist as not just a sacrament but the preeminent sacrament, the center of Christians' ritual and devotional lives; and, second, the sense among Christian theologians that their theological concerns about the body of Christ were shadowed by Jews (and by the things Jews supposedly said about the body of Jesus). In the twelfth century, the Eucharist "was emerging as the most frequently celebrated and attended sacrament," and people's behavior surrounding it was becoming more elaborate.[3] The process of actually producing the wafer that would be used in the rite was ever more regulated and "ritualized." Liturgists drafted a small library of guidebooks that instructed priests in the smallest details of Eucharistic practice; the penances to be undertaken should one fail those rubrics (if one, say, spilled consecrated wine) increasingly featured in penitential canons and decrees. The Eucharist became the object of new liturgical action—beginning in the twelfth century, for example, the host was elevated in the Mass (and simply gazing upon it was understood to be efficacious). By the mid-thirteenth century, the Eucharist was the subject of its own special feast day, Corpus Christi, on which a consecrated host would be carried through town in a monstrance. The Eucharist had become Europe's most fecund religious symbol.[4]

The Eucharist was not only becoming, in the twelfth century, the most ritualized sacrament. It was also becoming the "one which made the most outrageous of claims."[5] Those claims—specifically, claims about the Real Presence of Christ— energized tomes of theological scholarship, which traversed many questions about the Eucharist, not least the question of how Jesus was present in the bread and wine. In an article called "Bodies in Jewish-Christian Debate," Anna Sapir Abulafia argues that Christian theologians' parsing of Eucharistic doctrine—and doctrine about Jesus Christ's body more broadly—was inflected with Christian theologians' thoughts about Jews and what Jews said about Jesus. Abulafia's argument is worth reviewing in some detail. She lays out three registers on which Christian reasoning was shaped in part by Christian concerns about Jews. First, Incarnation, a doctrine whose denial defined Jews as much as its affirmation defined Christians: Christian theologians' new attentiveness to classical philosophy, argues Abulafia, prompted reconsiderations of how best to formulate the doctrine of the Incarnation, and theologians expended terrific energy trying to explain how the ineffable and infinite God could have become a man. The most famous of these considerations was Anselm's *Cur Deus Homo* (1090–99), and the arguments therein filtered down to other texts, many of which—Peter the Venerable's *Against the Jews* (1144–47) and Guibert's *A Treatise on Incarnation Contra the Jews* (1111), among others—were fierce in their vilifications of Jews. Jews, then, came to play a useful role in Christian worries about the Incarnation; they were figures who could be made to hold the concerns of Christians who were faced with philosophy's challenges to traditional doctrinal formulation. The Christian could displace his own concerns or confusions about the Incarnation by ventriloquizing (and then lambasting) Jews.[6]

A second register that finds Christians worrying about Jews is economic. To grossly oversimplify: In the twelfth century significant changes occurred in European economic practice, as a gift economy morphed into a monetary economy. Jews, not allowed to own land, sometimes turned to moneylending for their livelihood—thus Christians could benefit from the practice of moneylending without themselves practicing usury, and they could do so while disdaining Jews for the very lending that made Christian economic expansion possible.[7] (A partial analogy: Think of a man who hires a prostitute and then misogynistically upbraids women for their wantonness. The attack on women distracts the man from his own culpability and displaces his unease.) Thus host desecration tales borrowed one of its tropes from economic calumny, turning a story about Jews who made their living by essentially stealing from Christians into a story about Jews who stole the most precious good there was, the Eucharist.

A third register that finds Christians theorizing Jews is the Eucharist itself. Jews, as Abulafia explains, "stood accused of crucifying the very body through which God was supposed to have become incarnate. Christians for their part not only venerated that body, they believed they had a share in that same body when they partook of the host. And it was through their participation in the Eucharist that they conceived themselves to be united in the body of Christ, becoming his holy Church." Jews stood outside that body—the body that both made possible (fantasies of) Christian unity, and that invited Christian participants to recollect the Jews' role in crucifying the body of Christ.[8] Insofar as bonds of unity are predicated on another's exclusion, Jewish bodies could be drafted to serve Christian proclamation about Christian society; and insofar as outsiders undermine aspirations of unity, Jewish bodies could occasion contempt.

Taken together, these three registers suggest that, in the twelfth century, solving problems about the Eucharist became, for Christians, a task intimate with the task of solving problems about the Jewish bodies in their midst. Just what did it mean to say God had become man? And what did it mean to say that Christians could commune with Him through the host? How could the Jewish body of Jesus be regularly re-presented for the salvation of Gentile bodies? In Christians' minds, Jews lurked around seemingly internal Christian theological debates, for Christian unity—which was premised on chewing and swallowing the body of Christ—seemed to have no room for the Jews who simultaneously denied and murdered that body. As Abulafia explains it, Christians of the era put

> a great deal of emphasis . . . on the brotherly bond
> which was created between Christ and humanity on
> account of his willingness to die in order to save

man. And that bond was made explicit again and again when Christians felt united in the body of Christ through their veneration of and participation in the Eucharist. Interwoven into these discussions was the attempt to explain how it was possible for a transcendent God to become man and how Jesus Christ could be both man and God. . . . The concept of a universal Christendom was an illusion. But that did not make it any less real as a goal worth aspiring to.

And Jews, Abulafia argues, posed a special challenge to this goal:

Judaism . . . was seen as a threatening negation of the very essence of Christianity. . . . As non-Christians, Jews not only could not play any part in the religious manifestations of the church, but they also could not participate in the social activities generated by that religious ritual. To make matters worse, that ritual often entailed a great deal of anti-Jewish sentiment. After all, each time the Eucharist was celebrated, thoughts could easily turn to those who were accused of killing Christ.[9]

For Christians, then, Jews were a discomfiting reminder of the limits of the church's program of social unity, and a reminder of the apparent contingency of Christian understandings of who Jesus was and how Jesus was made present to present-day believers.

Christian worries about Jews, and Christian worries about the Eucharistic re-presentation of Jesus, surface in a coincident manner during the Fourth Lateran Council, convened by Innocent

III at Lateran Palace in Rome, in November 1215. Without much controversy or contest, the gathered bishops ratified the seventy proclamations presented to them, including an articulation of Eucharistic teaching and practice. At the level of practice, Lateran IV required the faithful to make an annual confession and to "receive the sacrament of the Eucharist at least at Easter" (unless a priest had instructed an individual not to). At the level of doctrine, it defined transubstantiation as *de fide: transubstantiatis pane in corpus et vino in sanguinem potestate divina*. This conciliar declaration ought not to be overread. What it tells us is not that conversation about the "how" of the Eucharist either began or ceased at Lateran IV, but that questions of Eucharistic mechanics were sufficiently in the air that the pope believed a conciliar declaration warranted. The council sanctioned the term "transubstantiation" and made the term an unavoidable part of Eucharistic conversation; it didn't offer a normative definition of the term or an explanation of how it worked.[10]

The prelates attending the Lateran council also devoted attention to sartorial regulation of Christian bodies' interactions with Muslim and Jewish bodies. As Canon 68 put it, because "through error Christians [sometimes] have relations with the women of Jews or Saracens," Jews and Muslims were required to dress differently from Christians: They shall "in every Christian province and at all times . . . be marked off in the eyes of the public from other peoples through the character of their dress."[11]

The Council, then, was concerned from two vantage points about encounters between Jewish bodies and Christian bodies. In a theologically regulatory key, the Council put words to the process whereby Jesus' (Jewish) body was made present over and over again for the salvation of (Gentile) bodies. In a socially regulatory key, the Council sought to mark Jewish and

Muslim bodies as visually distinct, so that Christians would not be deceived into bodily intimacy with them.

These two concerns—Eucharistic practice and the interactions between Jewish and Christian people in real space-time—came together in the second paragraph of Canon 68. "During the last three days before Easter and especially on Good Friday, they[12] shall not go forth in public at all, for the reason that some of them on these very days, as we hear, do not blush to go forth better dressed and are not afraid to mock the Christians who maintain the memory of the most holy Passion by wearing signs of mourning."[13] In this injunction, which aims to keep derisive Jewish bodies away from pious Christian bodies on the days when Christians recall the Last Supper and the execution of Jesus, there is again concern with the ways that Jewish bodies are visually, sartorially distinct from Christians' bodies. The sartorial distinctions reveal Jews' spiritual blindness: Christians know to mourn the death of Jesus, and Jews do not. In this injunction, we see a trope that will recur throughout church documents of the thirteenth century: restriction of Jews' movement in public space; segregation of Jews from Christians during Holy Days; the suggestion that Jews will "mock" the emotions and beliefs of pious Christians.[14]

Over the next few decades, councils and synods across Europe continued to regulate interactions between Jewish bodies and Christian bodies. Jews were, it was intoned, to dress differently from Christians. They were not to have sex with Christians. They were not to live near Christians. Jews were required to wear distinctive sartorial badges by Henreceian decree in 1217, by the Council of Oxford in 1222, by the Synod of Narbonne in 1227, by proclamation of the count of Toulouse in 1232, by the Council of Vienna in 1267. A 1233 letter from the pope censured the practice of Jews' employing Christians in their homes. These different kinds of regulations were linked to one another: Dress differently so that you can be identified as someone a Christian ought not to sleep with; don't employ a Christian servant because doing so might require you to live under the same roof. And don't live under the same roof lest you have sex.[15]

In addition to regulations that kept Jews residentially and carnally away from Christians, there were regulations about keeping Jewish bodies away from Christian bodies when the latter were in the presence of the body of their Lord. In Avignon, in 1243, all Jews over the age of nine were instructed to hide away, on penalty of fine, whenever a host was paraded in public. In Meissen, Saxony, Jews were required to stay inside during Eucharistic processions; if a Jew found herself on a street through which a consecrated host was being carried, she should go at once inside a house or to another street. The 1267 Synod of Vienna reiterated the point and gave an explicit interpretation, one that suggested Jews' craftiness and Christians' vulnerability, especially on points of opaque doctrine: Jews were to stay indoors when a Eucharistic procession passed by lest the clever Jews talk trash about the Eucharist and confuse their simple, devout, Christian neighbors.[16]

What we have seen in the twelfth and early thirteenth centuries, then, is increased devotional attention to the Eucharist, and the discursive interleaving of Christian concerns about the Eucharist with Christian concerns about Jews (concerns expressed on the register of theological discourse and on the register of social regulation). In the late thirteenth century, these interleavings turn more violent: Christians' accusations that Jews had procured a consecrated host and tried to destroy it became the discursive basis—the excuse, and the energizing rationale—for

Christians to kill their Jewish neighbors, burn down Jewish buildings, and replace those buildings with chapels devoted to Eucharistic miracles.

On Rubin's account, "the first fully documented case of a complete host desecration accusation, from discovery to punishment, occurred in Paris in 1290," seventy-five years after the Fourth Lateran Council. It was Easter, as well as the sixth day of Passover. In the parish of Saint-Jean-en-Grève, an economically marginal Christian woman has run to get her parish priest. She tells him that a Jew she knows—perhaps she owes the Jew money; perhaps she works for him as a maid—persuaded her to pocket the consecrated host she received on Easter morning. She delivered the host to him, and he then tried to destroy it, saying, as he did so, "I shall know whether the insane things which Christians prattle about this are true." As summarized by Rubin, it was said that the man struck the wafer with a knife,

> but it remained intact and simply began to bleed. He then picked up a hammer and anvils and pierced it through, but again the host remained whole and bleeding. He threw it into a fire, hoisted it on a lance and, attempting final destruction, threw it into a cauldron of boiling water. The water turned red . . . and the host was transformed into a crucifix which hovered above the cauldron.

The woman went running to her priest with this tale, and the priest summoned his bishop. The Jew was turned over to civil authorities and sentenced to burn. In one version of this story, he asked to hold his "book" (a volume of the Talmud) while burning. If he thought the book would, amulet-like, save him, he was mistaken; both he and his sacred scriptures went up in conflagration. His wife and children—"pliant," Rubin notes, not like the stubborn Jewish man; "impressionable" in their femininity or immaturity—converted. The historical record suggests that one of the surviving, now-Christian daughters of the executed Jew became a nun at Filles-Dieu.[17]

In the following centuries, similar tales would be told, and similar violence would ensue, throughout Europe: Korneu-burg in 1305. St. Pölten, 1306. Pulkau, 1338. In the second half of the fourteenth century, host desecration violence spasmed through Catalonia-Aragon. Brussels, 1370. Salzburg, 1404. Outside Vienna in 1421 (there, the Jews who didn't kill themselves or convert were burned at the stake on the banks of the Danube). Breslau in the 1450s. Regensburg in the 1470s. Sometimes, as in the Paris case, only one or a small number of Jews was killed. Sometimes, regional massacres followed in the wake of host desecration charges. In 1298, in Röttingen, for example, twenty-one Jews were killed after rumors of a host desecration circulated. The events in Röttingen sparked a wave of violence that eventually killed three thousand people and destroyed 146 communities.[18] Historian Mitchell B. Merback summarizes the impact of host desecration tales in "the south-ern reaches of the German empire in the two centuries before the Reformation":

> Such accusations shattered the patterns of Ashke-nazic life and permanently altered the social dy-namic of Jewish-Christian coexistence. . . . By the middle of the [fourteenth] century brutal religious riots in these regions had claimed thousands of in-nocent lives, with the host-legend playing loudly in the background.[19]

Often, as we have seen, after the Jew or Jews in question were killed, Jewish homes or synagogues were razed. In the 1290 case in Paris, for example, a chapel was built and an order known as the Brethren of the Charity of the Blessed Virgin grew up around the now sacred site; the order's job was to pray and to care for the chapel. The allegedly abused host was kept at the parish church, where a special liturgy evolved in its honor, and where the host desecration tale and its violence was materialized in liturgical implements including a reliquary decorated with a pearl- and diamond-encrusted sun. As late as 1602, those making an inventory of the church's liturgical implements knew how to read the reliquary: Displayed upon the sun, they wrote, "is the Holy Host mutilated by the Jews."[20]

Because of these shrines and special liturgies, host desecration dramas were not time-bound events; their sanctity was encountered (and vivified) again and again by pilgrims who made their way to commemorative chapels. Christians came to venerate the host, to recite special prayers in memory of the miracle, and to imaginatively place themselves near the perfidious Jew and the satisfying, Eucharist-confirming violence. Anti-Jewish violence and the memory thereof, mediated by the host desecration narrative, thus helped form and renew Christian practice; Christian practice mediated violence and in turn gave rise to new practices of pilgrimage, veneration, and remembrance.[21]

The usefulness of host desecration charges and their cults persisted long after the Middle Ages had turned toward reformations and early modernity. As Magda Teter has argued, in Reformation-era Poland, host desecration episodes flourished, taking on new polemical meaning: No longer were they only a tool for navigating the boundaries between Christian and Jew; they were also a tool of Christian differentiation in an era of competing religious reforms. By "flourished," I mean both that new host desecration accusations circulated in Poland through the sixteenth century and that older ones were ritually recalled with new vigor at memorial chapels whose (Catholic) agents sought to attract pilgrims and retain the religious attentions of men and women who might be tempted by Protestant upstarts. An instance of the first may be seen in an episode from the spring of 1556, when a Christian woman named Dorota Łazecka was accused of stealing an Easter wafer and giving it to Jews in Sochaczew. Łazecka "was promptly burned at the stake," recounts Teter, and her Jewish employer and three other Jews, charged with desecrating the wafer, were also "sentenced to death by burning." An instance of the second—the strategic revival of an old host desecration miracle undertaken by Catholics who were trying to bolster Eucharistic piety and Catholic ritual practice in the face of Protestant assault—may be seen in Poznan, where the celebrations of a 1399 host desecration episode were seen to have new salience after the Diet of Augsburg. In the context of Protestant growth, it was no longer just Jews who denied the ontology of the Eucharist—Protestants did, too. So in the sixteenth century, the local legend of a 1399 host desecration was revivified and embroidered as a way of navigating the Protestant-Catholic debate, and as a way of drawing visitors to the Carmelite church that had been built in the place where the Jews accused of the original host desecration had lived. At least until the 1920s, worshipers at that Carmelite church proclaimed not the traditional *kyrie eleison*, but this alternative prayer:

> Oh Jesus, unsurpassed in your goodness,
> Stabbed by Jews and soaked in blood again,
> Through your new wounds

And spilled springs of blood
Have Mercy on Us
The hearts of stone from the Jew Street . . .
Sank their knives in you
In the three Hosts, the Eternal God.
Have Mercy on Us, Have Mercy on Us, Have Mercy.[22]

It is a commonplace in considerations of the history of
Christian violence against Jews to note Christians' propensity
for enacting violence on Jews *during Holy Week*. Scholars have
addressed what it is about Holy Week—and Good Friday in
particular—that so often mobilized violence against Jews: Good
Friday liturgically reprised deicide charges and put the Johannine passion account, with its vituperative language about "the
Jews," before the people. More broadly (as David Nirenberg
puts it), "Read as a 'ritual sacrifice,' Holy Week violence served
to reinstitute differences and emphasize boundaries while displacing violence from the interior of the community."[23] If we
can ask what it is about the logic of Good Friday liturgies that
so easily funded violence against Jews, a similar sort of question
can be posed about the Eucharist: What is it about the *Eucharist*
that so easily allowed that sacrament to fund violence against
Jews? What is it about the Eucharist that allowed it to so easily
be harnessed to violent ends?

What is the Eucharist about? What is its form, and what
are its deformations? And what do its form and deformations
have to do with the history of Eucharistically funded toxicity
in medieval Europe? In offering one possible answer to those
questions, I am moving from the register of historical account
to the register of interpretive and suggestive juxtaposition. In
what follows, I am not arguing that when medieval Christians
received (or celebrated) the Eucharist, they often, or ever,

thought per se in terms of Jewish flesh. Neither am I arguing that there is a straightforward causal relation between, say, Lateran IV and host desecration narratives. Rather, I am offering a theologically motivated juxtaposition of things people did and things people wrote. I am juxtaposing theological questions with social and liturgical practices with the aim of showing not casual connections, but rather affinities—affinities that illuminate both thirteenth-century Eucharistic practice, and our own.

In pondering the Eucharist's propensity for violence, it is productive to think about the Eucharist as a place of great intimacy[24] between Christ's Jewish flesh and Christians' (principally Gentile) flesh. Lateran IV's articulation of transubstantiation as an article of the faith, its regulations governing the interactions and encounters of ordinary Jews and Christians, and various locales' subsequent reiteration and augmenting of those regulations may be seen as dilations on the same questions: How are (or are not) Jewish and Christian bodies to be intimate? How can Christians be intimate with the Jewish body of Christ when they are plagued by the nearness of Jewish bodies that in Christian accounts denied that body's divinity, killed it, and now mock it and its mournful devotees? How can Christians best guard against undue intimacy with Jewish bodies, while still organizing their devotional life around (and premising their unity with other Christians on) intimacy with the Eucharistic/Jewish body of Jesus Christ?

The overlappings of those questions at Lateran IV and in the decades and centuries after the Fourth Lateran Council suggest the usefulness of thinking about Eucharistic practice during the era of host desecration narratives with the postulate that there was slippage between Jews' "carnal" bodies and the body of Christ; that there was a lurking anxiety about Jesus, the Jew with a carnal body who becomes the Christ with a perfect body, a body he offers, over and over, for the sins of man. The murder of the Jew in Paris, and the murder of other Jews snared by host desecration tales, may be seen as the church's response to a problem about the relations among Jesus' Jewish body, Christians' Gentile bodies, and the Jewish bodies Gentile Christians lived near. It is, to be sure, not inevitable that such ferment turn violent. But when it does, the violence— sponsored by host desecration accusations and authorized by the Eucharist—is not connected to the Eucharist by happenstance. The violence depended on the centrality of the Eucharistic symbol. It was not incidentally Eucharistic but intrinsically Eucharistic.

Fundamental to the Eucharist is the reception of the Jewish flesh of Jesus by the typically Gentile bodies of Christians. Except in the rare instances where the gathered church comprises only baptized Jews, without the reception of the Jewish flesh of Jesus by the Gentile bodies of Christians, you do not have a Eucharist. The Eucharist is the consecration of bread and wine so that the bread and wine can be consumed as the body and blood of Jesus by the faithful. The principal good of the Eucharist is conformity to and intimacy with Jesus through ingestion. One of its characteristic deformations is a set of attitudes toward and practices about living Jewish flesh, a deformation that is predictable precisely because the Eucharist is about Jewish flesh, and about the kinds of claims Christians make about the particular (Jewish) flesh of Jesus. When something goes wrong with the Eucharist, the wrongness may unsurprisingly touch Jewish bodies, because the Eucharist's *aboutness* is Christian bodies consuming a Jewish body. This is not to say that the Eucharist must lead to host desecration charges and the murder of Jews (obviously, there are contingencies; obviously, there are many Eucharists that do not lead there). It is only to say that the Eucharist's funding violence against Jews is intelligible. The Eucharist becomes the moment when the church is most intimate with Jewish flesh; it is the moment when the church's faithful consume Jewish flesh. It is not unforeseeable that one of the Eucharist's characteristic deformations is the consumption of the Jewish flesh living in the neighborhoods of, and regulated by the conciliar and synodic pronouncements of, the church. To speak of the Eucharist's goods—the intimacy it made possible between (Gentile) Christians and their Lord—may also, and perhaps unavoidably, be to speak of the relation between Christian bodies and Jewish bodies under the rubric of supersession and exclusion.

In other words, this depiction of the Eucharist's form and deformations is closely linked to a more fundamental deformation within—indeed of—Christianity. One way to describe *Christianity's* form is to say that Christianity is the extension of relationship with the God of Israel to Gentiles through the Incarnation of Jesus Christ. The deformation most deeply characteristic of Christianity is supersessionism (by which I mean the belief that the church replaces Israel in God's plan for friendship with humanity and the salvation of Creation; I take this to be a view that has been held, explicitly or tacitly, by a majority of Christians for most of church history, and I take it to be a view that is untenable on a straightforward reading of Romans 9–11 and that has, since the Holocaust, been explicitly rejected by many church bodies, though it nonetheless persists in pulpits, in Bible study, in Sunday school classes, in prayer, and in many Christians' reflexive assumptions about the order of things). Christian supersessionism is precisely a distortion, a disordering, of intimacy; were there no intimacy between Christians and Jews, there could be no supersessionism. And given the abundant, confused intimacy between Christianity and Judaism, we ought to be on the lookout exactly for a distortion of Christianity that perverts intimacy into erasure, whether conceptual or fleshly. Because supersessionism is Christianity's characteristic deformation, it isn't adequate simply to cease repeating the anti-Jewish tropes that litter so much Christian speech over the centuries. Rather, what is needful is a Christian accounting of what it is about Christianity that has led us to those tropes—which is something other than a generic, free-floating hatred of the other. What has led Christians to these tropes is found not in Judaism but in the limits of Christians' own story, and in the ways Christians draft Jews and Jewish bodies to symbolize those limits. What has led Christians to those tropes is Christianity's intimacy with the God of Israel, the Christian hope that the reach of that God extends to include someone other than Israel, and Christians' lurking fear that perhaps the reach does not thus extend—therefore the church has to become Israel rather than simply be embraced by Israel's God. The tropes have to do, too, with the church's childish desire to be first, and with our nagging confusion about why the world is not yet fully redeemed—a confusion we easily displace onto Jews.

Alongside supersessionism, there is a second problem that dogs Christian accounts of Judaism. The church's fundamental narrative action is the taking over of another people's story and insisting, finally, that the appropriated people don't understand their own story as well as the appropriators do. We might call this second problem, borrowing from Harold Bloom, a theological misprision (or a creative misprision of Jewish testimony). Specifically, we might expect a form of tessera, which is a "completion and antithesis," in which a poet "antithetically 'completes' his precursor, by so reading the parent-poem as to retain its terms but to mean them in another sense, as though the precursor had failed to go far enough."[25] The creative

misprizing we find Christians doing to Judaism reflects, per
Bloom, anxiety of influence, but it also reflects a correct perception of incompatibility: Because my self-account is irreconcil-
able with yours, I claim to understand your own story better
than you do. Jews' and Christians' accounts of each other perforce cannot be accepted by the other—each will necessarily
make claims about the other that are incompatible with the
interlocutor's self-understanding and accounts. (An example
of this may be found two paragraphs back: It makes sense, in
Christian terms, for me to speak of "the abundant, confused
intimacy" between Judaism and Christianity; but this might
well be a claim that is incompatible with Judaism's account of
itself and its account of Christianity.) But our mutually incompatible claims about the other are incompatible in structurally
different ways. When Judaism makes claims about Christianity
that are incompatible with Christianity's self-description (and
unrecognizable as true to Christians), the claims are just that—
incompatible with Christian self-description and unrecognizable as true to Christians. When Christianity makes claims about
Judaism that Judaism does not recognize, there is not only a
description—there is a description and an appropriation. In
the one situation, I tell my friend that the kitchen in her house,
which she thinks is yellow, is really red. In the second situation,
I move into her house, and tell her the kitchen is red and that,
in my view, if she wants to keep living there, she will have to
accept the description as red, too. (Fortunately, neither de-
scriber is the keeper of the house.)[26]

Supersessionism and creative misprision of Jewish testimony are kindred deformations, and they are proper to Christianity. To say proper is not to say necessary, and it is certainly
not to say "not deformed." It is rather to say that they show
us—through their very distortion, as through an old, desilvered

mirror, what one of the chief goods of Christianity is: Gentile intimacy with Israel's God. And it is to say that the deformations are easy to miss, precisely because they are proper to Christianity; precisely because they are so intimate with Christianity's essential goods.

The history of host desecration is well known to historians. But it has been largely forgotten by twentieth- and twenty-first-century theologians, even those postliberal theologians for whose thought the Eucharist is so critical.

Postliberal theology has been keenly interested in the practices of the church, and how those practices form practitioners. At the center of the postliberal account of practices—the sine qua non of all that postliberal theology wants to say about practices more broadly—is the Eucharist, because it is, on this account, preeminently the Eucharist that carries within it a counternarrative, a story that has the power to refute the deadening and anomic stories of modernity. It is the Eucharist that makes possible an alternative politics—not merely by inviting practitioners to imitate the rite's logic but also by nourishing them and giving them solace, strength, pardon, and renewal. It is the Eucharist that offers a different way of arranging power, an arrangement possible only when the center of the arrangement is God's table, and only when the arrangers are there by God's invitation.

In the postliberal account, the Eucharist's politics can be seen in the Eucharist's disclosure of our end: Our end is to be a person who can and does eat with God, who is thus God's guest and God's friend.[27] The Eucharist thereby makes possible a kind of hospitality. It encapsulates and offers God's gracious hospitality to us, and—because God welcomes not only me, but also my neighbor—makes it possible for me to be hospitable. I may loathe my neighbor, but the Eucharist bids me—enables me—to welcome him as God does.[28] Hospitality writ large is peace, and the Eucharist makes it possible for participants—the body of Christ—to pursue peace. As Stanley Hauerwas and Samuel Wells have written, "The Eucharistic feast that Christians share is believed to anticipate the heavenly peace. Christians, therefore, seek the peace of the city in which they find themselves."[29] The Eucharist effects the transformation of participants into people of peace: "As we again and again are welcomed by this host at his meal of the kingdom of peace, we become people of peace and reconciliation."[30]

Postliberal theologians, in other words, ask the Eucharist to do a lot of work: to make possible a set of behaviors and actions that are decidedly at odds with the behaviors and actions invited by late capitalism and her coercive handmaiden, the nation-state; to make possible hospitality, abundance, and peace. If the church is an alternative polis (characterized by, among other things, an alternative economy), the Eucharist is that polis's authorizing ritual and its founding myth.[31]

Paris and Poznan suggest one of the chief virtues of the postliberal account: The postliberal account crucially recognizes that the Eucharist arranges power.[32] But host desecration narratives also suggest the limits—the curious optimism, almost magical thinking—of the postliberal Eucharist. Once acquainted with the history of Eucharistic violence, what can it mean to say, with ethicist Scott Bader-Saye, that "the Eucharist is a sacrament of peace whereby Israel's redemption is made present by the Holy Spirit in the body of Christ"?[33]

Nicholas M. Healy has astutely diagnosed this crucial flaw in the postliberal account of Christian practices: Often the account "relies too heavily upon the assumption that the practices of the church are at least for the most part performed according to their abstract and ideal descriptions. Ordinary concrete mis-performance or non-performance and its effect upon character formation and church witness are left out of the picture." Christian practices, writes Healy, "even when abstractly perfect . . . are performed by an often confused and sometimes sinful and faithless body."[34] The problem with the account whereby the Eucharist forms participants in a peaceable politics is not merely semantic; the problem is deeper than the account's continual cloaking of normative claims in descriptive language, and it will not be solved simply by converting all the descriptive declaratives to hopeful future-tense subjunctives. Nor is the problem simply that the account is altogether too rosy, generically failing to be chastened by the pervasiveness of sin. Rather: An account of a thing entails an account of its goods, and it entails an expectation of the ways those goods are likely to be perverted (that is, in a fashion proper to the thing itself). This is even—and perhaps especially—true about liturgical goods, which are the very things that seem to (and do, but incompletely) provide a road out of the blighted world and into heaven.

Peter Ochs's essay "Morning Prayer as Redemptive Thinking" provides a methodological caution that could help the church in its efforts to give an account of the Eucharist. Ochs analyzes the benedictions that observant Jews say daily in Morning Prayer, and argues that Morning Prayer prepares the practitioner to make different kinds of judgments than she would be capable of making had she not habituated herself to the liturgy—virtuous, countercultural, Godward judgments that reflect a chastened but still robust sense of agency, and that are attentive to "the world in its wholeness, amazingness, and blessedness . . . something much vaster and richer than what we are in the habit of discriminating within it."[35] Ochs could be charged with confusing normative prescription with description (that is, the liturgy might *want* to make its practitioners attentiveness to blessedness, but are practitioners in fact *made* more blessing-attentive by prayer?) until he wonderfully qualifies the entire essay at the end: Ochs notes that his essay has "examined only the logic of the [Morning Prayer liturgy]." After examining the logic of the words on the prayer book's page, writes Ochs, "the next step would be to test the logic ethnographically: to see if there are observable differences between the practices of judgment-making among those who are habituated to Morning Prayer, for example, and those who are not."[36] Christian liturgical scholar Don E. Saliers makes a similar point—perhaps a tad more pointedly—when he writes, "Liturgical theology suffers when it fails to acknowledge 'hidden' power issues and the malformative histories of practice. The point of normative questions, that is, what moral dispositions and ethical intention-action behaviors ought to be formed in us by liturgical celebrations of the teaching, life, death, and resurrection of Christ, can only be discerned when we gain an adequate descriptive account of what actually takes place."[37]

Ochs's analysis of the liturgy for Morning Prayer asks the same kinds of questions of Jewish liturgy that postliberal Christian theologians, contemporaries and intellectual siblings of Ochs, ask of the Eucharist: How does the Eucharist form practitioners? What judgments does it enable them to make? What countercultural postures does it prompt them to assume? What politics does it make possible? Similarly, Ochs's self-critical query might be aptly posed to postliberal accounts of the Eucharist: Certain judgments and politics seem to be encoded in the words and rituals that constitute Eucharistic performance, but are there "observable differences" between the judgments and politics of those who practice Eucharist and those who do not?

What "practices of judgment-making," to use Ochs's phrase, are found among those who are habituated to the Eucharist? In that most Eucharistic terrain of late medieval Europe, the answer would seem to include: violent practices, responsive to (and articulated within) deep problems about Christian intimacy with Israel and with Israel's God.

Host desecration events were "about" the Eucharist insofar as they were ostensibly undertaken in defense of the Eucharist. And at many subtler levels, the choreography of host desecration spoke to concerns, worries, and hopes that medieval Christians had about and for the Eucharist. Is the body of Christ broken in the breaking of the bread by the priest? wondered medieval theologians; host desecrations recounted a host not broken, despite the determined efforts of the torturing Jew. Does the body of Christ remain whole through chewing, digestion? Theologians answered yes, and host desecration tales staged a host remaining whole through attempted hacking and chopping.[38] Host desecration narratives also played with the Eucharistic choreography of take-give-receive. In a Eucharist, a priest takes the bread, blesses it, and gives it to a layperson, who faithfully receives and ingests. In host desecration narratives, a laywoman appears to receive rightly, but instead pockets the host. She then appropriates and misperforms priestly duties—instead of giving the Eucharist to a worthy recipient, she sells the Eucharist to someone who cannot receive it, because he is not baptized. (The economics of this transaction—which mocked participation in the divine economy, and which traded on the aforementioned associations of Jews with usury—was doubled by the material form of the host: small wheaten disks, coin-shaped, "not baked so much as minted," in the words of scholar John Parker.)[39] The Jewish man also parodies the priest.

His perverse manipulations of the Eucharist transformed a standard-issue consecrated host into an object of special veneration and pilgrimage—and backformed the Jew into a sacerdotal actor of sorts who had played a part in the creation of a sacred Christian object. Finally, host desecration inverted transubstantiation: Transubstantiation narrated a wafer that was acted upon with words, that didn't appear to change, but that did in fact change; host desecration accounts narrated a wafer that was acted on in ways that would change an ordinary wafer (it was sliced; it was boiled), but that remained unchanged—at least, it remained unchanged until it morphed into a crucifix or Christ child, or bled, or generated a crucifix or a Christ child that levitated from within the host.

Medieval Eucharistic practice casts the Eucharist as weirdly both strong and fragile, vulnerable and invulnerable. The Eucharist was so strong that simply gazing on it could convey a person to Christ's presence. On the other hand, it was evidently fragile, vulnerable to the mice who might nibble the reserved sacrament (concerned theologians pondered what the status of a host thus consumed was); vulnerable to being dropped by an elderly priest's palsied hands (concerned authors of penitential books cautioned priests against swaying with the host, or looking up at the elevated host in a way that might make the priest dizzy, and likely to drop the wafer). If the wafer weren't vulnerable, it wouldn't need protection from the mice or from lightheaded priests.

Host desecrations take up this dyad of strength and fragility and bend it. To take the Eucharist from the church and out into the world—in a procession, or simply on its way to a sick parishioner—was, it seemed, to court risk. Miri Rubin offers an almost disturbingly lovely description of this in her essay "Imagining the Jew": "At its most vulnerable, when out of doors, when carried in the hand of the priest passing through muddy lanes, sometimes in the rain, at these moments, any movement, gesture, even the mere presence of Jews could irritate and kindle doubts and anxieties, tensions that were inherent in the very nature of the Eucharist."[40] The host seemed exposed, bearing the weight of divine flesh through the crowded streets of town. (And indeed those simple Christian folk who were typed as so vulnerable to the Jews' clever polemics were also, in a sense, Eucharists: That is, some of those pliable Christians might themselves have just received—in which case, the Eucharist was not just borne in a monstrance in the hands of a priest; the people themselves were also carrying the Eucharist, in the occluded monstrances of their bodies.) Alongside this vulnerability came stories of the Eucharist's impossible strength: It warded off all those alleged attacks, all that alleged piercing and boiling. This is, again, distortion as in an old and wavy mirror. It is the disordered articulation of something true: The Eucharist really is, at once, vulnerable and invulnerable; if that were not the case, it could not be Jesus' flesh, which was both vulnerable and yet finally invulnerable—utterly ravaged on the cross and yet raised and ascended and glorified. Jesus' flesh is vulnerable and invulnerable, so if the Eucharist is to be his flesh, it must be those things, too.

Of course, vulnerability and strength characterize not only the Eucharist (qua consecrated wafer). They also characterize the Eucharist (qua rite). In a sense, this is my whole argument: The Eucharist—the rite, the sacrament, the practice—is invulnerable, and vulnerable, too.

Sacramental practice is tensive. A constitutive part of practicing Eucharist—and of an account of that practice—is the tension between acknowledging that, on the one hand, the Eucharist has gone, and inevitably sometimes will go, wrong, and, on the other hand, articulating the reason to go on doing it.

We participate in Eucharist neither because it forms us in particular ways nor because it habituates us in particular norms. We know this because of the kind of Eucharist we anticipate in heaven. Eschatologically, we will partake of a Eucharist,[41] and— since we will already be perfected—we will be freed from any hope or expectation that it will form us in any way at all. In that heavenly Eucharist, what will be left is the gift. Thus it is already a perversion of the Eucharist to speak about the rite as though it were intended principally for our educative remaking. This is not to say that, on this side of eternity, our formation might not result, second-order, from the Eucharist. Of course, the Eucharist *might* form us in particular goods (and perhaps it logically should, since Jesus is all good and all goodness, and since we are being conformed to, participating in, and—through our own bodies' incorporation of the Eucharist—being further incorporated into Jesus). A practice can make us (possibly) more good in some respects and (possibly) less good in others, even at the same time: Formation, growth, or damage may happen to us when we participate in Eucharist, although we do not undertake participation for those purposes. We undertake participation in the Eucharist—we continue celebrating and receiving the Eucharist— because the Eucharist is a preeminent and prevenient gift of God. It is that gift definitionally—by which I mean the Eucharist sets the terms for all other gifts from God, and also that the Eucharist's aboutness and goods turn on gift, rather than on formation, or even politics: More than the Eucharist being a means for God's giving something else, it is the thing given.

Perhaps another characteristic deformation of the Eucharist is human participants' failure to remember that we are not the Eucharist's agents. At the altar, Christians are being inscribed into the agency of God. We think we are celebrating the Eucharist in memory of—in memory of Jesus' death, resurrection, and ascension; in memory of the Last Supper. But maybe it is fundamentally not we but God who is remembering, and maybe it is the church's sometimes vicious deployment of this rite that God remembers.[42]

Indeed, one Eucharistic aboutness is memory. The Eucharist has a fundamentally memorial logic—anamnetic logic, in which more than merely recollecting, we allow the past to bear on the present. Given the strong claims the Eucharist makes about memory, it may be more than ironic that Christians have by and large erased the history of host desecration violence from our Eucharistic memory. This erasure—this "gap between corporate memory and corporate history," to borrow the words of theologian Katie Walker Grimes—may entail "the vice of nostalgic unknowing."[43]

Principally, the Eucharist remembers the events of the Last Supper. But it is possible to imagine bringing with us to the altar memories of our supersessionist and violent history, memories of the times we turned the Eucharist against itself. There is space for this kind of acknowledgment in the Eucharistic rite. As Donald Mathews has written, "The Eucharist, which is the Christian understanding of God's presence in history, dictates historical meaning because it includes the prayer of confession in which communicants confess in shame and guilt all that they have done and not done, something that is [or at least should be] sobering to all who kneel before that presence in remembering the past."[44]

Confession is not the only moment at which the rite itself corrects for our own incapacities. The key moment of the rite's recursivity occurs when partakers pray, "We are not worthy so much as to gather up the crumbs under thy Table."[45] That startling line comes in a prayer known as the Prayer of Humble Access. In my church (the Episcopal Church; the prayer is found in the Rite I Eucharist) we say this prayer just after the fraction and just before the distribution of the elements. The prayer should create a pause in the whole liturgy and in our confident proclamation about its politics. And the prayer should remind us whose worthiness and agency this practice entails: not ours.

For twenty years, I have prayed the Prayer of Humble Access and thought, in general terms, about the way it fittingly chastens. I have thought about how uncomfortable a thing it is to say. (Aren't I beloved of God? How can I be beloved of God and not worthy for God's crumbs? Why must we say this prayer, when the Scriptures make clear that God delights in spreading feasts for us?) I have thought about the way the prayer goes on to name mercy as proper to God—"but thou art the same Lord whose property is always to have mercy"—and how inside this claim about mercy, maybe it becomes apt, rather than just uncomfortable and strange, to understand one's self to be simultaneously beloved of God and not worthy to receive God's table's crumbs. "Grant us therefore, gracious Lord, so to eat the flesh of thy dear Son Jesus Christ, and to drink his blood, that we may evermore dwell in him, and he in us," the prayer concludes. I have thought about the great effort I make—an effort that reaches back to those medieval customaries and their worries about dizzy priests' capacity to drop God on the floor—to celebrate the Eucharist tidily. I try not to produce crumbs when I break the bread, and if I see any crumbs, I pick them right up and put them on my tongue. I try, in other words, to make the prayer's figurative language irrelevant, by doing my best to leave no bread crumbs behind.

It has been only more recently, as I have been looking at (and for) moments when the Eucharist recursively acknowledges its own potential deformations, that I have come to see that the Prayer of Humble Access points to something more precise than the generic impossibility of Eucharistic reception. We, the largely Gentile Christian church, pray this prayer just before we are about to receive the Jewish flesh of Christ. The recursivity lies precisely in the source of the words: The prayer was first scripted by two Gentiles—the centurion (Matthew 8:8; Luke 7:6–7) and the Syrophoenician woman (Matthew 15:27). So this is not a prayer, finally, about the bad things I did last week; nor is it a prayer broadly about the distance I maintain between myself and God. Rather, the Prayer of Humble Access *is about the rite to which it belongs,* and it shows, without removing, our tendency to expropriate Jewish flesh rather than accept it. It is a prayer first uttered by two non-Jews to Jesus, and when the church in turns repeats the prayer, for a moment all the supersessionism freezes, and we become again what most of us are[46]—non-Jews, saying to Jesus that we are not worthy of the God of Israel, and that we cannot intimately commune with Israel's God; and then, having remembered that God is merciful, we accede to God's offer, and precisely thus commune.

On Easter 1389, the Jewish community of Prague was massacred. Some of the massacre's origins lay in the calendar (that year, Holy Week, with its inflammatory Good Friday liturgy, intersected with Passover, whose last day fell on Easter) and in the people of Prague's anger at the king's reliance on Jewish moneylenders. But if structures of calendar and economy underpinned the pogrom, the presenting circumstances included charges of Jews disturbing a host. Specifically, on Holy Saturday, a priest was taking a consecrated host to a sick parishioner, and some Jews supposedly mocked the priest in the street, and perhaps threw stones at the monstrance that carried the host. It is hard to know how many Jews were killed in the ensuing butchery—the best estimate is four hundred to five hundred. The Jewish quarter was torched, property was stolen—and accounts were written. One of the accounts, known as the Limburg Chronicle, preserves a soft word of doubt about the idea that the Jews of Prague were interested in harming a Eucharistic wafer: The massacre began when a Jew threw a "small pebble" at the monstrance, says the Chronicle—or "so the Christians say."[47]

Doubts like the chronicler's dot the landscape of host desecration accusations. Another such dot is found in Pulkau, where a host desecration unfurled in 1338. John of Winterthur, who chronicled the Pulkau episode, claimed that the Jews had not been responsible for any violation of the host. Rather, the local priest, who was "of very slender means," had sprinkled a wafer with blood and tossed it near a Jew's house. Eventually— after around 150 people had been killed—the supposedly violated, supposedly miraculous host made its way to the church of the priest, who ultimately received many "offerings and oblations" from eager pilgrims. The bishop of Passau, sufficiently worried that the host desecration charge was a hoax and that people were thus venerating a nonconsecrated Eucharist, ordered a consecrated wafer to be placed next to the supposedly assaulted one. Despite all this, the doctor of canon law from Bamburg Cathedral who was eventually sent to investigate concluded that the host had indeed been assaulted.[48]

As in the case of Pulkau, when official doubts were registered about a host desecration episode, it was usually "well after the killing of Jews." Furthermore, the doubts were generally articulated not in terms of defense of Jews, but as worries over the (supposed) Eucharist—Was it really consecrated? Still, as Rubin has noted, these investigations "at least indicate that for some the stories did not work."[49]

This record of narrative failure is slight, compared to all the killing, but it is nonetheless a crucial part of an account of host desecration violence, for to name anti-Judaism as Christianity's characteristic deformation is not to argue that anti-Judaism is natural. (There is no such thing as a static anti-Judaism; insofar as anti-Judaism has threaded through church history, it has not been stable, but has been depressingly adaptive and protean.) The most saturatedly anti-Jewish moments in church history hold hints of Christian doubt about or shirking away from one or another of anti-Judaism's incarnations. As Barbara Newman has argued in her discussion of the Limburg Chronicle, these hints show that "resistance was possible and did sometimes surface."[50]

Miri Rubin has put the point eloquently:

> We can only understand anti-Judaism when we appreciate that it was *not* universal, and that it must be contextualized to be understood. . . . One looks around, guided by the single thing that anti-Judaism and similar social pathologies teach us loud and clear: that any attempt to categorize people, to place them in exclusive groups is a lie, and it requires an enormous effort of mendacity and persuasion to keep such lies believable. So much so that no claim can be coherent, that it cracks, and its cracks can become visible to us. . . . Anti-Judaic discourses . . . are full of such cracks and contradictions; and before they become our concern they were *theirs*, they belonged to those who lived and acted in the discourse in question.[51]

It is exactly the seeming ubiquity of anti-Jewish tropes (the sermons, the paintings, the Good Friday prayers, the biblical commentaries, the conciliar pronouncements) that testifies to that "enormous effort." The effort will always be exposed by a fracture, a fracture like the bishop of Passau's doubts; a fracture like "so the Christians say."

Those fractures should be remembered alongside the edifice they crack. And precisely because they are such a slender reed, we should remember them in the context of a larger re-membering, which is to say God's. Finally, any hope that might temper Christians' rightful, needful despair about supersession and the church's habit of creatively misprizing Jewish testimony will be lodged in God's memory, and in the *specificity* of God's memory. God does not generically remember. Rather, as the Psalmist tells us,

> He remembers his covenant forever,
> the promise he made, for a thousand generations,
> the covenant he made with Abraham,
> the oath he swore to Isaac.
> He confirmed it to Jacob as a decree,
> to Israel as an everlasting covenant. (105:8–10, NIV)

The Last Supper—which is to say, the first Eucharist—tells us forcefully that the Eucharist carries both gift and deformation. To remember the Last Supper is to remember the dominical gift of the Eucharist itself, and the gift of Eucharistic intimacy with Christ. And to remember the Last Supper is to remember the deformation of Judas's reception, followed immediately by Judas's betrayal of the One (whose Eucharist) he had just received.

A caveat: Judas's reception of the Eucharist is contested.[52] There is ambiguity in the Scriptures about whether Judas received, and different theologians and readers of Scripture have reached different conclusions. To read the Gospels as recounting Judas's receiving the Eucharist is therefore speculative; the Gospels don't require us to conclude that Judas received, but the synoptics leave open the possibility that he did, and it's permitted by the text to read Judas as a participant in the Eucharist. On the reading that Judas received, the first dominically given Eucharist is already malformed.

Most interpreters who argue that Judas received base their arguments in Luke and Matthew.[53] Augustine grounds his belief that Judas received Communion in Luke.[54] John Chrysostom, in a sermon on Matthew, also argues for Judas's inclusion in the sacrament: "How great is the blindness of the traitor! Even partaking of the mysteries he remained the same; and admitted to the most holy table, he changed not." For Chrysostom, Judas's crime was all the worse both because "imbued with such a purpose he approached the mysteries, and because he became none the better for approaching."[55]

Of the three synoptic accounts of the Last Supper, Luke offers the strongest and clearest suggestion that Judas partook. In Luke 22, the disciples have readied the upper room for the Passover. Jesus takes his place at the table and proclaims that he will not eat the Passover before "it is fulfilled in the kingdom of God." Then he takes the cup and the bread, says the words of institution, and immediately says, "For the Son of Man is going as it has been determined, but woe to that one by whom he is betrayed!" The disciples "began to ask one another which one of them it could be who would do this." There is not in Luke, as there is in Matthew and Mark, a suggestion that Judas ever leaves the supper. On the straightforward reading, Judas is there the whole time and partakes of the whole event. The key differences between the Lukan account and the other synoptics

are that in Matthew, Judas is named (he is not in Luke), and in
Matthew and Mark the announcement of the pending betrayal happens before the institution of the Lord's Supper.

The Johannine account is at once more ambiguous and
more pointed than the synoptics'. There are no words of institution in John; rather, in the place where the synoptics show
Jesus instituting the sacrament, John offers an account of Jesus'
washing the disciples' feet. After the washing, Jesus announces,
"One of you will betray me." The disciples wonder whom he
could mean, and Simon Peter presses the beloved disciple to
ask Jesus who the treacherous one is, which the beloved disciple
does. Then:

> Jesus answered, "It is the one to whom I give this
> piece of bread when I have dipped it in the dish." So
> when he had dipped the piece of bread, he gave it to
> Judas son of Simon Iscariot. After he received the
> piece of bread, Satan entered into him. Jesus said to
> him, "Do quickly what you are going to do." Now
> no one at the table knew why he said this to him.
> Some thought that, because Judas had the com-
> mon purse, Jesus was telling him, "Buy what we
> need for the festival"; or, that he should give some-
> thing to the poor. So, after receiving a piece of
> bread, he immediately went out. And it was night.
> (John 13:26–30)

John's is the only Gospel that states that Judas left the dinner,
and it is the only account to describe Judas's being identified
by his reception of a morsel. That morsel may be read as the
Eucharist. This is, admittedly, a reading that has been resisted
by most interpreters.[56] (Augustine says that those of us who

pursue it "negligenter legentes"—read carelessly—not because Augustine thought that Judas did not receive but because Augustine bases his belief that Judas did receive on Luke, and he thinks the Eucharistic distribution that Luke recounts came before this identificatory handing of the morsel that John recounts.)[57] But interpreting John's morsel as a Eucharist, while certainly a speculative reading that is not required by the text, is concordant with the text—and is worth entertaining, because on this reading John suggests not that the Eucharist happens coincidentally alongside Judas's betrayal, but rather that the Eucharist *is part of* both the betrayal's choreography and its unmasking (but not its prevention). Unlike Luke, in which Judas received and then is identified, on this reading of John, *Judas is identified as the betrayer precisely by receiving the morsel/ Eucharist.*

At its very inception, the Eucharist is fractured. One who receives immediately betrays the reception (and the Giver), and the betrayer's reception is inseparably the sign of his inability to receive; Judas's reception is about the fact that he will betray the reception. Christians' account of the Eucharist—our expectations of our own Eucharists—might well be grounded in Scripture's pointing, at the very moment of dominical gift, to the Eucharist's impossibility, to its inevitable corruption. In the ninth century, a French artist who was illustrating a psalter depicted Judas receiving the Eucharist: Jesus is holding a chalice with his left hand and is feeding Judas the host with his right hand. A black bird—a sign of the devil and of temptation, often found near Judas in medieval art[58]—appears to be about to fly into Judas's open mouth, and Judas himself appears poised to run. This striking image of Judas receiving Eucharist from the Lord accompanies and interprets Psalm 41:9: "Even my bosom friend in whom I trusted, who ate of my bread, has lifted the heel against me."[59] Even Jesus' bosom friend. Why do we imagine that any subsequent Eucharists will be less deformed than the first one?

Remembering—anticipating—the deformation will not, of course, remove it. The Klosterneuberg Abbey, as we noted at the beginning of this chapter, has, since 1181, been home to an altarpiece depicting, among other biblical scenes, Jesus giving the Eucharist to Judas[60]—that depiction of inceptive Eucharistic damage greeted worshipers each day. But that visual instruction in eucharistic wrongdoing did not adequately chasten the Christians of Klosterneuberg. At the end of the thirteenth century, a host desecration accusation whipped around Klosterneuberg. Ten Jews were killed, and a fraction of the host was preserved as a relic.[61]

Prayer

On the morning of October 19, 1860, Keziah Goodwyn Hopkins Brevard—a fifty-seven-year-old widow, and the owner of two plantations near Columbia, South Carolina—sat down at her diary.[1] After a brief word about the "boisterous" weather that might derail her plans for the day, Brevard turned to the subject that was exasperating her:

> Negroes such trying creatures you are—The first thing I saw like work this morning was Rosanna with a box of collards out of my garden—I have very few there, the hot summer prevented my saving but very few. I have a plenty of turnips, gave them as many as they wanted yesterday & the day before & intended they should have [more] when they wished. I made John stay in the Kitchen in wet weather & try to keep her [Rosanna] out of the rain—but she could leave my breakfast and go through the rain to deceive me. Oh I wish I had been born in a Christian land & never seen or known of

slaves of any colour. Negroes are as deceitful & lying
as any people can well be—Lord give me better feelings towards them. (Forgive me Lord, for unkind
thoughts & have mercy on me!)[2]

This was a subject, indeed, that *often* vexed Brevard: the insuf-
ferable, maddening behavior of her more than two hundred
slaves. On this particular morning, what happened was straightforward enough. One of Brevard's house slaves, Rosanna (who
inspired many of Brevard's diary rants) took a box of greens
from the vegetable garden. Brevard hadn't authorized Rosanna
to do so, so Rosanna was committing, in Brevard's eyes, simple
theft. She was "deceiving" Brevard—pilfering *and* sneaking out
of the house under the cloak of rain to do so. Brevard revealed,
but wouldn't herself have articulated, a third offense: By
taking the collards, Rosanna deprived Brevard of a chance to
do something that would make her, Brevard, feel good,
namely "giving" Rosanna vegetables. Rosanna took from Brevard not only collards but also the chance to feel benevolent
and generous.

This story contains plot points that show up again and
again in Brevard's diary: the slaves' small but pointed acts of
resistance; Brevard's wish to be away from the whole system of
slavery (a wish usually expressed in terms of strong support for
the colonization of American slaves in West Africa, and checked
by her equally strong resistance to the idea of emancipation);
and Brevard's abiding frustration with Rosanna and other
household slaves. Typical, too, is Brevard's tone—a combination
of annoyance and ferocity. And typical is her use of devotional
language. She articulated her relationship with her slaves, and
the work of managing a household that ran on slave labor, in
the idiom of prayer: *Lord give me better feelings towards*

them. (Forgive me Lord, for unkind thoughts & have mercy on me!)[3]

In none of this was Keziah Brevard unique. Complaints about slaves are commonplace in the diaries of slave-owning women of the antebellum and Civil War–era South. So, too, most of their diaries unwittingly preserve testimony to the slaves' acts of everyday resistance, like taking vegetables. Many diaries also recount their authors' praying about slavery: asking God to give them both "better feelings" about their slaves and slaves who were obedient. These prayers, I shall argue, represent a mode of household management. Slave-owning women probably learned about the centrality of prayer in household management from their own mothers and from widely circulated prescriptive literature, which enjoined women to make prayer a central part of household management.[4] An especially influential statement of this view could be found in the popular work *Letters on Female Character,* written by Virginia Cary and first published in 1828.[5] Framed as a series of letters to Cary's niece, the widely circulated volume contains the feminine commonplaces of the day: Women should find their chief consolations in religion and spurn ornate apparel. If a woman wants a happy marriage, she should aim for a cheerful disposition, because "A good temper hangs like a sunny sky over the conjugal atmosphere."[6] One letter points to the centrality of prayer in running a household with slave labor. Cary admits to having trouble managing her slaves—but her friend Emilia provides an example worth imitating. Cary had been impressed on a recent visit to Emilia's house by the dutiful and assiduous manner of Emilia's slaves: "I have never seen slaves look as they do in Emilia's family; and I am told, that she has the most moral and correct set in the country. This surely proves the propriety of her management." The key to Emilia's success, says Cary, is that she instructs her slaves in the Christian faith. "When [Emilia] is questioned on the subject, she says, that she became aware early in life, that the ordinary behaviour of these people would destroy her happiness. She therefore set herself to arranging a method of management which would have a tendency to remove these evils."[7] That "method" entailed tutoring her slaves in Christian hierarchy: "When we teach our servants to serve God," Emilia told her friend, "they serve us of course, for obedience to their earthly master is one branch of their duty to their heavenly King." In Cary's view, prayer was crucial to the harmonious relations in Emilia's household. "This method [of domestic management]," Emilia explains to Cary, "I digested prayerfully, and if I have succeeded in enforcing it, the Lord has been pleased to bless my supplications, for I always knew the work was too great for my feeble powers to accomplish, and I have left it to Him who does all difficult things for his creatures. I never omit to pray that God may give me good servants." A woman reading Cary's manual, then, would learn that if she wished to have an ordered domestic sphere, she should take her plan of household management to the Lord in prayer, and that part of the prayerful review of the plan should be petitioning God for "good servants."[8]

On my bookshelf sit about two dozen anthologies of Christian prayers. In them, I find many faithful and emulable things: Teresa of Ávila's so-called bookmark prayer, found in her breviary after she died ("Let nothing disturb you; Let nothing frighten you . . ."); John Chrysostom's doxology ("Glory be to Thee, O Lord; glory be to thee . . ."); Thomas Traherne's thanksgivings for the body. I don't find excerpts from the diaries of slave-owning women in the antebellum American South. My anthologies do not feature Elizabeth Foote Washington's prayer that God would "influence the hearts of my servants & cause them to treat me with respect."[9] Nor do they include Lucille McCorkle's importuning, after attending a prayer meeting in Alabama in 1847, that God would give her patience with her slaves because "As a *mistress* I so need patience *forbearance meekness* mercy."[10]

Prayer, Christians want to say, is the thing that delivers us to God. Prayer is the place of intimate communion between a believer and her Redeemer. Prayer is something God does in us, but also, we think (or, at any rate, we act as though we think), something we do. An account of Christian praying should make sense of Augustine's *Late have I loved you, O Beauty so ancient and so new.* It should make sense of Thomas Merton's *I believe that the desire to please you does in fact please you.* But it should also make sense of Keziah Brevard and Lucille McCorkle: *Lord give me better feelings towards them; As a mistress I so need patience forbearance meekness mercy.* The account of prayer implied in the anthologies that omit Brevard and McCorkle is inadequate, because it implies that all prayer is rightly formed; that people always pray for the things that the anthology editors think please God; that prayer is always in tune with the great Christian virtues; and that if prayer arranges power at all, it does so only in a way that fosters peace, concord, and the flourishing of all Creation. But sometimes prayer does not do those things—and then either we must name those prayers as "not prayer," or we must account for them. In this chapter, I read Keziah Brevard's prayers, as recorded in her 1860 and 1861 diary, to show how petitionary prayer carries within itself the possibility of its own deformation. This is to argue not that therefore we shouldn't engage in petitionary prayer but that we should do so knowing its potential for distortion, and do it in such a way that our knowledge informs our practice.

Central to the diaries of many slave-owning women is the question of household management, and such questions pervade Brevard's diary: How could Brevard most effectively control and motivate her slaves? Wresting labor from a captive workforce required dogged intent and constant supervision. Women in particular had to learn to hold together, on the one hand, the brutality that slavery required and, on the other hand, the genteel deportment that proslavery defenses of the slave system considered so essential. The fall and winter of 1860 was a time of heightened anxiety for Brevard as South Carolina seceded from the Union following Abraham Lincoln's election, and the nation plunged toward civil war. During these months, across the South, the challenges of managing slaves became more intense. As has been well documented by historians of the slave South, as rumors of war, and then war itself, reached southern plantations, slaves began to more boldly resist their owners. They increasingly talked back, and they more frequently ran away. As one mistress of a South Carolina rice plantation put it, as the war dawned, slaves more and more took "license." They "all think this a crisis in their lives that must be taken advantage of. . . . Times and slaves, have changed" because of the election of Lincoln and the coming of war.[11]

In their efforts to wring as much labor and deference as possible from their slaves, slave-owning women like Brevard drew on a large managerial repertoire, including gifts, emotional manipulation, sweet talk, and name-calling. Mistresses bartered material goods for docile behavior. Wrote one slave-owning woman to her daughter: "Your maid has improved so much that I have not had occasion to reprove her for nodding since you left; the promise of that new dress stimulates her to overcome the habit."[12] In addition to the occasional new dress, slave mistresses sometimes gave slaves burial shrouds, blankets, medicine, and provision for weddings—all as inducements to comportment and obedience.[13] Slave-owning women could fit "gift" as a management technique into the ideology of domesticity and paternalism—to "give" a slave a dress or a burial shroud was to fulfill the gendered role of taking care of the dependents in one's household.

But slave mistresses' managerial quivers contained less benevolent arrows as well. "Some we manage by kindness," wrote Keziah Brevard. "Some nothing but the fear of punishment will restrain in the least."[14] Sometimes mistresses controlled their slaves by threatening to sell them or send domestic slaves out to the fields. They managed slaves with dehumanizing condescension, using insults like "blockhead," "vile wretch," "black jip." One mistress called her household slave "nappy-headed bitch," and threatened to kill her for going up the stairs "like a horse."[15]

The threats and the name-calling were underpinned by brute violence. Slave mistresses confidently undertook those punishments, meting them out with frequency and regularity. There has been, since the antebellum era itself and continuing through successive generations of historiography, a widespread assumption that slave-owning women were not violent, or were only incidentally, exceptionally so. But as the historian Thavolia Glymph has decisively shown, that assumption is not consistent with the facts on the ground (which becomes especially obvious when one takes former slaves' testimonies, and not only former mistresses' diaries and nostalgic recollections, as "the ground"). The plantation household was both intimate space and political space, and it was saturated by mistresses' violence.

This violence was not occasional or spontaneous but systematic and integral to the working of the household. Mistresses themselves, cognizant of the gap between that violence and the serene, sanctifying, and benevolent face that southern domesticity and paternalism required them to put on slavery, could turn in a moment from brutality (directed toward a "favorite" slave) to tranquility (directed to, say, a suitor, a parent, or a friend).[16]

"Business negligently done & much altogether neglected, some disobedience, much idleness, sullenness, slovenliness. . . . Used the rod," wrote Alabama slave mistress Lucille McCorkle in her diary.[17] A range of physical gestures underlies the shorthand "used the rod"—and although slave-owning women's accounts of violence are, like McCorkle's, terse, interviews with former slaves give more details about the many actions that constituted slave-owning women's catalog of violence. Ida Henry recalled the afternoon that her mistress judged the potatoes served at dinner underdone. "What you bring these raw potatoes out here for!" she shouted at the cook; then she "grab[bed] a fork and stuck it in her eye and put it out."[18] Harriet Casey, who lived in Missouri, later told a white WPA interviewer:

> Mistress was cruel. Her brother would go down in the orchard and cut de sprouts and pile 'em up under de house so as de mistress could use 'em on us. She also used a bed-stick to whip with. One day we took de cows to pasture and on de way home I stopped to visit Mrs. Walker and she gave me a goose egg. And den when we got home de old mistress kicked me and stomped on us and broke my goose egg. Did'n mind the whipping but sure hated to break my egg.[19]

In recounting this story, Casey astutely managed to get the normalization of violence into the historical record while simultaneously playing with stereotypes both of strong black women and of black women's humor. As a result, the interviewer dutifully recorded the staggering, quotidian violence without feeling as defensive or uncomfortable or tense as he might have felt had Casey not displaced the brutality with the jokey suggestion that what she really minded was the loss of her egg.

Occasional gifts, name-calling, and, underneath that, physical brutality: Those were three of the tools slave-owning women used to manage the slaves in their realm. A fourth and vitally important tool was Christianity. Historians learned from Eugene Genovese four decades ago that Christianity shored up the ideology that made slave plantations work—and, as is made clear by Emilia's testimony that teaching slaves to serve God means "they serve us ... for obedience to their earthly master is one branch of their duty to their heavenly King," slave-owning women understood this long before their historians did. As Elizabeth Foote Washington put it, in a perfect expression of the Christian paternalism that featured on southern farms, "no one could have ... taken more pain than I have to perswaid my servants to do their business through a principal of religion—I have frequently told them that it was my most earnest desire they should do their duty as a servant for their saviors sake—not for mine—have instructed how they were to do it for his sake."[20] Slave owners held the whip firmly in one hand and the Bible in the other: The enslaved woman who could be convinced that she owed her mistress obedience because that obedience was one rung in a ladder of divinely ordained hierarchy was more useful than one who needed always to be monitored with the lash. Numerous historians have analyzed how this understanding of

Christianity's utility was imprinted in the texts of sermons white clergy preached to African-American audiences, and in the religious instruction free white southerners gave to enslaved southerners.[21] Scholars have paid less attention to the ways in which obedience intertwined with prayer on southern plantations—but intertwine it did. From these entanglements it becomes clear that slave owners' Christianity entailed not just an ideology of obedience but also a practice of obedience.[22]

Brevard's diary bristles with evidence that she was concerned—for reasons theological *and* ideological—with the religious disposition and Christian formation of her family's slaves. Brevard regularly prayed that God would kindle affection for God in the hearts of her slaves. "Make *my servants* (those who labor for me) to know thee & love thee is one of my constant prayers," she wrote on October 14, 1860. "May god give my servants true religion," she beseeched two weeks later.[23]

Why did slave mistresses like Brevard desire their slaves to love and know God? To be sure, many devout slave mistresses understood themselves to be moved by concern for the state of their slaves' souls. But this concern, and the specific kind of religious instruction it prompted, arose not from a kindly sense of shared baptismal kinship but rather because of mistresses' deep interest in promoting docility in slave society. When Keziah Brevard prayed that her slaves would know and love God, she did not mean the God who liberated the Israelites from Egypt or the God who, quoting Isaiah, preached release for the captives. She meant a God who ordered a hierarchical world and who would inspire and demand of any slaves who knew and loved him obedience both to him and to their earthly master, Keziah Brevard herself.

In order to shape their slaves' Christian sensibilities, slave mistresses prayed with their slaves and taught them Bible stories.

Although it was illegal to do so, some mistresses taught slaves to read. In teaching slaves about Christianity, mistresses sometimes relied on printed catechisms. Catechizing was a preferred method of instruction, in part because it could be easily adapted to teach people who were "strangers to the art of reading." When working with illiterate charges, the catechist was to repeat the catechism until the text was "imprinted" on the memory. (The same method of repetition and memorization could also be deployed to teach illiterate slaves set prayers—including ones that implored God for the gift of being obedient.)[24] Mistresses could, if they chose, use one of many catechisms produced specifically to teach slaves the basics of (a particularly docile form of) Christian faith. These catechisms included discussions not only of Creation, Christology, and soteriology, but also obedience. ("Will servants have to account to God for the manner in which they serve their masters on earth[?]" Answer: "Yes. Eph 6:8," followed by a lengthy elaboration.)[25]

Women were also encouraged by clergymen and by contemporary prescriptive literature to lead their house slaves in "family worship." Family worship was important because it, along with other forms of religious instruction, would "teach . . . slaves . . . an orderly and decent behavior; reclaim the roughness and fierceness of their nature; form their minds to modesty and mildness, and increase their love and respect to us, in a proportion as they advance in reverence and veneration towards Almighty God."[26]

In other words, this "worship" had as its chief goal not, in fact, worship of God. Its chief goal was to teach those praying about their lot in life. Of course, Christian life offers countless fairly benign illustrations of prayer being used to instruct other people while also (ostensibly or in fact) addressing God. Picture the mother, leading prayer before dinner, who thanks

God for giving her such good, obedient children, children who eat their peas—and then instructing her children to repeat after her: "Thank you, God, for giving me this dinner while so many go hungry; I will gratefully eat every bite." Picture the same mother, ten years later, praying aloud with her teenager before prom, thanking God for giving her a daughter committed to purity, a daughter who would never do anything to tarnish the family name. Or, in a slightly different frame, consider the church prayer chain that eagerly passes along urgent prayer requests: "Sally Jo's marriage is in real trouble—I think Rich is stepping out; we really need to pray for them"; "Mark and Susan's son was arrested last night for drunk driving; we really need to lift that family up in prayer." Might these morsels lead to prayer? Certainly. But they are also means of exchanging information about people, among people; they are gossip, and they arrange power in the way that gossip always does.

Corporate prayer has as its form communicating with God and others. The communication with others is found not only in free-form prayers about Sally Jo's feckless husband but also, perhaps more subtly, in structured liturgy. Prayers for the queen, for example, a commonplace of English Anglican liturgy, communicate to God some wish for the queen's good health. They also serve a socially regulatory function for the gathered body, reminding hearers of their status as subjects. Again, communication with other people is a proper part of prayer (otherwise Christians would not pray corporately) but it entails a characteristic deformation: Spoken, corporate prayer can become principally or exclusively a means of communicating with other people (and it can become a way of glossing gossip with piety) instead of principally a means of communicating with God. The prayers that slave owners attempted to pray with their slaves embodied this deformation: Corporate "family" prayer (that is, prayer in which master or mistress led bondsmen and bondswomen to pray) became principally a means of communicating something from one group of people to another, and (specifically) of reminding the subordinate group of their status.

Many ex-slaves recalled their mistresses teaching them how to pray, and at least one southern catechism was designed specifically for this purpose. Presbyterian pastor and slave owner Benjamin Palmer published *A Plain and Easy Catechism, Designed Chiefly for the Benefit of Coloured Persons, to Which Are Annexed Suitable Prayers and Hymns* in South Carolina in 1828. The tract included, after the catechism itself, a set of prayers that give some indication of the words that slave owners would have urged their slaves to recite, learn, and repeat with frequency. "O enable me to understand the greatness of my privileges, and to feel my obligations," the catechized slave was to pray. Or, in a prayer Palmer adapted from Isaac Watts's invocation for children to use in honoring their parents, slaves were to recite, "I praise thee, that I have a master and mistress to provide food and clothing for me, and everything else that I want. . . . Help me to honor my master and mistress—to be faithful in my performance of duty to them." Slaves preparing "to work in the Field" were to petition God that they might "go forth cheerfully and thankfully to my work and labour until the evening. Let me not be slothful in business, but diligent and industrious in the calling thy Providence has allotted to me. Deliver me from an indolent spirit." Throughout, the prayers explicitly narrate obedience to earthly masters as obedience to God. "Help us to perform the duties of our conditions as servants, faithfully as unto the Lord and not unto men . . . as knowing that the eye of God is upon us."[27] One way that slave owners put prayer to work in domestic management, then, was by teaching slaves prayers that the slaves themselves might be expected to pray. These rote

prayers reminded slaves of their status and gilded that reminder with the authority of Christianity.

Of course, slave owners could not control the prayers of
their slaves. The catechism evidences not enslaved African
Americans' prayer lives but rather the hopes slave owners had
for using prayer to serve the masters' political economy. The
evidence we have of what enslaved men and women actually
said to God suggests that slaves did not regularly pray that God
would infuse their cotton picking with joy. This is not to say that
enslaved people never prayed about social, political, and economic order; they quite often did. They prayed for strength to
endure slavery. Ex-slave Mary Reynolds remembered, "We prays
for the end of Trib'lation and the end of beatin's and for shoes
that fit our feet. We prayed that us Niggers could have all we
wanted to eat and for special fresh meat. Some of the old ones
say we have to bear all 'cause that's all we can do." Slaves prayed
"Set us free"—and, once the War came, "oh Lord, please send
the Yankees on and let them set us free," a prayer that Minnie
Davis recalled her mother praying inwardly, every time she had
to listen to a preacher preaching obedience.[28] Slaves, like slave
owners, saw connections between prayer and power.

Praying their own fierce prayers was one way that slaves resisted the regime of slavery—but there were other, more visible,
acts of resistance. Keziah Brevard's diary is littered with evidence
of that resistance, in particular the defiance of Rosanna and
Sylvia, who were, in Brevard's estimation, constantly insolent.
One page of Brevard's diary offers a very particular kind of
testimony to her slaves' resistance: A paragraph or two of the
text is crossed out and scribbled over. Beneath the defacement,
Brevard wrote, "I went out today & some of my mean little
negroes scribbled over this—sometimes I think Sylvia did it to

make me whip Dorcas."[29] Sylvia or Dorcas or whichever member of Brevard's household actually committed the scriptory offense was doing something bold and risky—both defacing her owner's private property, and briefly silencing her. Brevard believed she was, to a fault, kind to her slaves, which made their perceived insolence all the more galling. She complained about their "impudence" again and again. Impudence was a generic and ubiquitous charge—as Frederick Douglass put it, "one of the commonest and most indefinite in the white catalogue of offenses usually laid to the charge of slaves."[30] It does indeed seem indefinite in slave-owning women's writings, but the etymology, *pudere*, "to be ashamed," helps clarify a salient point. Lodged in the charge is the fault not just of insolence but of being not ashamed; that is, of acting like a human being.

Brevard and other slave owners believed that small acts of slave resistance, if left unpunished, could fester and grow into dangerous rebellion. Like many slave-owning women at the edge of the Civil War, Brevard feared slave uprising, insurrection, or murderous intent. When served coffee that tasted "dreadful," Brevard made her house slave Rosanna taste the coffee, fearing the slaves were trying to poison her. Although Brevard concluded that in this instance, "some of my lazy negroes" had simply gotten salt in her coffee, she noted, "So friends if I should be suddenly taken off after a meal,—remember the coffee."[31] On a Tuesday in March, Brevard was "in the kitchen noticeing the baking of cakes"—not baking them herself, but observing her kitchen slaves at work. "Rosanna struck up about three notes of a hymn—pretended she forgot I was near—*all deception*. I do wish God would punish deception with us at all times as he did with Saphira," Brevard concluded ominously.[32] Even in the context of Brevard's persistent anger with Rosanna and Rosanna's pattern of subtle resistance, this story is striking. First, Brevard has preserved for us some of the soundscape of slave resistance—the snatch of a hymn Rosanna was singing. Was it the fact of singing a *hymn* that Brevard found troubling, or, perhaps more likely, was it simply that Rosanna was making her presence audibly, musically, known, rather than working in silence and submissiveness? Underneath the singing, what appears to have angered Brevard was that, rather than acknowledge Brevard's presence, Rosanna *pretended* that she hadn't realized that Brevard was there, and the pretense showed disrespect. It was this "*deception*" that enraged Brevard—and "enrage" is not an overstatement. Brevard didn't just castigate Rosanna but compared her to the biblical Saphira. Saphira appears in Acts 5. She and her husband have sold a piece of property. They tell an out-and-out lie in order to deceive the church community into thinking that they have given all the proceeds to the church—in fact, they have held some back. Both Saphira and her husband Ananias are struck dead as punishment. In using this story, Brevard was assimilating herself to the church, becoming in her own mind a synecdoche of that righteous body to whom truth and fealty were always owed. She also revealed the intensity of feeling that perceived disrespect could provoke: Brevard wishes that as he struck down Saphira, God would strike dead Rosanna, and rid Brevard forever of Rosanna's three notes of hymn-singing, and her pretense.

For pious slave-owning women, the violence that their household management entailed—the whipping and blinding and "stomp[ing] on"—became inseparable from prayer. After whipping, after poking an enslaved woman's eyes with a fork, mistresses were moved to pray—for a more obedient workforce or for patience or for protection from what they perceived to be the corrupting influence of slavery. "I had little servant Jim whipped for fighting," wrote Susan Nye Hutchinson in her journal on January 3, 1832. "Father of the mercies, guard my heart and keep me from the seductions of evil. Oh how callous are the hearts of this people."[33] This praying for greater emotional self-regulation was not a *response* women had to being angry or violent; it was, rather, the final step of a well-worn choreography of violence and anger.[34]

Brevard's displeasure with Sylvia, Dorcas, and Rosanna's "impudence" regularly prompted her to both negatively assess her own emotional regulation and to pray that God would endow her with a different affective response to her slaves. One morning in September 1860, Brevard lodged in her diary an unspecific complaint about her household slaves: Whether her slaves had been singing in the kitchen or pilfering vegetables, Brevard yet again felt aggrieved. "I have so many little things to unnerve me . . . I wish to be kind to my negroes—but I receive little but impudence from Rosanna & Sylvia," she complained. "It is a truth if I am compelled to speak harshly to them—after bearing every thing from them I get impudence—Oh my God give me fortitude to do what is right to these and then give me firmness to go no farther."[35] What was she praying for, exactly? That she would verbally chastise but not whip Sylvia and Rosanna? That she would punish them with five lashes but not fifty? That we cannot know the answer from Brevard's record is part of the point. Rosanna and Sylvia were almost incidental to her prayer. She was praying instead for herself, that she would possess a set of desirable qualities—fortitude, firmness—that would enable her to act in a manner becoming a devout slave mistress.

On a Thursday in March 1861, another incident provoked Brevard to self-assessment and prayer. Brevard had entertained company all day, and she had presided over what she hoped would be a fine dinner of tongue, chicken pie, asparagus, two kinds of potatoes, rice, and soup, with ice cream for dessert. But the dinner did not turn out as she'd hoped, for "every thing had an odd taste." In this instance, she didn't confide fears of poisoning to her diary, but since this dinner occurred only three months after the coffee episode, one can imagine that Brevard remained dimly suspicious. Instead, she fumed that the meal had been a failure. "My anger rises in spite of all I can do," Brevard confided in her diary. "What is the use of so much property when I can't get one thing cooked fit to eat." But her *noticing* her emotional disregulation was not enough to check her anger. "I am mad when I think how mean my negroes serve me," she declared. "Oh my God help me to bear all of these crosses with more patience & Oh god fit me to leave them & take me to *Heaven*—there is nothing on *this earth* worth staying *one moment for* if we can only get to a better home—Crosses after Crosses is all I realize on earth."[36]

Prayer was put in the service of slavery, then, not only in direct petition for obedient slaves. Prayer was put in the service of slavery because it gave slave-owning women an idiom for navigating the gap between, on the one hand, the violence that was endemic and essential to the plantation household, and, on the other hand, the equable disposition that paternalism and domesticity demanded of women.[37] Slave-owning women hoped to be remade, through prayer, into people who could conduct themselves with patience and forbearance. They wanted to acquire equability and a spirit of moderation. "During the last week my mind has been too anxious about the things of this world. I have suffered my household cares, which are numerous," Lucille McCorkle wrote in her diary. "Have yielded too often to a spirit of fault-finding, a querulous complaining peevish disposition. I am sensible that I am deficient in firmness in stability of judgment in meekness—in patience. O for more spirituality of mind, composure of soul—diligence in everything! ... My heavenly Father, let this day be the beginning of better things." The concern was as much about managing their own emotions as it was about managing slaves. "I feel badly. Got very angry and whipped Lavinia," wrote Eliza Magruder, a plantation mistress in Louisiana. "O! for government over my temper."[38]

One entry from Lucille McCorkle, who wrote in her diary only on the Sabbath, reveals something of the tensions slave-owning women felt between their understanding of playing the role of the appropriate Christian woman, on the one hand, and the fury they felt at their slaves, on the other. Her child "Gamble was very fitful this morning," wrote McCorkle. "I left orders for Lizzy to stay at home with him. But when I returned from S School she was not to be found or heard of—and did not make her appearance till 11 oClock. My feelings were very much roused but I endeavored to defer anger till Monday." Anger, apparently, could be tolerated, but not on the Sabbath—the contradiction between Sabbath piety and anger was too great; the emotion (and its presumed violent consequences) would have to be postponed. McCorkle, of course, prayed for help with this temporary suspension of wrath: "O my Heavenly Parent give me grace, to control my self—and then the authority to control others."[39]

To say that slave-owning women used prayer to manage their emotions is simply to acknowledge, in a slightly roundabout way, that they used prayer to participate in the political economy of the slave South—for the management of emotions was part and parcel of the slave system. As the historian Michael E. Woods has argued in his study *Emotional and Sectional Conflict in the Antebellum United States*, emotional regulation was key to proslavery ideology. Or, rather, not much self-conscious regulation was supposed to happen because slavery itself was meant to regulate people's emotions. Proslavery theorists argued that slaves were happy, and that slavery in fact produced and inspired happiness in both slaves and in their owners. "The relation of master and slave generates the kindly affections by which it was intended to be maintained," wrote an anonymous contributor to the *Southern Review* in 1830. Or, as another author put it in 1857, "The connection of master and slave calls forth some of our noblest affections. Cool judgment, decision of character, self-controul, [and] benevolence" were, it was argued, both the fruit of the slave system and, in turn, part of what made that system function (and function more harmoniously than a free-market system that, the argument went, pitted worker against capitalist in a way that generated ill-will and rage).[40] When slave-owning women felt consumed by anger at their slaves—when slavery produced ire instead of happiness—something had gone wrong in a political, as well as an affective, sphere. Either the women were failing the system, or the system was failing them. When a woman prayed for a more cheerful disposition and for serenity, she was not just seeking a more pleasant interiority. She was also praying for validation of the political economy of slavery.

She was not alone in doing this. Literary theorist Lauren Berlant has analyzed "intimate publics"—that is, "the simultaneously flourishing logics of belonging that have, since the nineteenth century, been largely organized by the nation form insofar as the state, the law, and related institutions of social reproduction are prime generators of affective continuities amongst strangers both directly (in modes of social control) and imaginatively (in terms of their saturation of collective imaginaries of the social)."[41] The heuristic of "intimate publics" allows Berlant to evaluate the ways affect and sentiment are used publicly to arrange power, and the ways "the personal is refracted through the general." A variety of cultural products produces the imaginary of intimacy, which in turn authorizes fantasies of the apolitical while simultaneously forging a potentially (and ambiguously) political community of people brought together through affective ties.[42]

In the prayers of Brevard and other slave-owning women, we see the necessary sibling of the intimate public—we see political intimacy, twice over. First, prayer (an intimate approach to God) has been, as it often inevitably is, politicized—that is, it is used in the arrangement of power (as the Lord's Prayer suggests it should be). Second, as Thavolia Glymph has demonstrated, the very violence that galvanized slave-owning women to periodically salve their consciences was a pointedly *political* violence. This violence was made all the more frequent by the distorted intimacies between slave-owning women and their slaves (and also made too often invisible to historians because we have been captive to a romanticized ideology of the intimate relations between Scarlett and Mammy—an ideology that even a brief acquaintance with the relations between Keziah Brevard and Rosanna ought to unseat).

That Keziah Brevard prayed about her slaves, and about herself *qua* slave owner is, of course, unremarkable. It is unremarkable both because of what we know about prayer and because of what we know about slavery.

It is unremarkable because people everywhere pray about whatever is going on in their lives. If William James has it right—if prayer is the very foundation of religion itself—then prayer is predictably implicated in every aspect of human experience. Since religious people always pray about whatever they are concerned about, slave owners will pray about the slaves they find unmanageable and unruly and ungrateful and full of sloth. In a slave society, prayer will be laced with slavery. It is unremarkable, also, because of the kind of slave society the antebellum South was: a thoroughly Christianized one. In a thoroughly Christianized slave society, not only will prayer be threaded with slavery; slavery will be threaded with prayer. Seen from the vantage point of the historiography of the slave South, McCorkle's and Washington's use of prayer is one more instance of the ways that men and women of the slave-owning class joined religion and paternalism to run plantations.

So is Brevard's prayer a deformation of petition? Does it tell us anything about prayer at all? Maybe it just tells us about slavery, which, in Frederick Douglass's memorable formulation, could change "a saint into a sinner, and an angel into a demon."[43] Brevard's prayers are deformed, to be sure, but perhaps the deformation comes from slavery and is extrinsic to prayer itself. Some slave-owning women recognized the ways that slavery might deform them, the slave owners—they had discerned what Thomas Jefferson had recognized when he wrote in *Notes on the State of Virginia*, "There must doubtless be an unhappy influence on the manners of our people produced by the existence of slavery among us"—and they prayed that they would not be corrupted by the political economy in which they operated.[44] For her part, Keziah Brevard wondered whether slavery was responsible for what she perceived as her religious lassitude: "Lord help me to holy feelings," she prayed. "Make me love *thee* more & more for Oh I mourn this indifference—would I not be better in heart if I had no slaves? This is hard to answer—God has given them to us."[45] Brevard was, in effect, acknowledging that slavery might have deleterious effects on her, and she was praying for palliation.

Indeed, slavery in the American South deformed all manner of Christian gestures, starting with the sacraments. The white Anglicans of St. James Goose Creek parish in colonial

South Carolina once declared to their priest that they would "never . . . come to the Holy Table while slaves are Recd there."[46] The white parishioners of St. David's parish in King William County, Virginia, threatened the life of their priest, Alexander White, after White officiated at a baptism in which the baptizands included both free white children and enslaved black children.[47] Slavery likewise receives part of the credit for deforming slave owners' prayers. But just as, say, the aging body is deformed by pressures both intrinsic and external, so too in the case of petition, corrosion originates from within and from without. To say that "slavery" is responsible for deformations of slave owners' Christianity is to propose a tidy excision that can't possibly be possible. In the American South, there was no slavery without Christianity, any more than there was slavery without tobacco and cotton. Christianity became slavery's grammar; slavery ventriloquized Christianity so fluently that many didn't see the impersonation going on. To propose that "slavery" deformed "Christianity" is to exculpate the latter, to imagine some pure Christianity that existed outside of the very kind of deformations slavery made. In fact, slavery colluded with Christianity to produce this particular deformation—the deformation of commandeering petitionary prayer as if it were a neutral technology, usable in the service of anything.

Prayer, in the church's first approaches to it, meant petition, and there was anxiety about petition from the start. As Simon Tugwell has shown, as early as the third century, some of the fathers seemed "thoroughly embarrassed at the whole idea of asking God for things," and thus began redefining prayer in broad, even vague ways. For example, they used the expression "*homolia* with God" (which, Tugwell notes with a bit of barb, is "nicely ambiguous, as *homolia* can mean either 'talking' or

'communing' "). Only unvirtuous people, said Clement of Alexandria, pray to obtain what they don't have; this kind of
praying, said Clement, is probably a bad idea, because unvirtuous people are likely to ask for the wrong things.[48] And here we
can begin to draw a dotted line, from Clement of Alexandria
to Keziah Brevard.

Is it the content of Keziah Brevard's prayers—prayers that
God would kill her slaves as God killed Saphira—that makes
her prayers deformed? (And if so, is Brevard simply a variation
on George Lindbeck's crusader, crying "Christ is Lord" in a
circumstance—as part of a pattern, to use Lindbeck's preferred
trope—that turns a true statement into a lie?) Or is there something more exacting we can say about the way petitionary prayer
per se has gone awry? In one sense, of course, if praying for
something wrong or incoherent constitutes a deformation of
petition, then such deformation is to be expected, so much so
that it almost doesn't warrant exploration. Sin is misdirected
desire;[49] in petition, we pray for that which we desire; we and
our prayers are flavored with sin; thus sometimes we will pray
words that precisely do not draw us into the love of the Trinity
but harden our distance from it. This has long been a worry for
Christians' theorizing about petitionary prayer: the sure knowledge that if we get in the habit of asking, we are certain to ask
for the wrong things.

Petition is direct address of God by a creature, making a request
that entails something beyond "thy will be done." Philosophers
and theologians have relentlessly pursued a cluster of questions
about petitionary prayer: Does it act upon God? If not, is it in
vain? If God grants things in response to—or actually because
of—petition, would those things not have occurred without
the petition? These are questions about the mechanics of prayer

and about the freedom of God, and they are one way of getting at a description of petitionary prayer.

The early Aquinas, who worried about people praying for anything specific, hazarded a claim that would become familiar in such discussions: The main reason to pray for something is the impact the prayer has on the person praying. In his commentary on the Sentences, Aquinas says, in essence, that we pray for something in order to concentrate our own attention around it.[50] Prayer thus may be, in some instances, performative even if it doesn't act in any way on God. Dissecting (or predicting) the exact performative work prayer can do is close to impossible. Perhaps Keziah Brevard made herself a more patient slave owner by writing down an inventory of petitions about her own patience. Or perhaps her habit of taking her vicious emotions to God made her more at ease with her anger and her violence. Or perhaps both—to claim that her prayers might have made her occasionally more patient is not in tension with acknowledging that they also made her more easily a player on the stage of antebellum slavery.

Petition, in its ideal form, is a recognition of the self as the self really is—a creature, dependent on the Creator. There is, then, an intimate danger to petition: I am placing my desires before God, and in so doing I am rightly recognizing (some of) the limits of my own capacities. Yet precisely in the moment of that recognition I am asserting my will, calcifying it, reifying it. Petition initiates a tacit shaping of the self—I am always articulating the thing I desire or think I should desire. And sometimes there is an explicit self-fashioning: Lord, make me this, make me that; make me patient, make me disciplined, make me masterful.

In the topography of Christian prayer, petition may be the space where the self of the person praying is most overt. Thus petition offers the possibility of intimacy: Something close to my real self (or at least, what I perceive my real self to be) is now revealed before God. Of course, God already knows my real self, better than I will ever know it. The intimacy that follows my petitions is made possible not by God's new knowledge of me but by my new availability to God. Consider a mundane analogy: My best friend finally tells me about the infatuation she has been nursing for two months. Of course, I spotted the infatuation myself seven weeks before. Still, our friendship deepens, not because I have learned something new, but because in being willing to tell me about the crush, my friend has become more available to me. Similarly, even though God is the one "unto whom all . . . desires [are] known, and from whom no secrets are hid"[51]—that is, even though God already knew that I wanted whatever it is I am asking for—I become more available to God when I offer what I understand of myself before God. The promise of petition, therefore, is increased closeness, a deeper friendship, with God.

Indeed, friendship is petition's deepest good.[52] Aquinas in the *Summa* defends the rationality (and necessity) of petition by arguing that petitionary prayer does not move God to give us things that God wouldn't have otherwise wished to give us; rather, in response to our petitions, God grants us things-that-God-wishes-to-grant-us-in-response-to-our-prayer. Does this really make sense, interpreters ask of Aquinas? Is it not a rather circuitous way for God to accomplish God's purposes? It is circuitous only if the purpose is the granting of the thing I ask for, which God then grants. It is not circuitous, however, if the real intent is friendship. If, that is, God wants to reserve some things for granting only in response to prayer because God created me to be God's friend, and if my placing my desires before God is an effective way for God and me to grow in friendship— then the logic is not circuitous but direct.

What people get out of petitionary prayer, then, is not primarily the thing we think we are seeking. We might get that, as a second-order matter, but the first thing we receive is friendship. Friendship is a good that can come from petition, precisely because God has drawn us into conversation with God about our desires, and when we state our desires, we are offering intimacy with our desiring and vulnerable selves.[53] At the same time, petitionary prayer is characteristically deformed by the petitioner's failure to ask, "Is the direct object of my prayer—is the thing I desire—something I should want?" Such prayer is an intimate exchange, and it is when engaged in intimate exchange that we will forget (if we ever knew how) to wonder if a constitutive part of the exchange is good for us. This forgetting, or inability, to ask is characteristic.[54] It is the intimacy, specificity, and particularity of petitionary prayer that makes it easy to excise from petition the question, "Is this the kind of thing I should want, and should therefore be asking God for?"

Brevard's case highlights the inability of people to assess, or even consider, whether the object of their pursuit is the kind of thing they should be pursuing. Yet petitioning God for particulars isn't in itself wrong. Petition is arguably the most powerful means for us to gain intimacy with God. This is precisely the knot of petition and its friendship. One might say: Our prayers would be safe, protected from at least one sort of deformation, if we would refrain from asking God to give us the specific objects of our desire. We could pray only the last clause of Gethsemane and the third clause of the Lord's Prayer; we could pray only "thy will be done," and never hazard the presumption that our own desires are things the Lord might grant or endorse. But we cannot have the friendship that petition makes possible if we do not name our desires.

Disordered prayer can be part of our practicing what Lauren Berlant has called "cruel optimism." Optimism, in Berlant's glossary, is "the force that moves you out of yourself and into the world in order to bring closer the satisfying *something* that you cannot generate on your own but sense in the wake of a person, a way of life, an object, project, concept or scene." Cruel optimism is the state that obtains when "something you desire is actually an obstacle to your flourishing"; it is "the condition of maintaining an attachment to a significantly problematic object." There is a certain obsessive quality to cruel optimism—when in its grip, you return to the object of your desire over and over, because "the affective structure of an optimistic attachment involves a sustaining inclination to return to the scene of fantasy that enables you to expect that this time, nearness to this thing will help you or a world to become different in just the right way."[55] For the Christian, prayer can underwrite this obsessive return—prayer can be the wagon with which one keeps circling around a misbegotten object of desire.

Were optimism not deformed by cruelty—were optimism purely "the force that moves you out of yourself . . . in order to bring closer the satisfying *something* that you cannot generate on your own"—then the Christian would identify that optimism as God: God is the one who beckons, and God is the one whom "you cannot generate on your own but sense." The pursuit you undertake after being moved out of yourself by God, a Christian might say, is prayer in its pure form—the person praying is moved by God toward God. But our prayers go wrong, and we instead pray for "significantly problematic object[s]." That we are praying for these objects, rather than just talking about them with our wife or therapist, suggests that near our misdirected desire is or was some pull toward God—but now we pray as though our magnetic north has gotten yanked ten degrees to the east; we now pray pointed toward "obstacles to [our] flourishing" (and often to others' flourishing, too)—in Keziah Brevard's case, toward the obedience of human beings who properly owed her none.

Keziah Brevard's diary is disturbing to read. I have been reading antebellum slave-owning women's diaries for more than twenty years, and still I find being in the company of Brevard's mind unsettling. I feel shocked every time I read her caustic scathing; her desperate desire to send her slaves, and the abolitionists, off to some other country; her piety and her prayer.

One thing that shocks me is how deeply lodged in my brain a phrase from her diary has become: "Crosses after Crosses is all I realize on earth," she wrote on March 28, 1861. There is something unintentionally lacerating in her writing—and believing—that all her life yields to her is "Crosses," suffering. But the words are nonetheless beautiful; the repetition and the rhythm and the lack of subject-verb agreement make them so.

Part of what is disturbing, then, about Keziah Brevard's diary is this: Even she can be gifted by God with beautiful language that is, in its way, theologically profound.

The prayers slave-owning women prayed for patience and restraint may show forth something else about prayer—about Christian practice as a whole, and about how we talk about it. Their prayers resist a binary: We cannot say that the women's prayers are compromised without remainder just because they were part of slave society. Nor can we say that their prayers were fine merely because they aimed in part to reduce violence. By itself, to pray for less violence is a good thing. But this petition for decreased violence, less anger, and greater self-control is in fact a prayer that asks God to make the emotional logics of slavery work as the proslavery ideologues believed they should work, and the prayer thus fixes the petitioner more firmly into an evil system. Here, as so often in our blighted world, the reduction of one evil (say, the reduction of Lucille McCorkle's anger and violence on a single Sunday afternoon) is inextricably linked to the deepening of another. Brevard's prayers are a reminder that we cannot abstract a way of doing something from the ends it serves.

Keziah Brevard's entry for Tuesday, January 22, 1861, again opens with the weather: It had been "unpleasant" out for days, but now, at 2 o'clock in the afternoon, it was "as cold & disagreeable [a] day as any": cloudy, and the "wind is like ice." Brevard had spent the morning supervising the making of cakes for her fifty-five-year-old neighbor, Mrs. Wilson: "one large cake, lb. cake, though it had 1½ lb. of flour, butter, sugar each—eggs &c. &c.—One lb. of sponge cake, rather a large sponge cake, very near as large as the lb. cake." After describing the cakes, Brevard's attention turned back to Mrs. Wilson herself: "I only hope she may be as happy as she anticipates being—about one week from this her eyes will be opened to the reality of her folly." In other words, those cakes were for a wedding, and Brevard, whose own marriage had been unhappy and who enjoyed her widowhood, thought it foolish for her neighbor to remarry—whether because the man in question was a cad, or simply because remarriage meant giving up the rights to her property, she did not say.[56]

After this ode about marriage and cakes, Brevard turned to prayer, beginning with a lengthy prayer for her sister. Brevard had received a worrying note from her and had been tormented about it. Only in a later entry does Brevard go into enough detail to allow us to infer that the note had informed her that her nephew, her sister's son, was joining the Confederate Army.

Brevard petitioned God to remember and comfort her sister, in response to Brevard's petitions and for Brevard's sake if not for her sister's own. (There is an implication here that Brevard's sister was not the most pious member of the family: "Feel for her, if she has neglected her duty to thee, forgive her for Jesus' sake.")

A few hours elapsed, and Brevard picked up her diary again "at night": "I have seen a little of negro deception to night." Who can say what specific act of "deception" occasioned this entry? A theft? An illicit gathering in the moonlit cold? A lie appears to have been involved, but perhaps "lie" is shorthand for any kind of deception. Brevard continued:

> I wish the Abolitionists & the negroes had a country to themselves & we who are desirous to practice *truth & love to God were to ourselves*—yes, Lord Jesus—separate us in the world to come, let us not be together—it is encouraging to hope liars shall have no part in thee—let the goats be far removed from the sheep—Oh I am sorry when I find out any mean trickery in my servants—our lot is hard to be mixed up with such. Lord forgive me if I judge wrong.[57]

Brevard frequently prayed for her own death, asking that God spare her from the coming troubles by bringing her forthwith. "Take me to thee," she often prayed. But this is one of the few prayers in which she sketches a vision of her slaves' afterlife. Brevard begins by envisioning her slaves in the "world to come"—a heaven that will be segregated not racially but politically, with abolitionists and slaves in some other corner, far off from Brevard and her friends (her sister, her nephew,

Mrs. Wilson). Brevard has transposed her oft-articulated fantasies of colonization—that "Abolitionists and the negroes" would, in the here and now, have a country to themselves—onto the world to come. But quickly, with echoes of Matthew 25 and John 8, Brevard moves from a segregated heaven to a full-fledged eschatological segregation in which liars and deceivers "have no part" in Jesus. In other words, Brevard, who so regularly intones that she wishes her slaves had a deep Christian faith, moves from inscribing into heaven categories and divisions that are part of a fractured social order to bluntly damning her slaves.[58]

That our prayers go disastrously off course is not surprising. St. Paul tells us clearly that "we do not know how to pray" (Romans 8:26). At the same time, of course, we do know how to pray: the disciples asked Jesus how to do it, and he said, "When you pray, pray like this," and offered the Lord's Prayer. This doesn't mean that we are simply to repeat the Lord's Prayer over and over again. But it may suggest that the Lord's Prayer ought to be a model for all of Christian petition. As John Cassian put it in the twenty-fourth chapter of *The Conferences*, "We ought not to ask for other things, except only those which are contained in the limits of the Lord's Prayer."[59] We do not always pray the exact words Jesus gave us, but we follow the pattern of the prayer he gave. One question, then, we should bring to our petitions is "Can they be accommodated under the Lord's Prayer?" Of course, along the lines of the characteristic deformation already sketched, this is often almost impossible for the person praying to answer—the person praying will be too close to see; the person praying will have forgotten the opacity of her own desires. But from a distance we can see how a prayer sometimes cannot be held by the Lord's Prayer. (Historical distance, of course, is only one kind of distance. The distance of a skilled spiritual director is another.) Even with the caveat that the biases of the present age will sometimes yield assessments of past prayers that are simultaneously illuminating and distorting, it seems safe to hazard that Keziah Brevard's damnation of her slaves cannot be accommodated to the Lord's Prayer, which includes the petition "forgive me my trespasses as I forgive those who trespass against me." That petition makes it impossible for the person praying to elevate herself above other people, and it makes it impossible to carry unforgiveness with us into eternity—which, by damning her slaves, is exactly what Brevard was doing.

Four days later, on January 26, Keziah Brevard wrote another long prayer. She began with a perfectly sound phrase, which comports with the Lord's Prayer (and to Gethsemane, for that matter): "Help me to do thy will," she begins. Then there is an acknowledgment of blessing: "I am blest in worldly things." Still, Brevard notes that she is "often fretted by these *very things*" that bless her. Having acknowledged that she misperceives her blessing, feeling "fretted" rather than grateful or detached, she petitions God for the gift of reordered desire: that she may become unattached to her earthly things and focus on God alone: "Have mercy on me & teach me to love thee so I may count all things here as dust."[60] Brevard therefore begins with something close to the Lord's Prayer, with petitions that are not in themselves problematic. And even though we can rightly question her myopia at bemoaning her own sense of being burdened and fretted by slaves whose own, far deeper, burdens she never seemed to consider, we can recognize here that her pen initially seemed to form the right "thy will be done" words.

But after Brevard's expressed yearning to count all earthly things as dust, the prayer turns from the contours of the Lord's Prayer to an appeal patently deformed by her own desires:

> I have some good negroes & I wish them well—I
> pray God will place them in good places when I am
> taken from them—I have others who seem to dis-
> like me & never care to look at me—such I hope
> may one day know they were well to be under my
> care.... Negroes are strange creatures—I cannot
> tell whether they have any good feelings for their
> owners or not—sometimes I think they have—
> then I think there is nothing but deception in
> them—I am heartily tired of managing them....
> Lord help me to have patience while on earth.[61]

As soon as Brevard approaches the specificity of her own desire, she departs from the frame of the Lord's Prayer and, far from practicing detachment from her earthly concerns, slips into an extended grievance about those concerns. She holds forth a litany of complaints about her slaves, their perceived deception, and her own exhaustion from trying to manage them. Instead of becoming alive to the ways she is trespassing against her slaves, she focuses solely on the everyday strains entailed by stealing people's labor from them. And then Brevard ends her prayer with another petition for "patience," another prayer that God might reorder her emotions and make them more in line with what proslavery ideology tells her they should be.

Let's return to the anthologies of prayers on my bookshelf—imagining, now, a more complicated, more comprehensive anthology of Christian prayers that includes not just Teresa of Ávila and William Wilberforce but also the prayers of Keziah Brevard and Lucille McCorkle. How would the introduction to that anthology read? It would, I think, explicitly acknowledge that we do not know how to pray, and that we need an anthology not to show us only exemplary prayers (Jesus has already given us one, after all). Rather, we need an anthology to show us that since prayer is part of the human effort to connect our lives—which are shot through with all kinds of blight and blindness—to the divine, our prayers will be inevitably blighted, too.

Anthologies of prayers are generally intended for repetition. It is assumed that a person opens such an anthology and then borrows one of the prayers, praying it and making it her own. This anthology would have a different purpose: It would include not only prayers to be respoken but also prayers to diagnose our crookedness and chasten us for it. Where are my prayers—heartfelt as they are; making a moral sense inside my worldview and political economy as they do—thus deformed? And in the face of evidence about our capacity to wrongly pray, how shall we pray? To quote Keziah Brevard, "This is hard to answer." Even silent prayer, contemplative prayer, would not be exempt from the analysis offered here.

Perhaps confession—which, among other things, is diagnostic—should be the frame of all prayer. Confession can show us the characteristic problem of petitionary prayer: our tendency, when petitioning, to forget that we're likely wrong about what we're asking for. If confession should frame all petition, then perhaps the extent to which petitions aren't so framed, or to which the confession is cursory or flat, is the extent to which deformation will be pronounced.

But confession is hardly immune from deformation. Consider, once more, Keziah Brevard's diary. Intertwined with her complaints and her prayers for patience are prayers for forgiveness. To my eye, these pleas seem half-hearted and sometimes tacked on. They lack the rhetorical intensity of the statements she is repenting for. For example, on January 30, 1861,

Brevard introduces a narrative innovation into her diary by directly addressing the oft-criticized, "impudent" Sylvia:

> Sylvia, if slavery continues I hope no relative I have will keep you about them—nothing on this earth can change your heart—it is a *bad one*—The truth is, Sylvia *hates* a white face—I firmly believe this from the conduct of her whole life. Lord, if I judge wrong, forgive me.[62]

The vehemence and creativity of Brevard's animosity toward Sylvia is unmatched in intensity by her brief, formulaic, and conditional request for forgiveness (indeed, it is, almost verbatim, the same conclusion she used after prayerfully shipping off all African Americans and abolitionists to eternal damnation). On another occasion, Brevard lambastes Dolly, who thinks herself superior to white people, is "proud & ignorant" and "never would go to church unless as fine & fashionable as possible. Now she sits & does nothing too contrary almost to live." Warning that "the Lord punished those who are not thankful for their mercies," Brevard judges Dolly "very unthankful." The next breath is another conditional request for forgiveness: "Lord forgive me if I judge my poor negroes wrong." And then we are off again to castigation of her slaves and her own unchecked self-regard: "I know I treat *them* far better than they treat me—I am attached to those who do well—but they care nothing for me—*self is all.*"[63]

Most formal prayers of confession bewail the penitent's unworthiness, and petition for forgiveness—which, of course, the Lord grants. Some confessions even ask "thy will not mine be done." But the instances of Keziah Brevard and Lucille Mc-Corkle (not to mention the instance of myself, were I as willing to look as directly at my own prayers as I am at theirs) suggest the need of a confession that goes further. The confession my Book of Common Prayer guides me through should perhaps be supplemented by explicit lament for the fact that one's very desires (for patience, for self-control, for docile slaves) are unreliable, flawed, misapprehended. Part of what we ought to bewail in confession is our inability to discern what is good for us; part of what we ought to bewail is the state of affairs whereby what we think we want is often inflected with opposition to what God wants for us.

Baptism

In 1900, a particular christening party caused a great deal of problems. It was the christening party of a princess, one princess Melisande, and it was, in fact, a christening party that wasn't. Melisande's mother, the queen, "wished to have a christening party, but the King put his foot down and said he would not have it. 'I've seen too much trouble come of christening parties,' said he. 'How ever carefully you keep your visiting book, some fairy or other is sure to get left out, and you know what that leads to.'"

"Perhaps you're right," said the queen. "My own cousin by marriage forgot some stuffy old fairy or other when she was sending out the cards for her daughter's christening, and the old wretch turned up at the last moment, and the girl drops toads out of her mouth to this day."

"Just so. And then there was that business of the mouse and the kitchen-maids," said the king; "we'll have no nonsense about it. I'll be her godfather, and you shall be her godmother; and we won't ask a single fairy; then none of them can be offended."

"Unless they all are," said the queen. They all were.

All manner of tribulation followed from the king and queen's decision. Seven hundred fairies heard there was going to be a baptism to which they weren't invited. One fairy, Malevola, was especially piqued. "Don't begin to make excuses," she said, shaking her finger at the queen. "That only makes your conduct worse. You know well enough what happens if a fairy is left out of a christening party. We are all going to give our christening presents now. As the fairy of highest social position, I shall begin. The Princess shall be bald."[1]

Of course, it all turned out well in the end. But for our purposes what matters is: There was—or, more to the point, wasn't—a christening party. When the English Socialist and children's writer E. (Edith) Nesbit (she published some of her adult novels under the unsubtle *nom de plume* Fabian Bland) wanted to make a point about inclusion and exclusion, the christening party seemed to her the natural vehicle. Christian baptism has always done its work in the space between the exclusion of every guest but Jesus, and the inclusion of everybody by Jesus. These are its two characteristic deformations.

Our considerations of Eucharist and prayer contained explicit violence. There is a directness to the deformation of a Eucharist put to the service of murdering Jews or prayer put to the service of managing slaves. That kind of explicit violence has, to be sure, sometimes attended Christian baptism: most obviously, the history of forcing Jews and other non-Christians to be baptized.[2]

But—in part to suggest that deformations can be less blunt, more subtle, but no less characteristic—in this chapter we shall read late-nineteenth- and early-twentieth-century domestic christening parties, pointing to a deformation that is more understated than murder but nonetheless thoroughgoing.

The central claim is this: Baptism is the incorporation of a person into the body of Christ.[3] This incorporation requires baptizands to be *extracted* from their particularities (such as social location, language, history, and family; we can call the baptizand's particularities her *local*). At the same time, baptism superinscribes, rather than erases, particularities, and superinscribes them in a way that they are still legible. This superinscribing-while-retaining-legibility is characteristic of baptism; it is characteristic of all sacraments, and perhaps of all Christian practices: All sacraments feature particularity (the particularity of person, of material object, sometimes of place), and all feature a taking up into the Triune God. You have the granularity of here and now, and you have Jesus. The latter (God) doesn't erase the former (the particular, the local). That these two realities must be held in tension with each other is especially clear in baptism—because of the explicitness of the rite's extraction language and the unavoidability of the local (the baptizand in all her particularities, and her relatives and friends or their absence, are inescapably right there). One way baptism characteristically goes wrong is in its failure to express both—the failure to extract the baptized person from the local, while also affirming the local.

Baptism can easily deform in one direction or the other: It can erase wholly the particular; or it can evacuate the ecclesial into the local. In American history, the second iteration of this characteristic damage has been more common—specifically, the history of (infant) baptism in America is inflected with the evacuation of the ecclesial into the familial.[4] That deformation, on which I focus in this chapter, is, to be sure, less dramatic and ghastly than the murder of Jews or the managing of slaves. It is also, for many twenty-first-century Christians, closer to home. It is thus both less unsettling (because less ghastly), and more unsettling (because more immediately indicting). I will focus principally on one example of this deformation, one instance of baptism's failure to hold the affirmation of the local in judicious tension with the extraction of the baptizand from it: christening parties that became fashionable in fin de siècle America. In these parties, I read an instance of the local (specifically, the familial) wholly swamping the ecclesial (and even the divine). But before turning to the nineteenth-century christening party craze, I will argue that one can find, in the history of Christian worship, liturgies that both affirm the familial and extract the baptizand from it; and that the New Testament itself authorizes, encourages, and performs the simultaneous affirmation and extraction that baptism is meant to perform, too.

The history of baptism is an enormously complex topic, comprehending adult baptism and infant baptism, doctrine and practice, clergy and laypeople. In the midst of all that complexity, I will hazard one generalization: Normatively, in baptism, a baptizand's particularities (her locals) are taken up—affirmed, transfigured, superinscribed so as to remain legible; and the history of baptism shows that there has been much negotiation between the impulse to *emphasize extraction from the local,* on the one hand, and to *affirm the local* on the other hand.

The *locus classicus* for the claim that various locals are superinscribed in a way that preserves their legibility is Galatians 3. There, Paul names baptism as the ritual that clothes baptizands in Jesus. Then Paul states that Christ is clothing that utterly changes three locals: ethnos (Jew/Greek), legal ownership of one's own person (slave/free), and sex difference (male/female). Something dramatic and transformative happens to these three local identities in baptism. They are, in some sense, made to go away. But—as is evident from, for example, Paul's obsession with the relationship between Jews and Gentiles—Paul does not mean that these categories no longer exist. The Pauline corpus—with its persistent interest in how Jews and Gentiles relate to each other, with its discussions of marriage that suggest clearly that Paul thinks that "men" and "women" are marrying each other, with its request of Philemon—does not make sense if Galatians 3 means that the categories of Jew/Greek, slave/free, and male/female evaporate. Twenty-first-century readers may draw on all manner of resources, from brain science to queer theory, to push Galatians 3:28 further, but within the Pauline corpus, it seems that baptism changes rather than erases, for example, maleness and femaleness. Indeed, we see in Galatians 3 exactly the theme of this whole chapter—that there is, in baptism, a superinscription of the baptizand's particularities, but there is not erasure of them.

Here, instead of focusing on the three particularities named in Galatians 3, I will focus on the particularity of *family* or *lineage*. Just as other particularities are superinscribed but left legible in baptism, so too we can say the baptizand is extracted from family at the same time that her lineage or family is affirmed, transfigured, and superinscribed so as to remain legible.[5]

It is a regular feature of baptism to negotiate the baptizand's family: to address, through ritual performance, the status and significance of the baptized person's earthly family, and the relation of the baptized person to that family now that she has been adopted into the Christian *familia*. The particularity of being a member of a particular family is of special import—especially necessary, and thus especially vexed and vexing—when considering *infant* baptism, and we shall turn to infant baptism presently. But even the baptisms of adults often must take account of the baptizand's family. This is usefully illustrated by the famous two-part tale of Augustine's baptism. As recounted in book I of *The Confessions,* Augustine was almost baptized when he was young (and ill). His account shows that this near-baptism was inseparable from his identity as the child of two particular people—the mother who arranged for his baptism (and presumably forbade it after he recovered), and the father who, though not a Christian, did not interfere in Monica's raising Augustine as a Christian. At the same time, his account makes clear that Christianity makes claims on familial identity—Monica is Augustine's "physical mother," whereas the church is "mother of us all," and Monica "labored to convince me that you, my God"—and not his (physical) father Patricius—"were my father."[6]

So too Augustine's eventual baptism as an adult was a family affair—in that instance, Augustine was not child, but parent; he was baptized alongside his son, who was then "about fifteen years old." Augustine's account of his baptism in book IX of *Confessions* simultaneously affirms the perduring familial bond between Augustine and Adeodatus while securing the primary bond between Adeodatus and God—a bond Augustine is so concerned about precisely because he is the boy's father. Adeodatus was "my natural son begotten of my sin," but "You had made him a fine person" ("well had Thou made him," in the lovely if antiquated Pilkington translation). In Augustine's estimation, Augustine "had contributed nothing to that boy but sin," and Adeodatus's many staggering gifts (which were the same gifts his father possessed, including intelligence) came from God: "Who but You could be the maker of such wonders?" Augustine's son is thus extracted from his local context while yet being sponsored in his baptism by his father.[7]

Augustine's baptism illustrates that family features significantly even in the baptism of adults. But the centrality of the family is more overt in infant baptism. It is a matter of common sense, as well as of the historical record, that infant baptism cannot, in fact, wholly override the baptizand's family. Until such time as the church sends baptized children to a kibbutz to be communally raised, it is the family of the baptizand that is assumed to provide the child's Christian formation.[8] Precisely because of the infant's ongoing dependence on the family, the ritual performance of extracting the child from the family—of, for example, naming the child as the child of God the Father; of the liturgist's physically taking the infant from the parents, symbolically indicating that the church can do something for this child that his parents cannot—is particularly pointed.[9] Infant baptism throws into high relief the balancing act of baptism vis-à-vis the family: Baptism must extract from and affirm the thing from which is being extracted, all at once.

Throughout the history of the church, baptism has ritually staged the baptizand's incorporation into the family of the church. This incorporation is evident in the basic grammar of baptism: referring to even adult baptizands as children; speaking of God as Father and the church as Mother; speaking, as the fifth-century bishop Proclus did, of the "baptismal font [having] many children," and of the "painless birth pangs of the baptismal font."[10] In some early churches, baptismal Eucharists featured, alongside wine and bread, milk, which further cast the newly baptized person as an infant, feeding on the nourishment of Mother Church.[11] Baptism's power to incorporate the baptized into a new family is also suggested by the shape of baptismal fonts—as Robin Jensen has argued, in the fourth and fifth centuries, some were shaped like a womb:

> One very well preserved font [in the ancient North African city of Sufetula] appears to have been

designed to symbolize the Church's maternal organs
... concretely.... Found in the centre of a small room
attached to the eastern apse of the main hall of what
must have been the Catholic cathedral, the elongated
and undulating shape of the font looks much like a
woman's vulva. Candidates would enter from one direction (presumably the west) and stand in the well of
the font to be baptized. Emerging, then, from the
Mother Church's vagina, they would climb out on the
opposite side (the east), and present themselves, wet
and naked, as new-born babies, ready to join their
new siblings and perhaps to receive a symbolic swal-
low of sweetened milk along with wine and bread at
the altar rail.[12]

The parental language, the undulant font, the milk—all of this
ritually secured the baptizand's identity as a newly born member of the family of the church.

But in attaching the baptizand to her new family, baptism
does not erase all foregoing lineage. For every baptismal font
that recalled the reproductive organs of Mother Church, there
is a font that depicts the Holy Family[13] (signaling the perdurance of biological family even as a baptizand is pulled into the
family of the church that the Holy Family makes possible)—or
a font that features the coat of arms of locally prominent
families (as in a font at Santa Maria Novella in Florence, which
is decorated with the coat of arms of the Rucellai family).[14]
Baptismal words as well as objects remain attentive to lineage.
The initiation rite in the Bobbio Missal (circa 700), for example,
includes an explanation of each of the four Gospels. This explanation opens with the deacon proclaiming, about the Gospel of Matthew, "The book of the generation of Jesus Christ the

son of David, the son of Abraham: Abraham begat Isaac, and Isaac begat Jacob, and Jacob begat Judah and his brothers: now the birth of Jesus Christ took place in this way." (This affirmation of lineage appears shortly before the liturgy performs the extractive move of calling on God to "send forth the spirit of adoption.")[15] The Irish Stowe Missal (circa 800) ritually extracts the baptizand through language of regeneration and rebirth: The liturgist beseeches God to allow the baptized to "come forth from the unspotted womb of the divine font a heavenly offspring, reborn unto a new creature," and he asks that "grace may be a mother to people of every age and sex, who are brought forth into a common infancy."[16] This strong language of the baptizand's finding her regenerated identity as a child born of an ecclesial womb to a gracious mother follows shortly after the officiant's prayer that "in the homes of the faithful whatever may be aspersed with this water may be cleaned and freed from stain."[17] People's homes are affirmed and sanctified even as people are identified not as members of those homes but as members of the family of God and of grace.

Ritual gesture also stages extraction from and affirmation of family. In the Syriac-Maronite rite, for example, the ceremony begins in the vestibule of the church. There the mother stands holding the infant. The priest blesses the infant and then takes him from the mother, carries him through the church and into the sanctuary, and places him either on the altar or on the top step of the altar. While this is happening, a text recounting Mary's presentation of Christ in the Temple is sung or said ("Every child belongs to the Lord"). The baptismal liturgy proper (censing, sedro, trisagion, exorcism, anointing, dousing or immersion, chrismation) follows. The opening ritual choreography dramatically stages the removal of the child from his family (and some of the verbal prayer, such as the sedro's description of God as one who "called us to become spiritual children through Baptism," reiterates the theme). But the very first ritual gesture after the liturgy's concluding prayer underscores the perdurance of the family whence the child has just been (ritually) removed: The baptismal party processes around the church, with the celebrant first, and then "the godparents, the parents, members of the family, et al."[18] It is, really, no surprise that a liturgy that begins with a chant about Mary's making the *pidyon haben* in Luke 2 ends with a reinstantiation of the family: After all, Mary was not engaging in child oblation; she offered her turtle doves, then took Jesus home with her.[19]

Reformation-era Protestant liturgies tend even more than earlier Christian liturgies to stress ongoing familial bonds.[20] This stress was part of the broadly Lutheran project to make every family into a small church and every household into a small school of discipleship.[21] Protestant liturgies thus sometimes included a quartet of new vows in which the parents promised to raise their children in the faith,[22] and Protestant liturgies included robust and explicit enjoinments from pastor to parents about their important role in the child's formation— as in this instruction, found early in the Scottish Kirk's liturgy for baptism: "Ye that be fathers and mothers must take hereby singular comfort to see your children thus received into ... Christ's congregation, whereby ye are daily admonished" to bring the children up in the fear and knowledge of the Lord. After this exhortation, the baptizand's father recited a lengthy statement about his commitment to raise the child in the church.[23]

And one final example of liturgy's both unseating and underlining family: godparentage. The participation of godparents in baptism also bespeaks the both/and of extraction

and affirmation. We see this in the history of churches allowing
or forbidding parents to serve as godparents for their own
children. In the early church, when infants were baptized, it was
the norm for a parent to serve as godparent/sponsor. But that
had begun to change by the sixth century, and by the ninth it
was forbidden for parents to serve as godparents for their
children.[24] (This changed centuries later in Protestant churches, and there the change came in fits and starts.)[25] For at
least half of church history, then, and still today for the Catholic and Orthodox churches, someone other than a parent speaks
for the child at baptism. The pointed refusal to permit parents
to serve as godparents seems to suggest that baptism deliber-
ately and directly extracts children from their families—after
all, parents had no liturgical role; in many instances, the
mother, still lying in, was not even present at the baptism:
extraction.

However, in most cases, the delegation of the intimate
task of baptismal sponsorship to someone other than a parent
doesn't sever but serves family ties. One of the reasons that
around the sixth century parents began to decline to stand as
sponsors/godparents for their own children was precisely that
they perceived that both they and their children could benefit
from securing a close tie with someone else.[26] Sometimes, the
advantage lay in the shoring up of extended family ties, as when
an aunt, uncle, or grandparent served as godparent.[27] And when
the family looked beyond its ranks for godparents, this was
hardly in the interest of *eroding* the family unit or the baptizand's place in it—quite the opposite. Nonparental godparentage gave advantages to the baptizand and, indeed, to the entire
family. As David Cressy explains in his study of Stuart England,
"In practice the spiritual aspects of godparentage were easily
submerged beneath social and secular considerations. Many

families treated godparentage as a matter of social respect and esteem, rather than as surety for renunciation of the devil. To stand at the font was as much an honour to the parents as a favour to the child. . . . Parents were sometimes willing to delay the ceremony of baptism, risking censure before ecclesiastical officials, in order to secure a particular sponsor for their child." Far from obliterating social location, godparentage was attentive to it. Parents were keen to secure godparents who could be of some use, but they knew not to ask someone of "grossly disproportionate rank" to stand for their children. This sensitivity to the temporal benefits godparentage could provide was not limited to England. In nineteenth-century Swedish baptisms, it was typical that at least one godparent was a relative of the baptizand, and historians have found that parents were savvy in selecting the godparents who were not kin: For example, "shopkeepers often invited people from the stratum above them when they baptized their children, a particularly common practice when boys were baptized. The latter observation is interesting, because it tells us something about economic strategy. Boys represented continuity in the family business. It was the son who would inherit the shop, and therefore, it was important to establish strong links with groups in local society that could support the family business in times of economic depression." In nineteenth-century Brazil, enslaved parents often chose a free godparent for their first child's baptism, because "having free persons as godparents could bring to the family as a whole, including subsequent children, an important ally. . . . In particular, a free godparent could intervene on behalf of the slave in any dispute with his or her master."[28] This kind of "godparenting up" suggests how even in a moment when the liturgy insists that families—parents— cannot do everything for their children, the extraction turns back on itself to affirm the family and social location from which the baptizand has just been extracted.

This double emphasis on extracting Christians from family and affirming the bonds of family characterizes not only baptismal liturgy. It also runs through the Gospels, which here affirm family and lineage, and there extract us from it.

To say this is to argue against the tendency of recent North American theological scholarship to focus on the ways that Jesus challenges familial norms.[29] The scholarship in question carefully never says that Jesus destroys the institution of family, but it comes close, emphasizing the "radical" nature of Jesus' approach to family, and insisting that "Jesus' family values" are a lot weirder than James Dobson would like to admit.[30] This emphasis on the "radicalness" of Jesus' approach to family is understandable; the scholars in question are writing in a cultural context in which "Christianity" is regularly hitched to a socially conservative effort to shore up something inaccurately called "the traditional family" (and they are writing in a cultural context in which even good NPR-listening vegetarians seek to protect and perfect their own family units in a way that seems uncomfortably at odds with the hospitality and vulnerability the Gospel seems to invite).[31] In this context, scholars aptly insist that Jesus, and the New Testament broadly, can't persuasively be used to make an icon of June and Ward Cleaver. Yet in its sometimes singular focus on the "radical" things Jesus has to say about the family, this scholarship can seem to elide the ways that the New Testament also affirms the importance of family and lineage.[32]

Jesus' teaching both erases and affirms family bonds. Jesus castigates the new follower who wants to go home and say goodbye to his family before setting off to follow his new teacher; says he has come to set children against parents; and insists that marital bonds will dissolve eschatologically. On the other hand, Jesus explicitly reaffirms the commandment to honor one's parents; prohibits divorce in most circumstances; and, in the parable of the Prodigal Son, glosses penitential return to God as the restoration of a familial bond. Life as Jesus' disciple also involves extraction from and affirmation of family: The sons of Zebedee leave their father without hesitation to follow Jesus, but apparently they don't break ties with their mother, who later asks Jesus to place her sons at his left and his right in his kingdom.

Behind Jesus' teaching about family is Jesus' actual life, which (to put it mildly) both affirms and unsettles lineage and family. Family is both present and unstable from the beginning of Jesus' life: His parentage is decidedly odd, and the lineage through which the Gospels connect him to David is adoptive rather than biological (that is to say, the genealogies are Joseph's, not Mary's).[33] Jesus' very Incarnation requires extraction from family—that is, it requires him to leave his Father. And yet: Jesus is born to a particular family, and it seems to matter a good deal to the Gospel writers that he is. In different ways, the first chapter of Matthew (with its genealogy and its depiction of "His mother Mary" and "her husband . . . Joseph, son of David") and the first chapter of Luke (with its detailed portrait of Mary and of her extended kinship network; I will come to the genealogy in Luke 3 presently) make clear that Jesus' being enfamilied *in this lineage* is paramount. He could not be the messiah, descended from David, without it.[34]

Perhaps above all, Jesus' relationship with his mother, Mary, shows that his own life is characterized, from conception through death, by a perduring familial connection. In the Christian account, when God comes to earth, God does not plunk in from the heavens in the form of a swan, or dress up as a crone and flit in to pay a visit to the object of God's jealousy, or fall into a virgin's lap in the form of a shower of gold coins. Rather, the Christian God is born of a woman—a woman who herself has a particular lineage. This is the key to the puzzle-piecing together of Judaism and Christianity: if no Mary, then no Romans 9–11.

It has become commonplace to cite Jesus' instructions to Mary and the disciples about their fictive familial bonds as evidence that the kinship of discipleship erases the kinship of biological and legal family that defined Jesus' relationship with his mother before.[35] There are four passages in the Gospels that stage this discussion—three parallel passages in the synoptics, and a similar passage in John. Here is Matthew's version:

> While he was still speaking to the crowds, his mother and his brothers were standing outside, wanting to speak to him. Someone told him, "Look, your mother and your brothers are standing outside, wanting to speak to you." But to the one who had told him this, Jesus replied, "Who is my mother, and who are my brothers?" And pointing to his disciples, he said, "Here are my mother and my brothers! For whoever does the will of my Father in heaven is my brother and sister and mother." (Matthew 12:46–50)

Whether you read Jesus as saying something about the eschatological family or about what counts as "real" family on earth, it is easy to see why this passage is a favorite of people arguing that Jesus radically reshapes family. Jesus is redefining family not as a biological or a legal/nuptial/reproductive unit but as a group of people knitted together by discipleship. Family identity is found through one's relationship to Jesus, between and among other people who have a relationship to Jesus, regardless of whether those people are biological or nuptial or legal kin. If you want evidence of Jesus' weird family values, this is it. At the same time, as Rob Garafalo has pointed out, Jesus' appropriation of family language to describe relations among and between disciples is predicated on the existence of reproductive or nuptial families—if Jesus' intention was to wholly erase or "denigrate" preexisting family relationships, it would seem odd to use familial terminology to describe bonds he was lauding as most important.[36]

The synoptic accounts of Jesus putting his mother and his disciples in relation to one another should be read alongside the similar passage in the Gospel of John. John sets the conversation at the Cross:

> When Jesus saw his mother and the disciple whom
> he loved standing beside her, he said to his mother,
> "Woman, here is your son." Then he said to the dis
> ciple, "Here is your mother." And from that hour
> the disciple took her into his own home. (John
> 19:26–27)

This at first blush might appear to be another "transgressive family values" moment. But it more compellingly is read as precisely the opposite: Here Jesus is affirming family. Why does he entrust Mary in particular to the Beloved Disciple? Why does he care about what happens to her after he is dead? Why doesn't he make such pronouncements of familial reconfiguration higgledy-piggledy and writ large? Because Mary is Jesus' mother. Jesus entrusts Mary—and not, say Mary Magdalene, or Mary and Martha, other women who closely followed Jesus, who perhaps could have used some support—to the Beloved Disciple because she is his mother and her being his mother is important to him.[37]

Catholic doctrine takes this one step further: Jesus' familial relationships extend not only through the whole of his earthly life but beyond. They perdure eschatologically. Marriage may not exist in heaven, but at least one familial relationship does: the mother and son relation of Mary and Jesus. Mary is assumed not only because she is sinless but also because she is Jesus' mother and had a longing to be reunited with him (and he with her); this longing was particular to their filial-maternal relationship.[38] (Strikingly, according to Catholic doctrine, the saints don't yet have bodies, so the only enfleshed bodies currently in heaven—with the possible exceptions of Enoch, Elijah, and Melchizedek—are Mary and Jesus.[39] This makes the perdurance of the mother-son relationship even more arresting.)

So when we look at Jesus' teachings, his life, and his eschatological identity as Mary's son, we see the both/and of extraction from and affirmation of family. We see that same both/ and in Jesus' own baptism. At first blush, Jesus' baptism appears wholly extractive. The Gospels do not mention his parents being present (although, tellingly, the pictorial programs of some medieval fonts depicted the Holy Family or the Virgin Mary as present at Jesus' baptism)[40]—and the loudest mention of family is a voice from heaven, declaring Jesus to be *God's* son. Familial language seems to work in Jesus' baptism wholly to stage extraction and incorporation—there is no role for Jesus' parents, no blessing of his terrestrial family, no recitation of his Abrahamic lineage. But there is one strong instantiation of family at the baptism—the relationship between the liturgist and the baptizand. Jesus is baptized by John, who (as the Gospel of Luke has gone to great lengths to tell us) is Jesus' kinsman.[41] Thus, the liturgist who performs the ritual of extraction is in his very person representing abiding kinship ties. Vis-à-vis the familial, the local, Jesus' baptism models what every subsequent baptism should achieve: the both/and of affirming the baptizand's locality and particularity, and extracting him from it.

In Jesus' baptism, as in our own, both the extraction and the affirmation are in the service of incorporating the baptized person into the body of Christ. The extraction is in the service of my being incorporated because if I am not taken out of the thing I am in, I cannot be placed somewhere new. And the affirmation is in service of my being incorporated into the body of Christ because if all my particularities were *erased* (rather than affirmed), then I could not be incorporated into Christ (or into anything else)—because I would no longer be myself. Thinking of who we are after baptism is analogous to thinking about who we will be after resurrection: still ourselves, particularly and recognizably so, though metamorphosed, indeed made what we should be. The self at baptism isn't just analogous to the resurrected self—the self at baptism approximates the self upon resurrection. Baptism incorporates us, as much as we can in the here and now be incorporated, into the body of Christ; and resurrection will incorporate us completely.[42]

Notably, in the Gospel of Luke (the Gospel that establishes the familial connection between Jesus and the liturgist who will baptize him), Jesus' baptism is followed immediately by a genealogy. The genealogy itself both affirms and superinscribes lineage. It is Jesus' genealogy through Joseph, the man of whom, the Gospel writer tells us, "Jesus was . . . the son (as was thought)." The genealogy underscores the importance of Jesus' lineage while in the same breath reminding the reader of its fiction. Furthermore, the genealogy (unlike Matthew's) traces

Jesus back to Abraham, back to Noah, finally to declare Jesus "the son of Adam, the son of God." Luke turns the genre of family lineage into a genre that affirms the familial relationship between Jesus and God that readers just encountered in the baptism scene. Yet at the same time, Luke does not abandon, or even unsettle, the genealogical form, which he has allowed to show also that Jesus is human, that he is Jewish, and that he has this particular lineage. Luke has shown us Jesus' baptism, and then said, in effect, here is who Jesus is: He is still, importantly, the son and descendant of these men. His being the son and descendant of those men—his "inclusion . . . in the world of the fathers," to borrow the phrasing of Cleo Kearns—remains legible even as it is superinscribed by his being the son of God.[43]

The point of this overview of the Gospels' considerations of family is not to suggest that the status of the legal/biological/nuptial family is unaffected by an individual's (or a household's) conversion. Unarguably, the Gospels suggest that the family is transformed and transfigured by its members entering into friendship with Jesus: The Christian *familia* as such clearly frames the biological/nuptial/legal family; it would be difficult to read Mark 3:31–35 (and its synoptic parallels) otherwise. Rather the point of this account is to show that the Gospels neither leave the family untouched nor erase it.

Even as I write this account, I feel an impulse to add, constantly, "but on the other hand." (Perhaps you, the reader, feel the same thing.) That Italian missal may contain the earthly, covenanting lineage of Jesus; but on the other hand, many baptismal liturgies contain the litany of the saints. (Just so: terrestrial lineage *and* spiritual lineage.) Jesus may be closely connected to his mother; but on the other hand, he tells a bereaved son to abandon his father's corpse and follow him. For that matter, Jesus may be closely connected to his mother; but on the other hand, Jesus left his own Father (by whom I mean God, who was left by Jesus when Jesus came to dwell among us). (Just so: continued familial intimacy *and* extraction from it for the sake of the Gospel.) This impulse to unsay what has just been said by saying something that argues the other side of the ledger is the point. It is this maddening both/and that baptism holds. And it is baptism's characteristic deformation to tip over one way or the other.

As Balthasar argued, about some things, Scripture and tradition preserve different logics, either of which if pushed will make the other impossible. Our task, when we come to such logics, is precisely not to so push, but to leave "open the cleft between the two series of statements. It is not for man ... to construct syntheses here, and above all none of such a kind as to subsume one series of statements under the other."[44] Balthasar is writing about the Scripture's seemingly mutually exclusive claims about the universality (or not) of salvation, but, mutatis mutandis, the framework he suggests applies to Scripture's suggestions about the ongoing importance of, and the necessity of extracting disciples from, lineage and family. Scripture's statements about family seem to resist any effort to tidily systematize them exactly because the tradition preserves both strands. Somehow both must be right, so the interpretive task is to figure out a way to hold both—not by forcing away the contradiction but by admiring, if not flinging one's self into, the cleft. To put that differently, the epistemic task is to hold the two logics together without jettisoning one, and without eliding the jagged edges that make the holding together difficult and imperfect; and the liturgical task may be to find a way not only to preserve, but ritually to stage, the cleft.

Baptism, then, rightly operates in the cleft between extracting the baptizand from her locality and affirming that very locality. The rite's tendency to fail to hold open the cleft between extraction from and affirmation of family is a characteristic deformation. That failure can lean in one of two directions. It can overemphasize extraction, attempting to erase or elide all particularity that came before baptism. To do so is to move baptism in the direction of supersession (the capacity to hold together extraction from and affirmation of lineage is precisely the index of Christian nonsupersessionism).[45] Earnestly democratic Americans might bristle at the notion of affirming "lineage" (at least, those earnestly democratic Americans who haven't been bitten by the genealogy bug), but lineage is inseparable from election. All subsequent lineages after the call of Abraham—at least, all lineages that are legitimately Christian data—flow out of, and are predicated on, that election; for that election is not (as all genealogies inevitably are) a social construction but an act of God. The Gospels spell out Jesus' genealogy not only because the Gospels think genealogy is important but because the Gospels think election is important; when the Gospels speak of Jesus as "the son of David," they are taking the lineage of Jesus into the doctrine of election. If Jesus' baptism was only extractive—if his baptism erased that lineage—then the doctrine of election would be made null. The Gospels won't permit that nullification—just as they won't permit, in our baptisms, either the erasure of our particularities or the erasure of Jesus by our particularities.

In American churches, the tendency has been for baptism to go wrong in one direction—to deform into such a radical affirmation of lineage that Jesus is forgotten. (It is this tendency—the American assimilation of Christianity to "family"—that has produced scholarship that tends, by emphasizing extraction, to overcorrect.) In the following reading, I suggest that fin de siècle christening parties constitute one instance of the deformation of baptism whereby the ecclesial is wholly evacuated into the familial. If that reading is right, then there is an analogy between the deformations characteristic of the Eucharist and the deformations characteristic of baptism. In the Eucharist, the question is supersessionism; for baptism, the question—the point at which we expect the rite to go characteristically wrong—is family. At Eucharist, I have argued, the characteristic deforming tendency, which turns on the encounter between Jewish flesh and Gentile-Christian flesh, is a misprision of the relation of Christians to Jews. The deformation of baptism also turns on flesh—on the misprision of the blood of the birth family. The particular forms of that familial misprision can vary, of course; in the fin de siècle christening party, the bonds of familial flesh have wholly obscured the bonds of Christian kinship.

The nineteenth century offers examples of both versions of familial misprision—both an overemphasis on extraction from family and extraction's opposite, baptism as a way of incorporating the baptizand not in the body of Christ but more fully in her family. Although I will focus on the second deformation, I want to note two registers on which one finds a too-enthusiastic erasure of family in nineteenth-century Christianity. First, some of the "life of Jesus" scholars forcefully articulated the idea that (as David Strauss put it) Jesus "preferred his spiritual before his bodily relatives."[46] This Jesus cared not for earthly kith and kin. Rather, per Ernest Renan, "Jesus, like all men exclusively possessed by one idea, came to think lightly of the ties of blood. The bond of thought is the only one recognized by natures such as his." (There is an irony in *liberal* nineteenth-century scholars making claims virtually identical to those that postliberal and radical scholars make in the late twentieth and early twenty-first centuries. The same error, in other words, can be brought into being in more than one way, with more than one history. What nineteenth-century people like Renan cared about was the autonomy of the individual, the universality of ethical requirements—and the avoidance of enmeshment in things like blood; that is a different path to a dismissal of family than the path taken by the postliberals, but it arrives at the same place.)

At the same time that this early historical Jesus scholarship was being written, American evangelicals were performing a version of extractionism in their baptismal ritual, which often staged such a dramatic break with family that it shook even enthusiastic believers. Consider Wilson Thompson, who came of age on the Kentucky frontier in a thickly Baptist community (his father was a deacon and his uncle a minister). A revival swept through Thompson's community, and many teenagers, including cousins of Thompson, began to convert, seek baptism, and join the church. Thompson, however, was not touched by the Spirit, though he wished to be. The whole thing was upsetting and confusing to Thompson, and, as historian Christine Heyrman tells the story, "Not wishing to aggravate the boy's distress, his father told Wilson to stay at home when the rest of the family attended the cousins' baptism. As his relatives set out for the church singing, Wilson remembered, 'I really thought they were on their way to heaven. God was their father . . . and Christians were their brethren and sisters . . . and I thought as these Christians were now leaving me behind . . . so at the last great day they would thus ascend to heaven, leaving me to endure the just punishment due me as a vile sinner.' "[47]

Around the same time, a young Georgia woman named Caroline was converted, sought membership at a Baptist church, and was baptized. After giving a forceful testimony, Caroline was baptized in a creek at night. As an observer recalled the scene, "The banks of that little stream were lined with crowds of interested spectators. . . . Julia, of Monticello, her bosom friend and companion in her worldly course, seemed loath to leave her even for a moment, and clung to her till she reached the water's edge." Why did Julia thus cling? Because she understood the baptism as a ritual that would extract Caroline from her friendship. After a hymn, a short sermon, and a prayer, one of the ministers, Mr. Dawson, "took Caroline by the hand and led her down the shelving bank into the limpid stream. They had attained about half the desired depth, when she requested him to stop a moment, and, turning to those on the bank, waving her hand, she said, '*Farewell, young friends! Farewell, Julia!*' The effect was electrical. The whole audience convulsed. . . . Upon coming up out of the water, Julia rushed forward to meet her friend, embracing her, and crying out in agonizing tones, '*Oh, Carrie, you must not leave me! Mr. Dawson, pray for me! Mr. Mallary pray for me?*' "[48] Extraction for the sake of incorporation (Caroline's) neatly yielded the impulse for another person's extraction.

But within decades of the wave of revivalism that left Wilson Thompson worried about his eschatological orphanhood and Julia of Monticello requesting prayer, American Christians were performing (or reading aspirationally about, in the pages of etiquette guides and ladies' magazines) a quite different baptismal ritual, one that subsumed ecclesial bonds into familial bonds: the household christening party. An 1886 article from the *Art Interchange* (a periodical, founded in 1878, that sought to be a "combined art and household journal")[49] captures the flavor of such events. At five o'clock in the afternoon one December day in 1886, "all the members of a very large family," plus a "few friends," gathered in the two parlors of a New York home to witness, and celebrate, the baptism of a newborn. The location was au courant: As the *Art Interchange* informed its readers, it was "much more fashionable to have babies christened at home, and to give a small entertainment after the ceremony, than to carry them to church." The christening itself, which utilized a silver bowl flanked with smilax and white rosebuds, was dispatched fairly quickly;[50] thereafter, the baby, in his or her white lace and satin sash, was "kissed, and sent off to the nursery with the nurse," and the guests enjoyed one another's company in the elegantly appointed parlors. Like the baptismal bowl, the dining room table was decorated with roses and smilax, and among the flowers, the charmed guests found "ices in various forms," one shaped like Santa Claus, the others shaped liked babies, all "resting in spun glass." Spiced cakes, coated in white icing, were served, as was caudle (a spiced gruel or oatmeal, typically diluted with Madeira, or with "a pint of brandy, a pint of mulled sherry, half a glass of rum and a quart of scalded milk").[51] Each guest received comestibles to take home: a piece of cake, "wrapped in white papers and tied with white ribbons," "with a pretty little baby's face pictured on its top," containing the white almonds that were "conventional," "always used at these entertainments." Additionally, the guests received one token that was neither edible nor typical:

> Each guest was presented with a large artificial rose
> and rosebud upon one stalk. . . . Hanging from the
> stalks were small foreign gold coins, and each
> rose had in its centre a little child, cut out of silver,
> with the name of the baby and the date of its birth

> engraved on the back, to serve as a reminiscence of
> the occasion. . . . These roses and trinkets, being a
> novelty, caused much amusement and pleasure,
> and the guests dispersed promising not to forget
> the pleasure received.

This baptism represents the characteristic deformation of the familial overtaking the ecclesial—or, to put it differently, *generation* (or generations) displacing *regeneration* as the ritual's sign event.[52] The liturgy replaced ecclesial symbols with their domestic doubles: the sacred space in which baptism was celebrated was now a home, not a church sanctuary; the gathered faithful comprised only family and friends; a church's baptismal font was replaced with a family's silver bowl; and the Eucharist was replaced with imitatively sacramental foodstuffs (cake and caudle, or, as one contemporary etiquette guide's discussion of domestic christening suggests, "the most refined form of refreshment, is a good wine passed with cake in the parlor").[53] All of this caused the meaning of baptism to congeal, not as a ritual of incorporation into the body of Christ but as a reiteration of the family; not as a ritual of sacramental regeneration but as a ritual of the continuity of generation.

In particular, four features of the baptism cemented the centrality of the local and familial meanings of the rite, over and against the extractive and ecclesial meanings. First, the location. Location carries meaning, and different meanings will be made possible or emphasized when a baptism is celebrated in a home, in a hospital room, in the pastor's study, in a church sanctuary, or by a river. One might want to argue that a certain collection of sacred meanings is most likely—perhaps possible only—in the public *consecrated* space of a church. Others might argue that to baptize at a river is to connect the baptizand and the gathered community more fully with Jesus, who was baptized at a river; or that to baptize in a river is to stage more dramatically the way that baptism calls you out of the world. In a modern (nineteenth- or twentieth- or twenty-first-century) landscape of churches and rivers, it is hard to mount a strong theological case for the baptizand's residence as the place of baptism—such a location will almost always slant the meaning of the event toward family and away from ecclesial community. That said, houses have had different meanings at different times—sometimes they tilt more toward private space, sometimes more toward public space (and sometimes those categories are anachronisms).[54] The deep problem with the *Art Interchange* baptism is not, finally, that it happened in a residence—the problem is that the residence was bounded, rather than porous; that it was closed to the larger ecclesial community rather than pushed open, by baptism, to the ecclesial community.

This takes us to the second feature of the baptism that solidified the event's familial meaning: the guest list. Domestic christening parties were small, private affairs. The guest list typically included only "the near relatives of the infant, and the most intimate friends of the parents."[55] Indeed, part of the definition of the christening party is the guest list's intimacy and exclusion. "Invite only your most intimate friends," Frances E. Lanaghan instructed readers of *The Ladies Home Journal* in 1892. *The Good Housekeeping Hostess: An Old-Fashioned Guide to Gracious Living* (in which "christening" is listed in the table of contents under "social life"—sandwiched between chapters on "cards" and "children's parties") spelled out the same point in 1904: "My lady first meets the friends of her family when they are bidden to gather for her christening, or, in case that ceremony may not be part of her inheritance, she may be introduced at an old-time caudle party. . . . On either occasion it is the most intimate of all the family feasts, only those people you really care for being honored with the engraved cards, or the notes asking their presence." Emily Post reiterated the instruction eighteen years later: "Invitations to a christening are never formal, because none but the family and a very few intimate friends are supposed to be asked." The explicit limiting of the baptismal event to only family and a few friends evades the extraction from familial identity and social location that baptism requires. Baptisms could, perhaps, properly happen in people's houses if the owners of the house allowed the ritual to remake their house into a (satellite) church (as would have been the case with first-century house churches), but when families hold household baptisms without allowing the baptism to transform their house into a church—when they limit the guest list, as Frances Lanaghan instructed—they turn baptism into a rite not only for the making of family but also for the replication of social class.[56]

In addition to the guest list, two pieces of material culture that featured in domestic baptism bespoke the familial meanings of the rite: the silver bowl that stood in for the font, and the white gown worn by the baptizand. In domestic baptisms, bowls—as Emily Post, with telling punctuation, flags—mimicked and replaced ecclesial vessels: "The 'font' is always a bowl—of silver usually—put on a small high table." The conventional use of *silver* bowls in domestic baptism recalled church silver. Whether silver or not, the bowls were often inscribed with family markers; as Mrs. Frank Learned spelled out in her 1906 guide *The Etiquette of New York To-day,* it was fitting to use a bowl "which is valued from family associations."[57] The Hall family of Charleston, South Carolina, used for its baptisms a 1793 silver bowl engraved with the family's coat of arms;[58] the Randolphs of Virginia used a chinoiserie punchbowl "mounted upon a black wood stand upon which is a silver plate bearing the noble historical names of its past owners";[59] a Pennsylvania family used a "huge" silver punch bowl, inscribed with the names of generations of women (in the words of a 1920 report on the bowl, "On the bowl are panels with spaces for inscriptions and the names and dates of baptism of a good many Sarahs have been registered there").[60] The repurposing of punch bowls located the christening fete in a repertoire of family occasions—and the genealogical inscriptions gave a different account than did the ecclesially evocative silver and the liturgical language that named the baptizand as a child of Father God.

If the engraved silver bowl replaced the church font, the "usual white lace and satin sash" in which our Knickerbocker baptizand was clad also represents the replacement of an ecclesial object with a familial object. Fin de siècle baptizands wore family-owned (and often family-made) baptismal gowns, and they wore them *before* the actual baptism. These gowns displaced the medieval and early modern infant's ritual baptismal garb, the chrisom. The chrisom was a white cloth placed on the infant's head or wrapped around the infant immediately *after* baptism. The chrisom was owned by the church and was usually given back to the church at the mother's churching. Variations on this practice continued through the early eighteenth century, by which time the chrisom was being displaced by the family-owned christening gown.[61]

Historians of fashion, textiles, and the material culture of childhood usually explain the emergence of the christening gown by pointing to larger changes in the theory of child rearing, and concomitant changes in children's dress. Specifically, through the mid–1600s, children were swaddled at birth. When, in the late seventeenth and early eighteenth centuries, pedagogues began to argue that children needed to move more freely and experience the world, parents stopped swaddling children and began dressing them in looser garments; with this sartorial change came the replacement of the chrisom, which (except when placed only on the infant's head) had overlaid swaddling, with the christening gown.[62] This general shift in children's clothing is no doubt part of the explanation. But these historians have not attended to the shift from common, ecclesial property to individual family property.

To replace a chrisom cloth with "white lace and satin sash" was to replace communal, ecclesial-owned garb with a private, family possession. Christening gowns were normatively passed down through the generations. (As one nineteenth-century etiquette guide spelled out, the baptizand is "dressed in the finest and softest gown that can be afforded, all the better if it has been handed down from other family christenings.")[63] Just as the shift to the family christening gown took place during the decades when norms of children's clothing were changing, so it also took place during the decades of enclosure—the decades when, in England and America, land that had been previously held in common was (sometimes literally) enclosed, now marked off by fences and private property rights.[64] This general shift away from the common to the private and family-owned seems as germane to the change in baptismal clothing as changes in children's fashion (after all, church-owned chrisom cloths could in theory have been replaced by loose-fitting dresses that belonged to the church, not by loose-fitting dresses owned by individual families).

Thus all the Knickerbocker christening gown had in common with the earlier chrisom cloth was color: Both were white, and thus carried the suggestion of purity.[65] In contrast to the chrisom cloth, the christening gown was not ecclesial property; it was self-consciously private family property. And whereas the baptized person received the chrisom cloth *after* baptism, the family gown was (and is) typically worn throughout the whole ceremony. Thus the sartorial marker of transformation, of new identity through incorporation, was lost. Clothing no longer marked the ritual transformation that occurred during the ceremony; rather it marked the baptized throughout as a member of the family that owned the gown.

Thus the baptismal ritual itself, with its silver bowls and its satin gowns and its socially replicatory guest list, performed affirmation more than extraction and incorporation, generation more than regeneration. At the *Art Interchange* baptism, the party following the prayers underlined the theme of family reproduction. For example, the roses that decorated the baptismal bowl, and the rosebuds given to guests: by the late nineteenth century, flowers—which had long been understood as symbols of reproduction—had become part of an energetically consumerist floriculture. Thus the roses evoked both fertility and the family's capacity to generate money—a meaning made more explicit by the coins that dangled from the rosebuds' stalks. Each rosebud also featured "in its centre a little child, cut out of silver, with the name of the baby and the date of its birth engraved on the back." The silver betokened the prosperity that was hoped for the baptizand, and the name and birth date pointed toward generation. The ices of babies and the pieces of cake stamped with a baby's face multiplied the signs of procreation. The one sign of baptismal metamorphosis—the baby—had been whisked away. In the absence of the baptizand, the celebrating family stood around looking not at the sign of regeneration but at itself.[66]

Elegant christening parties, reported in the periodicals of the day, made for aspirational reading among the middle class.[67]

Nineteenth-century readers were also fascinated by stories about royal baptismal celebrations: Published accounts of the baptisms of royal families in Russia, Germany, and England dwelled on the fine clothing the royal families wore and the gifts babies received (middle-class kids received porringers; royal children received "jewels and land"). When Princess Beatrice's daughter was baptized, readers were treated to details about the "aristocratic group of guests." When the prince of Wales was christened in 1842, the newspaper noted the choir and more than thirty-one instrumentalists who performed.[68]

Periodical readers also encountered descriptions of the domestic christening celebrations of immigrants and working-class people. These reports were quite different from the respectful and admiring accounts of silver bowls, smilax, and Santa Claus ices. When reporters (and readers) turned to New York's tenements, they saw not refinement but rowdiness and violence. Immigrants' celebrations were described as unruly, drunken affairs that often degenerated into brawls and attracted the attention of the police. One representative newspaper account described a domestic baptism that took place in an apartment "on the fourth-floor of a tall tenement house." ("It is high life indeed," quipped the sarcastic reporter.) In this baptism, far from being the well-behaved (or largely absent) baby, the tenement baby joined into the "general hilarity with a jubilant crow and a reckless throwing out of pink little arms and legs." The reporter dictionally mocked the baptism, contrasting this tenement party with the baptism of royalty: "The aristocracy of Avenue A and Tompkins square is well represented," "The instrumental music for the occasion is furnished by a local orchestra, consisting of a capacious accordion in the hands of an energetic youth with an inexhaustible repertory of tunes." Most accounts of immigrants' christening parties stressed the violence that broke out. For example, in April 1887, in an article entitled "Beer, Baby, Bullets," readers in Denver learned that at a "Swede House" "Riot and Murder Take the Place of the Christian Sacrament to Be Administered. The Baby is Lost Sight of in the Beer and Blood and in the Ensuing Row." One man was shot, two wounded, but eventually "The police, by skillful work, arrested twenty-one of the Swedes, Poles, and Hungarians who assisted at the ceremony." In 1899, readers in Springfield, Illinois, reading an article entitled "Row at a Christening," learned that during an October 15 christening, a "riot" broke out between "Hungarian and Pollack miners." As the paper went to press, "a sheriff and several deputies" were en route to the christening but it was expected that "the foreigners will resist arrest and a fight will ensue."[69]

This yellow copy suggests a cultural trope in which baptism was used to underwrite broad social distinctions. Baptism operated not only to stitch the Knickerbocker baby into her family and its small circle of appropriate friends. Additionally, baptism operated discursively to articulate and endorse social identities more broadly: Middle-class readers of these newspaper accounts were being treated to reports of low-class foreigners' mangling even baptism (if they can't get baptism right, they won't get citizenship right either). Rather than writing over social location, still leaving the location legible though transformed, these accounts represent the use of baptism to *create* and sustain social location.[70]

Domestic baptisms are no longer "fashionable." But many Americans are still attached to the material props of baptism, and their engagement with these props reveals the extent to which the fin de siècle overtaking of regeneration with generation reigns in American Christian practice. One twenty-first-century family's encounter with a baptismal bowl is illustrative. In August 2008, Lyle Danielson of Johnston, Iowa, was participating in an annual cleanup of the Des Moines River. Danielson was taking a breather on a sandbar when he was approached by a homeless man known as Turtle. Turtle chatted with Danielson for a few minutes, then handed him a Homan Silver Plate Co. bowl engraved with thirteen names and dates. Then Turtle vanished.

When he got home, Danielson Googled the thirteen names engraved on the bowl, but didn't turn up anything. Later, he described the bowl to a friend who, knowledgeable about antiques, identified it as a christening bowl, and said the thirteen names were probably family members who were baptized in water the bowl held. Enter here the Iowa Genealogical Society, which upon learning about the bowl, set about finding the descendants of the owners. The genealogical researchers determined that the first children to be baptized in the bowl and have their names engraved on it were Erma, Leta, and Iola Runyon, who were born between 1892 and 1899 to Edith and Harry Runyon, a Des Moines–area grocer. Erma Runyon married Guy Shaw, and their daughter Katherine Shaw was baptized in the bowl, her name engraved thereon. She married John V. Synhorst and had her children, Julie, Susan, and John Synhorst, baptized in and engraved on the bowl. Diane Dinsmore, the genealogist working on the bowl, located a Des Moines address for John V. Synhorst. She wrote to him, explaining her research, and then asked, "Are you this John V. Synhorst? If so, we would like to return this bowl to you and your family." Indeed, this was the right Synhorst; the bowl was returned to him, and a few months later his great-grandchild was baptized in the bowl, the first time it had been used (at least by the Synhorsts) since 1963.

When the participants in the recovery of that bowl told the story, the theme they underscored was family. Anticipating the baptism of her child, the then pregnant Katie Snook, granddaughter of John Synhorst, said, "It will be the reintroduction of the bowl into the family." Even more striking is the way Danielson, the man who first received the bowl from the homeless Turtle, later made sense of his encounter with Turtle. Danielson told a reporter that he was surprised that Turtle took so much trouble over the bowl: "I can only assume he recognized this as a way to get it back to its owners," Danielson said. "I'm astonished he cared that much about it. Homeless people may be in hard times but they once had families and remember the good times."[71] Danielson, in other words, cast the bowl's recovery in normative and nostalgic notions of family. He imputed to Turtle a concern for family, a concern that Danielson grounded in the happy familial past Danielson imagined Turtle had. Katie Snook and Lyle Danielson named family as the register of baptismal meaning: Baptism and its objects have become wholly familial, rather than ecclesial, signifiers.

Christening gowns also provide an index of the continued evacuation of ecclesial meaning into family meanings. (Imagine the woman who wants her child to be baptized *so that she can use the family gown*.) The christening gown, which has wholly replaced the chrisom in a way that bowls have not replaced fonts, is inevitably described in terms of familial, rather than ecclesial, significance. For example, in the midst of a discussion of how baptism "connects the newborn child with the history of the church and previous generations of the family, extending the circle of belongingness and strengthening the core of identity," Fuller Theological Seminary psychology professor Frederika Vande Kemp explains that in her family "the christening gown was a family heirloom that made the baptism a 'linking' event."[72]

Robyn Covelli-Hunt illustrates baptismal gowns' carrying *generative* rather than *regenerative* meaning in a poem called

"The Lineage Maker," which she wrote for her daughter Delaney. The lineage maker in question is a christening gown, named in the poem's first line:

> To see my grandmother's christening gown,
> on the body of our tiny daughter, is to drink from its
>   linen bowl
> one broad sip at a time.

This forty-eight-line poem recounts the family identity the dress, with its "hem reinforced to outlive us," carries:

> Our girl, not yet princess, sits
> in this precious drape and hears the whispers
> of those who crawled inside this tent before her.
> I wore this dress and my mother wore it.

The sacramental meanings are largely absent, almost wholly displaced by familial meanings, legible (barely) only when the author speaks of herself and her mother as "white tuberoses in our parents' arms / for submersion into certain communion." The dress, "smelling of cedar wrapped in tissue," is "testament to the mothers and fathers who came before." The whole of the family's journey westward, their labors at the family grocery store and their weekly appearance at church to sing "Protestant hymns," are held by the dress with its "necessary hem." The lineage has been "made," and, Covelli-Hunt is sure, it will continue: "One day my daughter will pour her baby into this crinoline waterfall / and history will hitch itself to her shutter finger."[73]

Sometimes, people procure a christening gown because they want a family heirloom. In a 2010 Columbus, Ohio, newspaper article, Rachel Dilley explains that "the baptismal gown

worn by both of my daughters was seemingly kissed by destiny."
When Dilley was a girl, her family vacationed with another
family, whom they knew through church, on North Carolina's
Outer Banks. Dilley and her sister enjoyed playing with the
three boys from the other family. During a day trip, the two
mothers became "enchanted" by a boutique called Maria's,
which included "a selection of Maria's beautiful, handmade
baptismal gowns." The mother of the three boys fell in love with
the gowns and wanted to purchase one, but she left the store
"empty-handed and misty-eyed." The next summer, the family
with the boys could not make it to the beach—but the mother
asked the author's mother to buy one of Maria's christening
gowns for her. "No, she wasn't planning to have any more children. Instead, she intended to save the dress for her first granddaughter, even though she knew that a decade or two might
pass before she had one." Years later, the author grew up to
marry one of those three boys—and her two daughters were
baptized in the prematurely purchased gown. "Destiny made
sure of it."[74]

Both forms of familial misprision in baptism appeal to me. The
fantasy that baptism utterly erases one's family appeals to me,
deeply. This is, surely, to do with my own history—my familial
history (fraught), and my baptismal history (as an adult, an
ocean away from any member of my family). Those histories
dispose me to frankly recoiling at the principle that baptism
has to somehow hold the tension between human family and
ecclesial family, between baptismal kinship and other kinships.
I prefer (mistakenly) to imagine that the former does wholly
away with the latter.

    And then too, the fin de siècle christening party appeals
to me—I write about it because I like it. What I like: the central

role of laypeople broadly, and women in particular, in shaping the rite; the flowers, the food, and the fact of the other baubles (if not the particulars of the creepy silver baby faces).

These things, I think, are good to like. The flowers and food and baubles are good to like because they are a kind of unofficial "sacramental"—objects used for devotional purposes; objects that, among other things, make invisibility visible, and draw the senses of the participants fully into the event (the participants are smelling the rosebuds and tasting spiced cake). Christianity, at its best, hallows the material and delights in the delight that Christians take in material objects. (Furthermore, I believe that God felt delight that December evening in 1886, looking down at all those ices. The ices, the Madeira-infused oatmeal, and the flowers, real and fake, were offerings of a sort, and Christians, hoping we are Abel and not Cain, always hope that our offerings are delightful and acceptable to God.) From this perspective, the materiality of the rite is not to be bemoaned as a consumerist distraction but rather appreciated as part of how the rite works.

And the centrality of laywomen to the event is good to like, too. As Irene Elizabeth Stroud, the leading historian of domestic baptismal fetes, has noted, domestic christening parties were events over which women presided—women planned them, women made the guest lists, women organized the food; women wrote the etiquette guides that served as the domestic counterparts to prayer books; the whole event unfolded in domestic space, which was firmly marked as feminine by the late nineteenth century.[75] This is an important corrective in a history of a ritual whose liturgies have been largely crafted by and presided over by men. (At many points in church history, mothers, observing the dictum that women should not enter a church for forty days after childbirth, were absent from their own children's baptisms.)[76]

The effort to read baptism theologically raises questions of authority: Does the archive whereby we can discover the theological meanings of baptism comprehend only the written texts of the liturgy and the gestures the liturgy's rubrics direct, or does it comprehend the dress and the cake? (Given the history of the church, these questions are perforce gendered questions.) What counts, and how does it count, in an account of baptism?

I like both deformations I have depicted, and I wish to flag a worry—that my reading of these baptismal archives reinscribes my own social location (as one who reads from the academy) just as firmly as that Knickerbocker christening party reinscribed the baby's. By which I mean that it would be easy enough to quote a line of maternal doggerel, say very little about it, and leave the snobbish mocking to the interpretive space between the reader and me. That would be easy not because of the quality of Covelli-Hunt's enjambment, but because of shibboleths of my class and profession, which suggest I should identify the commercial and the sentimental with the feminine, and castigate them all.

And so, recognizing my own biases, I want to ask how Covelli-Hunt and Dilley and the woman who hosted that 1886 christening party can instruct me. Their poetry, cakes, and dresses are in the service of one fundamentally right thing: the affirmation of lineage as proper to the baptismal act. There's nothing wrong with their cakes and dresses per se. What's wrong is not what they are, but what they exclude—which is the same thing that is wrong with blunt declarations about Jesus' radical overturning of family.

How might they instruct me? Consider one last baptismal gown.

Really, this gown is not a gown but an undergarment, a slip—"embroidered with family tree to wear under baby's

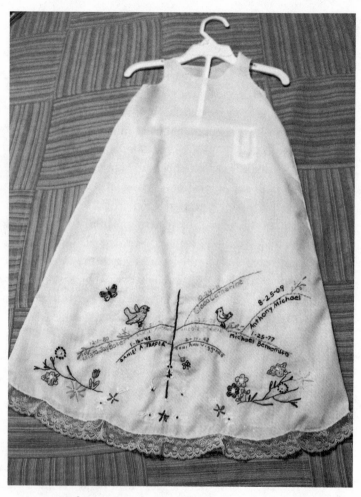

A twenty-first-century baptismal slip, whose brightly colored, embroidered family tree might show through the baptismal gown that would be worn atop it.

christening gown," meant to be "pass[ed] down from generation to generation for each family member to wear." The mother who posted the picture on Pinterest worried that the "bright colors"— the green of the tree's branches, the yellows and pinks of the birds, the oranges and blues and pinks in which baptized kiddos' names are stitched—"are cute, but might show through."[77] She concluded that were she to make the slip, she'd probably choose lighter colors. I like it with bright colors, of course, because it makes a nice sartorial metaphor. In baptism, the child will be clothed with another garment over this slip—neither a christening gown nor a chrisom cloth, but the garment (according to Paul in Galatians 3:27) of Christ himself. That garment will overlay this orange and blue family tree, just gauzily enough for the tree to show through.

Damaged Gifts

Eucharist, prayer, baptism: These things are blighted. Why keep doing them, then? If they are subject to characteristic deformation and collapse upon themselves, or overflow with violence, or order the world in a distorted way; if it all will inevitably sometimes go wrong, why do we carry on with prayer and Eucharist and baptism (and silence and marriage and celibacy and song and all the other good, damaged ways we have to place ourselves somewhere where we might be found by God)? Because they are the only things we have, and because they are gifts from the Lord.

A gift has at least three characteristics. First, it comprehends the troika of giver, recipient, and object given and received. Second, the object must be transmitted between giver and recipient in a particular way. Third, there can be no recompense required—or even possible.[1]

To elaborate: For there to be gift, there must be an object (of the gifting action). If I intend to give something to you but have nothing to give ("What shall I give him, poor as I am?"), there is no gift. If I realize I can give my heart, then *gift* becomes possible. Similarly, *gift* requires the object to be given and received.

If I pluck some habañero peppers from my garden and steep them in a vat of vodka, and as the vodka is steeping, I harvest and juice the tomatoes from the next bed, and I do all of this with the intention of giving my friend Peter a Bloody Mary starter set on his birthday next month—the vodka and the tomato juice aren't yet a gift. They aren't a gift until I actually give them, and until Peter receives them. (There are other ways, besides giving and receiving, that Peter could come into possession of the starter set. He could break into my kitchen and steal the vodka, or he could write me a check for the market value of nineteen tomatoes and persuade me to take the check as payment for the tomatoes; either case—expropriation or purchase—would interrupt, and wholly derail, the process by which the habañeros and tomatoes were becoming a gift.) If any of these three things is absent—the object, the giving, and the receipt-of-gift-qua-gift—we have something other than a gift.

This troika of object, recipient, and giver is part of what makes a gift—but, of course, troikas make other kinds of exchanges, too (the cash, the confidence man, and the mark; the mortgage, the newlyweds, and the banker). What distinguishes a gift is precisely that it is given and received without any reciprocation; this is what it means to give or receive something *as a gift*. The gift-object is given by a giver whose motive is to give a gift, and either because of the nature of the object, or because of the conditions of the object's giving and receiving, the gift-object definitionally is not and cannot be recompensed; it cannot entail an obligation to offer (in the anthropologist's argot) a countergift; it cannot incur debt. By this definition, many things that we think of as gifts are exactly not because, as Mauss has taught us (even as he claimed this as a characteristic of gift), they oblige the recipient to give something back. On Derrida's account, the many "gift exchanges" pondered by Mauss are precisely not gifts. They are, rather, a complex form of ex-change that creates webs of obligations, which is just what gifts do not do. As Derrida put the argument, "If there is gift, the given of the gift must not come back to the giving. . . . For there to be a gift, there must be no reciprocity return, exchange, countergift, or debt."[2]

In these terms, only things you cannot reciprocate can be gifts. Thus death is a gift (for Derrida, the only possible gift), as is being, and *agape*. Something intended for the generations, and therefore not recompensable in any straightforward way, can be gift: a bequest; land.[3] I am on a spiritual (psychoana-lytic, familial, emotional) quest to learn to give things to my sister (help with her kids, praise, understanding) without expect-ing anything back; if I can learn to do this, I will have given her a gift. In these terms, many of the things God gives are gift: Eucharist, church, the seven gifts of the Holy Spirit (not to men-tion existence; that is, the fact that there is anything at all). These are all gifts that cannot be reciprocated. They are only things that can be received, and enjoyed in the mode appropriate to their kind, with no hope of return.

Gifts, like all other created things, can be damaged. Derrida's aporia may be one way of naming the gift's characteristic deformation—its tendency to immediately create a circum-stance of exchange that undoes its gift-ness.

Indeed, there are many ways a gift can be damaged. If any part of the gift's constitutive troika—giving, receiving, object—is damaged, the gift itself is damaged. The most straightforward kind of damage a gift can sustain is damage to the object given and received: The object can, simply, be dented, cracked, faded, ripped, or chipped. It can be misaligned or burned or fraying. The book I give you can have two pages printed upside down.

The tomato juice in your starter kit could have soured. But damage doesn't prevent an object's being given and received, and an object's damage doesn't prevent the gift's being, still, a gift. To wit, the opening pages of Louisa May Alcott's *Little Women*. It is the Civil War, and money is dear, but—because "Christmas won't be Christmas without any presents"—the four March daughters determine that each will give beloved Marmee a gift. Jo decides to give her mother a pair of shoes, Amy a flask of cologne, Meg a pair of gloves, and Beth a set of handkerchiefs. Beth purchases the handkerchiefs and then marks them herself, in charmingly "uneven letters" that "cost her" a great deal of "labor." But Beth has made a mistake—instead of embroidering the handkerchiefs "M. March," she marked them "Mother." (Jo is only too happy to point out the defect.) The handkerchiefs are flawed, but they are nonetheless a gift; Marmee receives her present from Beth gratefully, and straight away puts a handkerchief into her pocket for later use.[4]

So gifts are damaged when the object is damaged. But there are other ways for a gift to be damaged. A second kind of damage comes when the giver or the act of giving is damaged. Among human givers, gifts are typically damaged in the giving *to some extent,* but there is a continuum of damage, and a gift partially damaged in the giving can retain some of its gift characteristic. Typically, the damage-in-the-giving of gifts given by human givers can be indexed to the giver's motive. For something to be pure gift, the giver must have purely the motive of giving a gift, and this is rarely (perhaps never) a human giver's whole and pure motive. Sometimes the motive is so unrelated to giving that the gift is wholly damaged. Say I take a colleague out to lunch. Theoretically, I might be giving a gift of lunch. But I hate this colleague, and I wish him ill. In my perfect world, he would get run over by a bus. Why, then, am I buying him lunch? Because he has a vote on my tenure case and I want him to feel warmly toward me. This giving is so damaged that the entire character of gift has been eroded. With my singular focus on what I want in return for this lunch (not to mention my drenching the whole thing in false bonhomie and friendliness), I have transformed what might have been a gift into a gift's opposite: calculated and manipulative exchange; no gift.

But there are other examples in which the damage-in-giving is less pronounced. I pick out a present for my sister—a pair of earrings. I really think she will like the earrings, and I really want her to like them. I remember how extravagant our mother used to be with gifts, and how much Leanne loved the extravagance, and I hope I can re-create a bit of that experience. Where's the damage? As with my colleague, I want something in return. Only here, the balance of my motives is different, and even the thing I want is less univocally self-serving—I want the gift to somehow improve things between me and my sister. I'd like this gift to help my sister set down the story she's been carrying around about me for twenty-five years, the story in which I am a selfish jerk who never extends myself for her. My motives, in other words, are mixed, but not so much as to erode all the character of gift. This is a gift whose gift character is still evident, even though shot through with my wish that I might indeed receive a return. Or finally a third gift: My friend's daughter is in the hospital for a minor procedure. I give the gifts of time and food—keeping my friend company for a long while and bringing an elaborate lunch. This approaches pure gift, but it doesn't quite arrive. Mostly, what I want is to give my friend and her daughter my time and these gourmet sandwiches, but even this impulse is tinged by other motives: I want my presence at the hospital to solidify my place in this friend's life; I delight in telling myself that I, and not friends X and Y (by whom I feel threatened, with whom I feel competitive), am the one who has gotten the friend-when-kid-is-in-the-hospital slot. Here the gift character is only barely—but still—occluded. In my own life, the tarnished hospital-giving is as close to pure gift as I get. Giving is damaged when the giver has motives beyond gift—and among human givers, giving is usually, perhaps always, mixed or cracked in some way.

A gift can also be damaged in the *reception* of the gift. You can give your niece a pottery planter and she drops it while taking it out of the box. You didn't give her a damaged platter, but you did give her (and she received) a damaged gift. You give your wife a negligee and she receives it with every intention of wearing it next weekend when she meets her lover in Paris. You haven't given her damaged lingerie, but the gift—the troika of object, giving, and receiving—is damaged by her reception. Or, receiving, just like giving, can be damaged in such a way that turns gift into exchange—I allow my colleague to buy me lunch, and jokingly (but not) say, "This just obligates you to have lunch with me again, so that I can pay." In saying that, I have explicitly turned the gift into something that creates obligation, and I have thus eroded the gift character. People often damage gifts in just this way. We damage them because we are uncomfortable—not uncomfortable being in someone's debt, but uncomfortable with not being in someone's debt. So I receive a gift I cannot possibly repay: My novelist friend generously reads *seven drafts* of the novel I am trying to write, and helps me learn how to shape the plot and make the characters a little more believable. Exactly the qualities that make it possible for him to give me this gift (he is an accomplished novelist and I never will be) mean that I will never be able to repay him in kind. Rather than simply receive the gift, I awkwardly say something about "paying it forward" or "gift karma." To say this, rather than simply to receive, is to (slightly) damage the gift in reception.

Gifts, then, are damaged when any one of their three component parts is damaged. And there is a fourth way in which gifts can be damaged: the damage sustained not because of any particular damage on the part of the gift or the giver or the recipient. Rather, this fourth kind of damage happens when each player in the gifting is flawlessly what or who he is, but a recipient like *this* cannot help but damage a gift like *that*. A grandmother might give her three-year-old granddaughter a Meissen figurine. The granddaughter will not receive the gift well, not because she is damaged but because she is three; she will gleefully hurl the figurine down and shatter it. J. R. Ackerley might give his German shepherd Tulip a copy of *A Room with a View* (the author of which was Ackerley's best friend). Tulip will not be able to receive the gift well. She'll probably try to eat it.

The large library of fairy tales that explore what happens when people are given the gift of a wish (or three) begins to illustrate the kind of damage that occurs because human beings can't help but use this kind of gift badly: The wish is perfect, and so is the sprite or magical fish that gives it, but the receipt of the wish—by people who inevitably wish injuriously; the recipient wishes for everything he touches (and so also his food) to turn to gold, or he wishes for an extra pair of hands, which he aims to use to earn money, but his manual grotesquerie so repulses his neighbors that they kill him—is damaged. The wishes that fairy tale people receive are perfect in themselves— they are flawless gift. But it is in the nature of human beings to damage a gift like a wish—there is no way a human being could not receive the wish damagingly (and thereby wish for the wrong thing). The damage comes when a perfect giver (in the case of the fairy tale, a sprite, or a fish, perfect in its kind) gives a perfect gift to a particular kind of recipient—not necessarily a recipient who is damaged, but rather simply a recipient who in her nature cannot help but mangle the gift.

What kind of givers are Ackerley and the grandmother and the fish with his wishes? What kind of grandmother gives a toddler something breakable? With this question, we have arrived at theology proper: What kind of God gives us a gift we can't use well? Divine giving is not like Ackerley's gift to Tulip—God does not give gifts that the recipient simply does not know what to do with. But the grandmother might be like God—if (and only if) she is not in fact an incompetent, stupid, or inadequate grandmother, but rather if she knew beforehand that the child would break the figurine, and knew that this breaking would bring about good that otherwise would not come about. The child, possessed by the memory of the Meissen figurine, grows up to become the most renowned porcelain artist of the twenty-first century, the Michelangelo of porcelain—and the grandmother, gifted with foresight, knew this would happen. What kind of God gives gifts we can't use well? The God who gives felix'd gifts.

Of these four kinds of possible (and possibly interlocking, simultaneous) damage, gifts given by God can be damaged only in the latter two modes. They cannot be damaged in or by the Giver (who is perfect), and they cannot be damaged in the object itself (because that Giver gives only flawless gifts). They can be damaged only in or by the recipient—either because the recipient is damaged, or because a recipient like *this* (a three-year-old) will be likely to receive a gift like *that* (a Meissen ornament) badly.

Thus it can be said that God gives damaged gifts. The only gifts of God that could be otherwise are gifts given and received in the eschaton, and gifts given and received among and between members of the Trinity.

In the present age (postlapsarian, preeschatalogical), people are damaged, and will therefore receive things in a damaged way (I drop the platter, I harbor adulterous intentions for the negligee). Indeed, the essence of the Fall is exactly that human beings received gifts in a damaged way. God's giving the gift of being and existence to us was like giving the toddler that Meissen—we didn't receive the gift properly. Give a thing like *that*—a perfect wish; perfect being—to creatures like *us*, and we receive it damagingly. At the beginning of creation, none of the three parts of the gift troika was in itself damaged—the gift (being) and the Giver (God) were perfectly what they were, and the recipients (Adam and Eve) were perfectly what they were. But because of the kind of creature they were, Adam and Eve did not receive the gift they had been given without mangling it. The toddler shattered the figurine.[5]

If Creation and Fall can be glossed in terms of gift, so too can redemption. Torah is precisely *given* to (not, say, sold to or, as with Prometheus and his fire or Tantalus and his nectar, burgled by) Israel. There are two midrashim on the revelation at Sinai that (especially when put together) may be read as a comment on people's incapacity to receive gift. In one midrash, God attempts to give the Torah to numerous peoples—the Edomites, the Ishmaelites, and so forth. None of the peoples will accept the gift; instead, they all ask about the Torah's details, and, finding something objectionable (the dietary codes, say, or the way of marking holy time), they refuse to accept the offering. And so at last God comes to Israel. Israel accepts the gift without parsing its particulars.[6] Couple this midrash with a second midrash, which glosses the phrase *b'tachtit ha-har* ("at the foot of the mountain") in Exodus 19:17. In this midrash, God offers Israel the Torah and Israel accepts—because God holds Mt. Sinai over the people's heads, threatening to crush the people with the mountain if they do not.[7] This midrash could be read to say covenant is not gift at all, but coercion; or it may be read as a sign that the people is not constituted so as to receive the gift as gift. The revelation of the Torah is perfect gift by perfect Giver. Yet the people receive it in a damaged way.

The Prophets record, over and over, people's capacity to misuse the gifts God gives. The book of Hosea describes people's misusing agricultural gifts—corn, wine. (The form of misuse was to offer these gifts to a foreign God; the circumstance that made possible the misuse was the people's ignorance of the identity of the giver: "She did not know that it was I who gave her the grain, the wine, and the oil, and who lavished upon her silver and gold that they used for Baal" [Hosea 2:8].) Ezekiel records misuse of the gift of the Sabbath and the land (Ezekiel 20:11–13).

A third gift people misuse in Scripture—one that has direct implications for understanding Jesus as gift—is kingship. The scriptural account of kingship seems, at first blush, to be preeminently a record of misused gift, gift damaged in the reception. In 1 Samuel 8, the people petition God for a king. *We want to be as other nations are,* the elders say to Samuel; *we don't want to be governed only by judges; we want a king.* God explains to the distressed Samuel that it is not Samuel the people are rejecting; they are, in fact, rejecting God, and have been doing so ever since God led them out of Egypt. The Lord then instructs Samuel to tell the people how it will be—what a king will demand of them, what a king will take from them. Samuel does so, but the people insist they want an earthly monarch. So God says, "Listen to them and give them a king," and the results are, let us say, mixed. There are, in the Samuel account, multiple gifts, made damaged by multiple botched receptions. Foremost, the people cannot rightly receive the gift of God's kingship—the kingship itself is perfect; the reception of it damaged. Second, the people do not receive aright God's gift of human political structures. They are dissatisfied with the judges God has given them, because they want to be like other peoples (this means, too, that the people are failing in some way to receive their unique identity, also a gift from God). And once God gives them what they think they want—a king—they deform and distort that form of governance too, as seen in the long chain of pockmarked monarchy that follows.

Yet even this gift has profoundly positive consequences, and the Scripture is keen to preserve both the good (say, Josiah's reforms) and the bad (say, Manasseh's abuses); in the span of just two chapters (8–9), the book of Judges both agrees with 1 Samuel 8 that the request of kingship can rightly be interpreted as a rejection of God and acknowledges that kingship was a gift that helped order a disordered society. The psalms warn people not to put their hope in princes (Psalm 146). Yet on the other hand, the king is a recipient of divine blessing who enacts great victories (given to him by the Lord) (Psalms 20, 21)—and who in turn mediates divine blessing for the people (Psalm 72). What goods can come out of the kingship? Social goods: The monarchy and its attendant ideology justified nationalism, but also emphasized the king's duty to provide justice for the marginal. As J. J. M. Roberts notes, the same ideology that animated imperialism also "lies at the base of the great prophetic visions of universal peace." Also, theological goods: Ironically, it was precisely human kingship in Israel that helped fully develop the theological (and devotional) notion that the Lord was indeed king of kings. And, as Roberts has argued, "The royal theology's claim that God has chosen David and his dynasty as God's permanent agent for the exercise of divine rule on earth was the fundamental starting point for the later development of the messianic hope," a hope that Christians see fulfilled in Jesus. Roberts acknowledges the underbelly of kingship—"No one will deny that quite human and sometimes sinful motivations played a role in the formation of the kingship and of the imperialistic royal ideology that was developed to undergird it"—and then aptly questions the significance of this acknowledgment: "Theologically one must ask, So what? The God portrayed in the Bible has never seemed averse to working through human agents who were less than perfect." Just so.[8]

It should thus be no surprise that the gift of Jesus-as-king is misreceived. At first—that is, in both Matthew and Luke's accounts of Jesus' conception and birth—the biblical texts seem to suggest the gift will be received rightly. The Gospel of Luke opens with a dispatch about gift reception, showing two people (Mary and Zechariah) receiving the same gift (news about an unexpected pregnancy) from the same giver (the angel Gabriel). What distinguishes the two pictures is the way the recipient receives. Zechariah receives damagingly, asking the angel for proof, for evidence that he, Zechariah, can trust his senses. Zechariah's response precisely illustrates the damaging of a gift in its reception (and Zechariah suffers a direct consequence— muteness; the temporary uselessness of the orifice through which the damage came). In contrast, when Gabriel comes to Mary, bearing news of Jesus' conception (and specifically of Jesus' kingship—Gabriel names Jesus as the one to whom "the Lord God will give . . . the throne of his ancestor David. He will reign over the house of Jacob forever, and of his kingdom there will be no end"), Mary asks a question that seeks deeper understanding (not a question that seeks proof or an epistemological account), and then she says, *Fiat mihi.* She is told about a gift;

she asks a question that will deepen her appreciation of the gift; and then she accepts it, perfectly.

Matthew also begins with the suggestion that Jesus' kingship will be received in an undamaged way. The first line of Matthew's Gospel tells us we are reading about a king—one born, that is, in the royal line of David. Then, after that king is born, Matthew shows us a picture of people, the magi, receiving the gift of Jesus-as-king perfectly. The story of the magi reads like a kind of fairy tale—an idealized portrait in which three mysterious and magical figures are able to follow stars and receive messages through dreams and recognize that the ruler of the world has been born to a seemingly ordinary young woman in Bethlehem. Upon arriving "at the place where the child was," the magi are "overwhelmed with joy," kneel down before Jesus, and present him gifts: gold, frankincense, and myrrh. The "meaning" of these gifts has been much pondered in the history of the church. As early as Irenaeus and Clement of Alexandria, Christians read the gold as a gift that designated Jesus' kingship, frankincense as a gift that designated his divinity, and myrrh a gift that pointed to the significance of his death. Biblical scholars question this interpretation, arguing that the gifts are better understood eschatologically, and also noting a connection between Jesus and King Solomon (who was also given gold and myrrh by foreigners).[9] The Solomon connection points to what the text (specifically, Matthew 2:2) straightforwardly says—that the magi understood they were searching for a king; presumably, they packed gifts that would be appropriate for terrestrial royalty. Regardless of the particular symbolism one finds in the three gifts, the magi's gifts are ineluctably a sign that the magi have received the gift of Jesus-as-king. In turn, their gifts are received by Jesus and his mother. (Yet the gold, frankincense, and myrrh are patently not countergifts. Rather than giving out of indebted obligation, the magi are simply doing what people who understand Jesus as a kingly gift do—responding to that gift with recognition and gratitude.)

The reader of these gospel stories might reasonably conclude that the ambiguity around kingship in the Hebrew Bible has resolved into a gift of kingship that would be rightly received. Alas, the magi and Mary are the only people who receive Jesus' kingship in an undamaged way. During Jesus' life people do perceive and respond to Jesus' kingship—but always with damage. This happens in Matthew and Luke's accounts of Satan's testing Jesus in the wilderness. Satan has a gift to offer to anyone he likes—kingship. (The language of giving and gift is especially pronounced in Luke's account.) He offers Jesus the chance to be king of endless kingdoms—but the kind of kingship Satan has to give is not consistent with the kind of king Jesus is. Satan has, in his way, recognized that Jesus is a king—but, of course, to say that Satan has done this "in his way" is to say he has done it with damage. (Satan's particular damaged recognition immediately entails his trying to get Jesus to renounce his kingship. This attempt to remove Jesus' kingship and replace it with another kind of kingship turns on Satan's having recognized that Jesus is king, but it is the very opposite of receiving that kingship as gift.)

The Gospel of John also records damaged reception of Jesus' kingship in John 1.

> Jesus decided to go to Galilee. He found Philip and said to him, "Follow me." Now Philip was from Bethsaida, the city of Andrew and Peter. Philip found Nathanael and said to him, "We have found him about whom Moses in the law and also the prophets wrote, Jesus, son of Joseph, from Naza-

reth." Nathanael said to him, "Can anything good
come out of Nazareth?" Philip said to him, "Come
and see." When Jesus saw Nathanael coming toward
him, he said of him, "Here is truly an Israelite in
whom there is no deceit!" Nathanael asked him,
"Where did you get to know me?" Jesus answered, "I
saw you under the fig tree before Philip called you."
Nathanael replied, "Rabbi, you are the Son of God!
You are the King of Israel!" Jesus answered, "Do you
believe because I told you that I saw you under the
fig tree? You will see greater things than these." And
he said to him, "Very truly, I tell you, you will see
heaven opened and the angels of God ascending and
descending upon the Son of Man." (John 1:43–51)

At first blush, this appears to be a perfect reception of the
gift of Jesus' kingship—Nathanael, a man of no deceit, declares
boldly, "You are the King of Israel!" But read more carefully,
this passage begins to sound similar to Luke's story about
Zechariah. Zechariah (unlike Mary, who assumed that what the
angel predicted would happen; she just wanted to know how)
asked an epistemic question. He wanted reasons to think that
the angel was right. Zechariah's question—the wrong kind of
question—is like Nathanael's question to Philip, "Can anything
good come out of Nazareth?" With this question, Nathanael
identifies himself as one who is confused about the kind of
evidence he needs and the circumstances in which he needs it.
This character trait is displayed again when Nathanael asks
Jesus an even more epistemically pointed question—How does
Jesus know what he knows? Upon hearing Jesus' answer, Nathanael quickly comes to see that Jesus is king. But he has received the gift of Jesus' kingship on the basis of the wrong

thing—on the basis of the "evidence" of Jesus' having seen him under the fig tree. For his wrong reception, Jesus rebukes Nathanael, essentially saying, *If that's why you think I'm king . . . well, it's certainly right that I am, but that's a misguided way to come to know it.*[10]

Finally, the Gospels depict damaged reception of Jesus-as-king at the crucifixion (revealed with special pointedness in the Gospel of Mark, where Jesus is not identified as a king until his trial, and then is named as king six times in thirty verses). When the soldiers and the chief priests refer to Jesus as king; when the soldiers clothe him with royal purple and crown him; when he is identified by a sign as "King of the Jews"—all of this is ironic, but it is also true. In their very parody, the soldiers and priests are in fact acknowledging Jesus' kingship.[11] Or, to put it more strongly: They are not *acknowledging* Jesus' kingship so much as they are *receiving the gift* of Jesus' kingship in an almost untenably damaged (and damaging) way; the contrast between their reception of the gift and Mary's reception of the gift could not be starker. Mark's account of Jesus' death concludes with a softer reiteration of the irony and the damaged reception, telling us that Jesus' loyal follower, Joseph of Arimathea, "was also himself waiting expectantly for the kingdom of God." This represents a codicil to the Gospels' portrayal of people's inability to receive Jesus' kingship in an undamaged way: Joseph of Arimathea, Mark is telling us, is generally oriented toward the good; he loves Jesus, and wants to bury him properly; he has rightly received him as a teacher, perhaps, or as a friend. But even he has failed to properly receive Jesus' kingship—he is "waiting expectantly for the Kingdom of God," not understanding (as Mark expects the reader to understand) that this kingdom has already begun to dawn in Jesus' death.[12] As codicils go, this is a gentle and hopeful one. Joseph of Arimathea shows the reader that there is a spectrum of gift reception, and he is much closer than the Roman soldiers to a reception of Jesus' kingship that is not especially damaged. There is hope for Joseph of Arimathea, and for the reader, too.

Given the Bible's testimony to people's damaged reception of gifts, is it any surprise that the church's reception of Jesus was, from the start, also damaged? Jesus—who comes as gift to redeem the act of gift-gone-wrong-in-Eden—is a gift given by the Father, and is also Giver. What he gives is foremost himself, and then he gives signs that recall and re-present that gift. His redemption is precisely redemption of the act of giving, which went wayward in Adam and Eve's fruited exchange. Yet here, at the moment Christians name as greatest gift, the church's reception was characteristically damaged—damaged by supersessionism, the telling deformation of Christianity. In the person of Jesus, the church has been given the gift of Jewish flesh—specifically, the gift of the Jewish flesh that knits Gentile flesh into the family of God. The Christian reception of the people of Israel is the paradigm of Christian people's expropriating (rather than receiving as gift) a dominical offering. Aptly, the category of gift ought to help the church articulate precisely that God's giving Jewish flesh to the church in the person of Jesus does *not* entail the abrogation of God's covenant with Israel. After all, a distinguishing feature of some gifts is that once you have given the gift, you, the Giver, still have it, and can give it again: so God can give covenant to Israel, and still give covenant to someone else. (If I give a student knowledge about Jean-Luc Marion's phenomenology of gift, I nonetheless retain the knowledge and can give it again to a second student without having to take it back from the first.)[13]

Jesus is gift, and from the start, the church receives that gift in a damaged way, insisting, as we hold out our hands for

Jesus, that our reception of him entails God's withdrawal of gift from the people of Israel (that is, from the people that makes it possible for Jesus to be who he is, the people into whom the gift of Jesus stitches the church). This same Jesus will give gifts, and as we have seen, the nature of the recipient makes it nearly certain that in the act of receiving the gift, the gift will be damaged. Dominical gifts are not damaged in the way that Beth March's handkerchiefs are damaged. They are damaged the way that fairy tale wishes are damaged. Eucharist, baptism, and prayer are perfect in kind, and are given by a flawless giver. But any gift given by a Giver like that to a recipient like us will be damaged.

In the eschaton, these problems will resolve. Those who receive resurrected flesh (which is to say, in my view, everyone) will be *imago Dei* transfigured—and thus able to receive the gifts we are given. In the time in between, the gift shouldn't be refused. Rather, one should receive the gift with gratitude, and with a dual certainty that it is for good as well as for ill.

But not only with gratitude. There are other practices and affective postures that ought to accompany Christians' receipt of damaged gifts from God: confession-repentance and lament.

In confession, Christians expose to God the ways they have been pulled away from and have turned away from the goods proper to them, and in repentance, Christians turn back toward the goods and the God who forgives. This choreography is a fundamental response to the recognition of our agency and complicity in damage.

Repentance entails, or houses within itself, other practices: cessation (and, where apt, prevention), and redress and repair. The penitent, definitionally, intends to cease doing the sinful act of which she repents. She may adopt new choreographies, habits, or discourses that will help her avoid repeating the sinful act, and if the sin belongs to a community of which she is part, she will encourage her community to likewise adopt habits and discourse that will help prevent the community from repeating its sinful act. An account of characteristic damage can help a community be alert to the kinds of damage its hallmark practices are likely to extend; thereby, an account of characteristic damage can help the community sometimes avoid extending such damage in the future. If a church knows that baptism constitutionally tends to go wrong by either overemphasizing or underemphasizing the extraction of the baptizand from her family, the church community can scrutinize its baptismal rites with an eye on extraction, realize that celebrating baptisms on a Tuesday night in the pastor's study with only immediate family present is not a great idea, and determine to baptize only at Sunday congregational worship or at deathbeds. If you know that Christianity's characteristic damage is anti-Judaism, you can look for hints of anti-Judaism in your reading of Scripture, and you can try to scrub your hermeneutic clean of anti-Judaism's stain. This is one reason to ponder a practice's characteristic damage—predicting, and thus meaningfully intending to avoid, arbitrary damage is difficult; but characteristics can be foreseen, and, sometimes, dodged.

Repentance also involves trying to redress the harm you caused when you turned away from your proper goods. Although there is never a one-to-one correlation between repentance, on the one hand, and redress and repair on the other, redress and repair often index the sincerity and depth of repentance, and some effort at redress is usually a sign of repentance to one's larger community (even if that community is no larger than the priest hearing your confession). Or, to put the point with more nuance, redress and repair can index repentance, and the penitent ought to pursue them—in cases where redress and repair are possible. Sometimes they are possible only to an extent wildly disproportionate with the crime: The Jew you murdered is dead; you can divest yourself of the wealth you earned by setting up a touristy chapel where (before you torched it) his house stood, and give that money to his orphaned children; that is partial reparation; but he is dead, and your reparations are limited. The disproportion shouldn't stop the murderer from pursuing what redress she can, but she shouldn't imagine that her redress is adequate to the harm. Sometimes, redress and repair seem, or are, not just disproportionate but impossible. To consider an example less grave than the murder of Jews: The insults your daughter screams at you from the foot of the stairs move you to feelings of deep penance about the cruel comments your twenty-six-year-old self made to your mother. But your mother died of congestive heart failure in 2003. You can confess your regret to God, but you cannot repair the pain you caused Mom. Or less grave still: Your procrastination and your insouciance about deadlines made your editor's hair turn white; you can pledge to abide deadlines in the future, but you cannot recompense your editor for his stress.

The choreography of repentance, then, involves intent to prevent the sinful action's happening again and it involves attempted redress. The worship committee at your church, which you chair, realizes that your congregation has been praying, each Sunday, that "all citizens of this nation experience peace"— the citizens, and no one else. Penitently, your committee asks the pastor to change the words of the prayer to "the people who live in this nation," and the pastor agrees to the change (that is, the committee tries to prevent the congregation's praying the problematic words in the future). Further, your committee writes a note explaining the reasoning behind the change and publishes the note in the church newsletter; organizes a parish-wide reading of a book about the daily lives of aliens living in the United States; and takes up a monetary offering for the alien family that lives down the block (that is, the committee attempts to meliorate the harm done by the congregation's previous prayerful focus on "citizens").

Of course, repentance has its own deformations. The characteristic damage of repentance is the presumption that having repented, one can become cavalier about the thing repented of; or the characteristic damage of repentance is the riotous activity that follows repentance, in the cases where that activity makes things worse, often in unexpected ways; or the characteristic damage of repentance is the mistaken thought that because I have apologized for my action, the effect of my action is as naught; or the characteristic damage of repentance is the prideful presumption that, having been penitently seared and having seen what the light of penitence shows me, I can make everything alright.

Or the characteristic damages of repentance is the inability of the penitent to see that she will, in fact, repeat the act of which she repents. Like all characteristic damage, this failure to predict the future does not always obtain. Sometimes, the penitent can escape it—when she does, her repentance is tinctured by her relative certainty that she will again be an agent of or again be complicit in the act of which she is repenting, even if she intends the opposite. Repentance thus tinctured is repentance that carries with it the recognition of its own incompletion, and thereby opens out onto lament.

Lament is the third practice and posture that properly accompanies the receipt of damaged gifts. Because the gifts are gifts, and because the gifts in question are given by God, we receive them with gratitude; because we've done damage to and with these gifts, we confess and repent. And third, we receive the inevitability of the gifts' sometimes carrying damage in their train with lament.

To invite lament is not to sidestep penance. It is, rather, to situate repentance's prevention, redress, and repair in a frame of lament. For example, when I place prevention in the frame of lament, I can see that the inconsistency of my efforts at prevention is itself lamentable. As suggested earlier, an account of damage can show a community some of the kinds of damage its hallmark practices are likely to extend, and thereby help the community be on the lookout for, and sometimes avoid, such damage. But the best possible outcome is the reduction, rather than the wholesale prevention, of future damage—a best outcome that is worthy of lament.

To invite lament is to recognize that lament is a needful response to, among other things, those damages of which I, the lamenter, am not morally blameworthy. Repentance involves recognizing discrete responsibility, and it is limited to the things for which I am responsible (which might include long-past actions of institutions of which I am a part, especially the ontologically charged institution that is the church—although, to be sure, it can be difficult to assess when the dynamic of responsibility across centuries is in play). Lament, by contrast, expands to include the damages of the cosmos for which I am not remotely responsible—the sinfulness of the world, the brokenness that we are born into and inherit, the principalities and powers by which we are trapped.

To invite lament is to recognize that human creatures cannot wholly repair the world. I can repent of my habit of praying only for citizens; I lament the sin-soaked structure of misbegotten desire that means I will sometimes inevitably pray for the wrong thing. Perhaps lament, which does not issue in anything beyond itself, is the content of repentance in cases where there's no remedial action to be taken, cases where the only possible practice of repentance is lament.

Christianity's twinned practice of repentance and lament is the way Christianity holds together original sin and moral responsibility. I believe lament is needful because I do not trust my own capacity to set aside damaging practices. Consider the case of Christian anti-Judaism. Although no particular form of Christian anti-Judaism is inevitable, the propensity for some form thereof is so tightly woven into the fabric of Christianity that Christians will always have to lament it. We can—we must—abjure anti-Judaism. But can the church abjure its anti-Judaism and be quite sure that it will never come back again?

Christians undertake lament in the context of a doctrine of providence that instructs us that the all damages will be taken up into God's healing. That is, our laments are sung on the register of *felix culpa*. That register is, or should be, uncomfortable, given the characteristic damage to which *felix culpa* itself is subject—the propensity to justify horrors by saying they will be better by and by. God takes horrors up into healing; that doesn't make them anything other than horrors that will be taken up into healing. Consider, once more, the question of how beauty may be wrested from damage, a question answered by *kintsugi*, those damaged and golden-repaired pots that are more before now than they were before they broke. Murdering Jews is, of course, not a beautiful golden crack in the Eucharist; neither is disciplining slaves a beautiful golden crack in prayer. Rather, it is our acknowledgment of damage, and lament about that damage, that might be turned, by God, into a golden vein. Host desecration narratives do not make the Eucharist more beautiful than it would have been without them, and healing does not make the damage something other than healed damage—but lament might be part of what makes a healed Eucharist more beautiful than a Eucharist that had never suffered or extended damage.

Of course, lament, too, is subject to deformation—we self-congratulate about our lamenting, or we look past the edge of lament to what lament will accomplish, or we lapse into quietism, mistaking as wholly lamentable sinful systems or sinful circumstances whose remedies we should pursue, and saying complacently "sin made me do it" about those things for which we are responsible and whose recurrence we should try to prevent.

It is thus with awareness that we cannot purely or perfectly lament that we nonetheless take up lament as one of the postures in which we receive God's gifts. After we have considered—faced—an account of the damage that inheres in our most elemental practices, we can (imperfectly) lament the inevitability of damage, and we can ask God to repair it. Any pursuit of repair must be grounded in our asking God to repair because the healing that we sometimes do comes tautologically through our cooperation with God. So we ask God to repair the damage. And then we ask God to allow us to participate in the repair.

Henry James's 1904 novel *The Golden Bowl* is about marriage and adultery, and about one woman, Maggie Verver, embracing knowledge and forging subjectivity. It is also a book about how to speak about damaged gifts.

The plot turns on the relationship between Maggie's husband and Maggie's stepmother, Charlotte. Before Charlotte and Amerigo married into the Verver family, they'd had an affair—and not long into their marriages, they resume it. The eponymous bowl first appears in the novel just before Amerigo and

Maggie marry. Amerigo and Charlotte are on a shopping expe-
dition, with the aim of buying Maggie a wedding present. In an
antiques store, they spy a crystal bowl which, the shop's owner
says, was gilded according to "some beautiful old process," "a lost
art."[14] Charlotte is drawn to the bowl and wants to talk to the
shop owner, but Amerigo, apparently bored with the shopping
trip, tells Charlotte he will wait for her outside. Charlotte and
the shop owner, who has a bit of the huckster in him ("the little
swindling Jew," Amerigo calls him at one point),[15] haggle a bit
over the bowl, which she wants to buy and give not to Maggie
but to her once-and-future-lover. Finally, Charlotte concludes
that she can't afford the golden bowl and goes outside to find
Amerigo. She admits to Amerigo that she wanted to buy the bowl
for *him,* and laments that she couldn't afford to. But Amerigo
has spied the bowl's flaw and tells Charlotte of it: The bowl has
a crack, and it is good that she didn't buy it.

> She thought again. "Thank goodness then that if
> there *be* a crack we know it! But if we may perish by
> cracks in things that we don't know—!" And she
> smiled with the sadness of it. "We can never then
> give each other anything."
>
> He considered, but he met it. "Ah, but one
> does know. *I* do, at least—and by instinct. I don't
> fail. That will always protect me."[16]

They are, of course, talking about the bowl, and also talking
about themselves. The damaged gift sits at the heart of every
love story: I give myself to you; I am damaged, flawed, and
contorted. To one who loves me, I am still a gift—received as a
gift, precisely because loved. Amerigo is wrong—not only to
believe that one can always detect flaws and that such knowledge

is protective, but in fact to seek protection itself. And Charlotte is wrong to think that, given the likelihood of an unknown flaw, "we can never . . . give each other anything." To the contrary, in every gift (of love) there are flaws, some of which we are perforce ignorant of and some of which we have caught sight of, and we give and receive nonetheless.

Later in the novel, in a stagy bit of plotting, Maggie herself buys the bowl—she intends to give it as a birthday present to her father. Unlike Amerigo, she has not detected the crack, and the shop owner, feeling guilty, decides to visit Maggie at home and confess the bowl's flaw. While on this errand of integrity, the shop owner sees pictures of Amerigo and Charlotte, and tells Maggie that he had met them together in his shop several years before. Maggie quickly understands that Charlotte and Amerigo have been having an affair, and a series of confrontations begins, with Maggie in pursuit of happiness that is undamaged; Maggie in pursuit of happiness that is like "the golden bowl—as it *was* to have been . . . The bowl without the crack."[17] This is always an impossible pursuit.

Over and over, *The Golden Bowl*'s principals are mistaken when they speak about the bowl. Perhaps the only one who says something exactly right is the ambiguous antiques dealer, who is at once slick dissembler and necessary truth-teller. The most important thing he says is not the dramatic truth he gives Maggie, but rather his (slightly unctuous?) offering to Charlotte about the need to disclose an object's flaws: "Does one make a present," Charlotte had asked the shop owner, leadingly, "of an object that contains, to one's knowledge, a flaw?" "Well, if one knows of it," the shop owner replied, "one has only to mention it."[18]

This is a call for a kind of account—an account that speaks of the flaws and damages that we know to be inherent in the beautiful things with which we surround ourselves (or, better, the beautiful gifts with which God has seen fit to surround us).

An aside: The golden bowl is not original to James, but appears first in Ecclesiastes 12, as a figure of death: "Remember your creator in the days of your youth, before the days of trouble come," writes the Ecclesiast, ". . . before the silver cord is snapped, and the golden bowl is broken, and the pitcher is broken at the fountain, and the wheel broken at the cistern, and the dust returns to the earth as it was, and the breath returns to God who gave it." James's biographers tell us that James placed a golden bowl—rather, than, say a blue vase or a red tea service, or a pitcher or a wheel—at the center of his novel not merely (or perhaps not at all) because he was inspired by Ecclesiastes but because he was inspired by an actual bowl that he had seen in a bank vault in 1902. The bowl was tied to Lamb House, the Rye estate where James had lived since 1897, and in which he wrote *The Golden Bowl*. George I had visited Lamb House in 1726, and during his visit, he attended a baptism held at the house. George I gave the golden bowl to the baptizand, a kingly christening gift.[19]

Giving an account of a gift's damage is one needful response to damaged dominical gifts. Another response is anticipating that even damaged gifts make possible goods that would have otherwise been impossible.

Toni Morrison's *Jazz* is, like *The Golden Bowl*, a novel of an affair (its etiologies and its aftermath) and a novel of a woman's knowledge and emerging subjectivity. Joe, a middle-aged black man in 1920s Harlem, has been faithful to Violet their whole marriage, but in middle age he takes up with Dorcas, a younger woman whom he meets in the course of his work as a cosmetics salesman. As the novel opens, Dorcas is dead, shot by her lover. Violet is furious, Joe is bereft. Husband and wife are together, but isolated; Violet wants to be close to Joe again, and he to her, but they can't seem to find each other. Months pass. Trying to draw near to her husband, Violet becomes obsessed with his dead mistress, putting a photograph of her on the mantel and sitting with Joe, staring at the photograph, both of them crying. (Like her biblical eponym, this Dorcas is well mourned.) Unsurprisingly, this is not a successful recipe for marital repair.

In time, Violet meets Dorcas's best friend Felice (from *felix*, as in *felix culpa*). Felice has come to Violet and Joe's apartment looking for an opal ring that Felice had lent to Dorcas, and which Felice suspects Violet may now have in her possession. The ring came, originally, from Tiffany's, where Felice's mother had been sent one day on an errand for her employer. The clerk treated Felice's mother abominably, and, burned by his racist rudeness, Felice's mother swiped the ring, and then gave it to Felice. She told Felice the ring had been given to her by her employer, but, says Felice, "I know my mother stole that ring."[20]

The ring cannot be extracted from the sin that attended the giving of the gift—the sin of racism, which produced the clerk's hideous behavior; the lie Felice's mother told to explain the ring's provenance. The ring was a stand-in anyway for what Felice really wanted, which was the kind of relationship that her mother, working away from home to keep bread on the table, didn't have time to give. Still, the ring had a boldness and an importance; it was a real inheritance, not because of its material value but because of what Felice's mother's theft showed Felice about her mother, and about how to be. Felice's mother was a notoriously deferential and law-abiding sort, "so honest that it makes people laugh."[21] Stealing the ring was out of character, and the ring became encrusted with Felice's mother's brave anger. The ring was a gift in itself, but more important, "the Gift never coincides with the object of the Gift":[22] The ring was a gift of a mother's teaching her daughter how to get along in this world; it was a token, or a cipher, a relic of courage and rare, righteous fury. "She gave it to me, and I love it," Felice explains.

It is the hope of recovering her ring that sends Felice to Violet's. When she gets there, she finds only Violet and Joe—the ring, it turns out, was buried with Dorcas. Oddly, the three like each other. Oddly, Violet and Joe stop looking at the portrait of the dead girl on their mantel and befriend Felice, and through her, each other. Through their friendship with Felice, Joe and Violet are able to find each other again and settle into a lovely kind of love. Felice's search for the opal ring her mother gave her—a ring tarnished by racism and untruth; a ring, perhaps, that was part of the adornment that held Joe's eye and prompted Joe's brashness at the party—has led somewhere good.

Sometimes damaged gifts lead not only to damage. And so we carry on with them, always hoping that, despite the damage, they will return us to one another, and to the Lord.

Appendix
Depristinating Practices

One of the most striking developments in Anglophone Protestantism over the past four decades has been Protestant theologians' adoption of the category of "practice."[1] *The Dangers of Christian Practice* can be read as an attempt to prise a fissure in recent (postliberal-high-theological and popular-Christian) accounts of practices, and to suggest that many current discussions of Christian practice are too rosy—are pristinated—and fail to acknowledge, let alone account for or respond to, the sin entailed by those practices.

"Practice" has come to do a particular kind of burnishing in the Anglophone theological landscape. Put in the bluntest terms possible, when a Christian theologian (or a "popular" Christian devotional writer) writes about a "Christian practice," she is almost always commending something to you. She is not usually warning you about the ways your practice (say, fasting) might entwine with the gendered social sin of eating disorders, or the way your practice (say, silence) might intersect with a generous Quaker anthropology and a charitable Early Republic reformist zeal to produce the practice of solitary confinement. For the Christian theologians of the past two generations who have been drawn to the category, "practice" is neither a label, neutral with respect to ends, for thinking about how people organize life, nor a code for hegemony. It is, much more often, keen endorsement.[2] To put this another way, there is a significant gap between, on the one hand, Bourdieu's contention that practices often function as "officializing strategies, the object of which is to transmute 'egoistic,' private particular interests ... into disinterested, collective, publicly avowable, legitimate interests"[3] and, on the other hand, practical theologians Dorothy Bass and Craig Dykstra's assurances that "practices, therefore, have practical purposes: to heal, to shape communities, to discern. Oddly, however, they are not only treasured for their outcomes. Just taking a full and earnest part in them is somehow good in itself, even when purposes that are visible to the human eye are not achieved"; and that "practices are filled with meaning, and the meaning goes far beyond our own spiritual life to touch all the suffering of humanity. Taking part in Christian practices can cultivate qualities we did not have before and open our eyes and hearts to the activity of God's spirit in the wider world."[4]

The recent Protestant theological recovery of "practice" conversation has two abiding hallmarks: First, Protestant theologians have turned to practice to redress a lack of attention to what Christians do and have done in the recent past—that is, the Protestant stance vis-à-vis practice has in no small measure been a stance of *recovering* practices. Second, when Protestant theologians write about Christian practices, they are almost always *extolling* the practices. This pristination of Christian practices occurs not because the theologians of practice are naïve but because of the particular work theologians are calling on Christian practices to do: counter other practices that (in their estimation) malform. Theologians frequently offer a Christian practice as a superior alternative to some other practice. (Sometimes the other practices that are being countered are [narrated as] external to Christianity, and sometimes they are internal to Christianity.)[5]

Those two hallmarks can be seen clearly in specifically postliberal Christian theology's use of practices that had either been ignored, downplayed, or simply not exploited for their formational potential. This is best explored via George Lindbeck and Stanley Hauerwas. For Lindbeck, the "abiding and doctrinally significant aspects" of religion are found neither in free-floating propositional truths nor in inner experience but in a religion's grammar. Because a religion definitionally comprehends its own grammar, sentences that sound like propositions ("Christ is Lord") become first-order propositions that make ontological truth claims only when they speak within a set of practices, only "as . . . used in the activities of adoration, proclamation, obedience, promise-hearing, and promise-keeping, which shape individuals and communities into conformity with the mind of Christ." When considering religions, then, it is the case that a person has to know how "to use its language and practice its way of life" before she can intelligibly affirm or reject any of the statements the religion makes about the nature of things.[6] Underpinning all this is Lindbeck's reading of Wittgenstein. Wittgenstein is principally attentive to language as a thing that people do, so to arrive at an analysis of language, he looks at practices of language (although he prefers the term "game" to "practice"). (Given the preponderance of structuralists and positivists who preceded Wittgenstein in linguistics, this was a polemical move.) What Wittgenstein does in the linguistic sphere, Lindbeck and Hauerwas do in the Christian sphere, and this Protestant deployment of Wittgenstein is a continuing thread in the fabric of the Protestant recovery of practices.

For Hauerwas, Christian community is a narrative and performative (or, perhaps better, narrating and performing) community.[7] It is through the "shared commitments and values of a community" that are "found in our inherited languages, practices, and institutions" that Christians are formed and sanctified. Those inherited practices and languages are a lot like bricklaying. To lay a brick, you have to learn a set of skills, and the attendant language (what is "frogging mud"?). You'll "make mistakes," and be "confronted with new challenges." You need to learn from a master bricklayer. Anyone who can follow this metaphor, Hauerwas argues, will end up with a fairly reliable "picture of what it means for the church to be a disciplined community ... what it means to be saved, what it means to be a Christian." And if bricklaying isn't your thing, another practice will do: "The most determinative moral formation people have in our society is when they learn to play baseball, basketball, quilt, cook." Grasp any of these practices, and you will have grasped something of the shape of the Christian life.[8]

Though Hauerwas rarely engages the nitty-gritty of historical accounts, he argues that the Christian community is also a historical community. It is the history of the church that allows Christians to have gotten and to get the church's practices right: To learn to lay bricks is to be "initiated into a history." More broadly, "theological ethics is not a 'creative' discipline; rather, it is parasitical on the form of the moral life that Christian men and women act out in their historical context. Christian ethics cannot create the form of Christian life and existence, it can only analyze and conceptually articulate what Christians have found to be the nature of the good in their actual living." Central to Hauerwas's account of Christianity is that habits can steward the story of God amid the many failings of sinful people. Without a community continuing to perform, through practices (habits), some semblance of discipleship, no one would ever have a chance of excelling in virtue; hence Hauerwas's oft-quoted observation that "saints cannot exist without a community, as they require . . . nurturance by a people who, while often unfaithful, preserve the habits necessary to learn the story of God."[9] Why carry on with habits or practices, given the likelihood of their (and our) going wrong? Hauerwas doesn't ask that question per se, but one answer may be found in his insistence that if we don't, we will erase the possibility of anyone's ever becoming a saint.

It is, perhaps, obvious from the very moniker "postliberal" why the category of practice appealed—and why the designation of something as a Christian practice/habit came to have an inoculatory effect in postliberal usage. The language of practice allowed postliberals to constitute religious identity around something sturdier than the porous weft of "belief"; and the language of practice gave theologians a way of describing and recommending Christianity that would make Christianity capable of doing something for people—capable of forming them. Theologians cared to do this precisely because they were aware that there were powerful forces—post-Fordist capitalism, American empire—that were malforming people, forming them away from Christianity and toward shopping malls and church sanctuaries bedecked with American flags. As Hauerwas put it in *A Better Hope*, "the time that is America is a time no longer shaped by the hope made possible by God but rather is the time shaped by quite different presuppositions [of the logic of capitalism]. As Christians confuse our time with American time we lose the ability to be patient in a world of injustice and war." Practices ranging from Eucharist to baptism to prayer can, on this account, combat capitalism's practices. Even marriage: because "you cannot have both marriage as lifelong monogamous fidelity in which children are desired and capitalism too," the Christian practice of marriage "may well prove to be one of the most powerful tactics we have to resist capitalism."[10]

Indeed, throughout his oeuvre, Hauerwas uses Christian practices to counter practices (and their goods) external to Christianity, such as militarism and late capitalism. For example, in "Why Gays (as a Group) Are Morally Superior to Christians (as a Group)," he offers prayer and bodily gestures of corporate worship as antagonists to war. "Christians are asked to pray for the enemy. Could you really trust people in your unit who think the enemy's life is as valid as their own or their fellow soldier? Could you trust someone who would think it is more important to die than to kill unjustly? Are these people fit for the military? Prayer, of course, is a problem. But even worse is what Christians do in corporate worship. Think about the meal, during which they say they eat and drink with their God. They do something called 'pass the peace.' They even say they cannot come to this meal with blood on their hands. People so concerned with sanctity would be a threat to the military."[11]

But theologians (including postliberal theologians) have also used Christian practices to counter—and reform, or reveal as other than we thought—things that are *internal* to Christianity. This is precisely what Eugene Rogers does in his discussion of marriage: He uses Christian practices to show the church something about its practice of marriage, and to argue forcefully that in light of what has been shown, the church should enact that practice differently that is, open it to same-sex couples (in his preferred language, recognize that gay and lesbian marriages are no more "irredeemable" than heterosexual marriages). Specifically, Rogers shows the church marriage's nature and goods by referring at once to the church's practice of monasticism and to its practices of marriage. He calls on Evdokimov's narration of Christian marriage as a monasticism *à deux* and a "mutual kenosis" to show the church something of marriage's *aboutness:* On the church's own terms, marriage is "not about procreation." Or put in positive terms, Rogers uses the practices of monasticism to show the church that the practice of marriage is "about a mutual satisfaction by ascesis"; marriage is an "ascetic practice," one form of the "universal ascetic vocation of Christians" (and although it entails hospitality, the hospitality in question is not necessarily the hospitality of parents to biologically produced—or any—children).[12]

Rogers's move—using one Christian practice to show the church something about another Christian practice—is articulated to a pneumatology that is attentive to how the Holy Spirit works in and through (and also despite) Christian practices. As he writes of his essay "Trinity, Marriage, and Homosexuality," "theologically, the essay claims to acknowledge the work of the Holy Spirit in mobilizing signifiers for the production of grace," marriage being the signifier in question here. Embroidering this pneumatology is Certeau, who helps Rogers show Christians that we have allowed marriage to be "policed by meanings generated at other sites," and inspire in Christians a desire that marriage "become once again a site generating transgressive meanings of its own." Also embroidering Rogers's pneumatology is Judith Butler. Rogers is fond of quoting this passage from Butler's essay "Contingent Foundations": "To deconstruct the concept of matter or that of bodies is not to negate or refuse either term. To deconstruct these terms means, rather, to continue to use them, to repeat them, to repeat them subversively, and to displace them from the contexts in which they have been deployed as instruments of oppressive power. . . .

[My procedure] does not freeze, banish, render useless or deplete of meaning the usage of the term; on the contrary, it provides the conditions to *mobilize* the signifier in the service of an alternative production." In "Trinity, Marriage, and Homosexuality," Rogers adds "[or marriage]" to Butler's "matter." Read as articulated to marriage, Butler's statement of method illumines Rogers's strategy: not to "negate or refuse" Christian marriage, but through the Spirit to "continue" it (and to continue with and within it), and to (in Rogers's case use another Christian practice to) "displace" marriage from a terrain on which it has been an instrument "of oppressive power" and return it to a terrain where it can be, more aptly, *the practice of marriage*.[13]

Feminist theologians (generally liberal feminist theologians) likewise have turned to "practice" as a positive, recuperative resource to recover something inadequately present in the recent Christian past, and to counter other practices that malform. In many instances, feminist theologians argue that practices *both* counter practices that are external to Christianity *and* can be a tool for transforming or rehabilitating practices *within* Christianity. If postliberal theologians began using practices in part to antagonize militarism, jingoism, and capitalism, many feminist theologians see in Christian practices a way to antagonize toxic body practices—both ecclesial and extraecclesial toxic body practices. Marcia Mount Shoop's *Let the Bones Dance: Embodiment and the Body of Christ,* for example, proposes that Christian practices can counter negative body practices "in the larger culture," and counter damaging practices (and attendant beliefs) *within* the church.[14] Mount Shoop explains that, in distinction to the widespread Christian "worship practices and patterns" that "silence" the body, she offers an "embodiment theology" that attempts "to expand and enrich, to deepen and to discern how Christian practice can not only embrace bodies but also stretch into the embrace of difference." Mount Shoop laments "the dearth of practices, both liturgical and otherwise, that allow us to live into embodied fullness of life." But "dearth" does not mean a complete lack of such practices. To the contrary, those ecclesial practices that *do* emphasize, or can emphasize, the incarnational aspects of our faith are a deep resource, inherent in Christianity, for realizing the "promise of the Christian life," that "we are transformed by God's embodied proximity to us. That transformation re-forms us most deeply when it seeps into the ways we inhabit our own bodies and into the ways we respond to the bodies of others." In particular, Mount Shoop, a Presbyterian minister, finds in "the rhythms of Reformed worship . . . the capacity to awaken and stretch our bodies into worshipful encounter with God. Confession, the Lord's Supper, and music each have this potential for bodies to take up more space in how we lean into God's sacred promise to be with us."[15]

Feminist theologians have also recovered practice as a category in order to argue that practices not often seen as Christian per se, or as devotional, may be narrated as exactly that. Thus such practices (and the women who practice them) can be drawn explicitly into the life of Christian faithfulness, rather than being seen as adjunctive to, irrelevant to, or at odds with said life. In particular, feminist theologians have brought the lens of practice to bear on motherhood, and a host of possible practices entailed therein. For instance, in "Mary Kept These Things, Pondering Them in Her Heart: Breastfeeding as Contemplative Practice and Source for Theology," Elizabeth Gandolfo makes "a case for breastfeeding as an empowering spiritual practice of contemplation." Noting that her "argument grants pride of place to practice as the starting point and goal of theological reflection," Gandolfo argues both that "the experience of nursing an infant, especially in the early weeks and months of life, can offer spaces and places for . . . more traditional contemplative practices of silent prayer, reflection, and meditation," and that breastfeeding fits nicely under a "broadened definition of contemplation" of entering into divine Eros (this "broadened definition" draws on Wendy Farley). Influenced by theologians ranging from Farley to Janet Martin Soskice to Elizabeth Johnson to Sarah Coakley, Gandolfo shows how breastfeeding can function as an act of contemplative *kenosis* and *ascesis*.[16] Similarly, in her book *In the Midst of Chaos: Caring for Children as Spiritual Practice,* Bonnie J. Miller-McLemore argues that people usually think "religious practice" means "a special ritual action with a structured format." By that measure, parenting is not a religious practice. But if instead practices are those things that "sustain faith in daily life, embody deep religious values, and preserve and convey faith across generations," then parenting very much is. Playing with kids in the afternoon, talking around the dinner table, reading Dr. Seuss—these are the practices of parenting, and they are practices that "train our eyes to see God amid change and time." Miller-McLemore draws on insights of the tradition to reframe parenting: picking up Simone Weil's notion of prayer as paying attention, she argues that the basic acts of parenting require and develop the skill of paying a particular kind of focused, loving attention. But Miller-McLemore doesn't always gloss a parental activity as fitting some previously definition of a Christian spiritual practice. Sometimes she uses parenting to challenge the tradition. For example, noting that "Living with children . . . thrusts one into change," she argues that the parent who is immersed in changeability might criticize the church fathers' assumption that, because God is impassable, "the spiritual life" is "about the pursuit of the eternal and unchangeable."[17] The logic of Gandolfo and Miller-McLemore is to leverage "practice" to argue for a new appreciation of maternal practices that have been disdained and ignored both within and without the church. The lens of practice allows them to articulate the spiritual and devotional possibilities of routine maternal tasks, and to expand what the Christian tradition thought it knew about what constitutes spiritual and devotional life.

Perhaps the most audacious use of "practice" in recent theological writing has been that of Sarah Coakley. Coakley, an intellectually idiosyncratic figure not easily assimilable to either the postliberal or the (liberal) feminist trajectory, nonetheless offers a reading of pristine and pristinating practice. In Coakley's case, the commended practice is contemplative prayer—specifically, prayer undertaken in "silence or near silence," which, it seems, Coakley practices daily.[18] The "silence of contemplation is of a particular, *sui generis,* form," writes Coakley, and it provides a privileged kind of access to the divine other: "Authentic contemplation . . . in its very practice of gentle effacement allows communication with the 'other' at a depth not otherwise possible, indeed perhaps not even imaginable."[19] While she does not wish to reduce contemplation to its effects, Coakley holds that contemplative prayer, if pursued faithfully will (and *alone* can) begin to reorder the desires of the person praying.[20] As she put the matter memorably in her essay "Prayer as Crucible":

> No less disturbing than the loss of noetic control in prayer and all that followed from that was the arousal, intensification and reordering of desire that this praying engendered. Anyone who has spent more than a short time on her or his knees in silence will know of the almost farcical raid that the unconscious makes on us in the sexual arena in

such prayer, as if this is some sort of joke that God
has up God's sleeve to ensure that "ourselves, our
souls and bodies" are what we present to God and
not some pious disembodied version of such.[21]

To reorder desire is to accomplish something of evident psycho-
analytic import—but that pales alongside the more urgent
theological and spiritual significance that emerges when one
considers Coakley's preferred articulation of sin as "misdirected
desire." Perhaps even bolder than the suggestion that contemplative prayer is a place in which "grace and the Spirit" might attend
to "desires [that] are strongly inflected by sin"[22] is Coakley's
argument that contemplative prayer must underpin the practice
of writing theology. The task of theology, writes Coakley, demands "the practices of prayer, contemplation and worship."
Because "a particular set of bodily and spiritual practices . . . are
the *precondition* for Trinitarian thinking of a deep sort," if one
does not participate in those practices, notably contemplative
prayer, "there are certain sorts of philosophical insights that are
unlikely, if not impossible to occur to one."[23] Contemplation is
necessary for theology, for Coakley, at two levels. First, contemplation is necessary at the level of methodological defense: It
protects *théologie totale* from the critique that systematics will
collapse into hegemony, because contemplation fosters un-
mastery, and constitutes an "appropriately apophatic sensibil-
ity," a "vertiginous free-fall [that] is not only the means by which
a disciplined form of unknowing makes way for a new and
deeper knowledge-beyond-knowledge; [but also] the necessary
accompanying practice of a theology committed to ascetic
transformation." More narrowly, a theology grounded in prayer
is demanded by our culture's obsession with sex and the "ecclesiastical paroxysms" that obsession has unleashed. Arguing that

"only engagement with God who had been ineluctably revealed and met as *triune* could hold the key to contemporary anxieties about sexuality, gender, and feminism," Coakley posits that "prayer and renewed asceticism . . . [must] be at the heart of any attempt to solve the profound question of desire with which the churches" struggle.[24] Ultimately, on Coakley's account, contemplative practice is necessary for writing theology because "the task of theology is always, if implicitly, a recommendation for life. The vision it sets before one invites ongoing—and sometimes disorienting—response and change, both personal and political, in relation to God. One may rightly call theology from this perspective an ascetical exercise—one that demands bodily practice and transformation, both individual and social."[25] This is, like other turns to practice, postfoundationalist, but, stresses Coakley, "what distinguishes this position . . . from an array of other 'post-foundationalist' options that currently present themselves in theology, is the commitment to the discipline of particular graced bodily practices which, over the long haul, afford certain distinctive ways of knowing." Having defined theology as a task that "involves not merely the *metaphysical* task of adumbrating a vision of God, the world, and humanity, but simultaneously the *epistemological* task of cleansing and reordering the apparatuses of one's own thinking, desiring and seeing"; and having claimed for contemplation a unique and privileged capacity to give access to God and to reorder desire, Coakley then concludes that not only is the latter necessary for the former, but that "the interplay of theological investigation and ascetical practice" reforms the practitioner's "very capacity to see." Through this interplay, "one is learning, over a lifetime—and not without painful difficulty—to think, act, desire, and see aright."[26] Contemplative practice, then, uniquely reknits ascetical and dogmatic theology. Contemplative practice is the means by which the Triune God who is the object of theological study takes practitioners into the Trinitarian ontology of desire—into the Triune God's hallmark desiring of God's self—and thereby regenerates practitioners' capacity for *theologically* approaching God. (Thus one might say that, on Coakley's account, it is contemplative practice that allows God to be, or shows that God is, not only the object but also the subject of theological study.)

Practice, as a category, is malleable, and has been fruitfully taken up by theologians for a variety of purposes—to constitute Christian identity against the backdrop of late capitalism; to make a theological case for same-sex marriage; to reveal the spiritual potency latent in seemingly extrareligious practices; to frame theological study. Recovered practices have been deployed for certain good (according to the deployers) purposes, including countering practices that malform, whether those practices are internal (as in the case of Rogers) or external (as in the case of Hauerwas) to the church. What unites these projects is that in each, practices have been embraced as a way of fixing something in or for the church; practices have been embraced as strategy of recuperation, repair, or reform.

But there is another way of talking about practices—to suggest that Christian practices carry with them their own deformations. If recent Christian discourse has engaged in a certain repristination of the category of Christian practice, my effort to show that it is internal to these practices to form those who practice them away from the practices' own goods may be considered a depristination.

Notes

Characteristic Damage

1. The question of nonhuman animals' sin is an interesting one. Traditionally, the church has attributed sin only to what Jesus assumes and can redeem; thus the church has not attributed sin to nonhuman animals. The reasoning whereby some nonhuman primates might be included in the category of creatures-with-agency-who-sin goes something like this: if nonhuman primates (or extraterrestrials, or any other living creature) share some quality with us that means they can sin, then they share that quality with Jesus, too.

2. My use, throughout this book, of the category "damage" is indebted to Griffiths, *Intellectual Appetite*, 29–49; Griffiths, *Christian Flesh*, 19, 28, 30–38, 106–7, 142; and especially to the formulation that "liturgy is celebrated in a devastated world, and is itself therefore damaged and imperfect," in Griffiths, *Decreation*, 101.

3. Why the language of forms? I use it not to summon, in the strong sense, an Aristotelian taxonomic version of Platonism, but rather because Genesis 1–2 suggests that God's creative action was involved with kinds, and to sort the world into kinds, you need the language of forms. In other words, instead of indicating, by use of the metaphor "form," a broadly essentialist Platonism (which is to say a thick Aristotelianism), I use "form" to indicate instead a Wittgensteinian heuristic of family resemblances. The language of "form" is useful because, although it is philosophically and historically complicated to say precisely what, for example, "Eucharist" or "chair" or "father" means across time, "Eucharist" means *something*—that is, the use of signifiers across time is not an empty device. The Eucharist is not in every instance identical across time, and to speak of the Eucharist across time is not to say that every Eucharist from the Last Supper to last week is identical in every

particular—but that is no reason to avoid using the word "Eucharist" to denote phenomena widely separated in time and space (or to avoid thinking about what makes it possible to do so).

4. On this point, it is useful to engage Annabel Wharton's recent work. As Wharton's title—*Architectural Agents: The Delusional, Abusive, Addictive Lives of Buildings*—suggests, she argues that buildings perpetuate and often are the agents of harm. Wharton discusses "sick buildings"—buildings that make their residents sick. True enough, buildings (their lousy ventilation, the chemical compounds they comprise, and the microscopic lifeforms they harbor) can and do "make those who occupy them ill"—but when we speak of buildings "making" someone ill, are we really indicating the building's agency? Rather, the agents of the residents' illness are surely the fashioners of housing policy that forces people to live in such buildings; the fashioners of the health care policies that prevent people from having access to preventative care; the fashioners of economic policy that makes people unable to afford nutritious food that would in turn bolster their immune systems; and so on. Wharton also offers the Cloisters as an example of a building with agency. The Cloisters had to destroy other buildings in order to exist. It is true that the Cloisters is "a synthetic whole constructed from the transplanted parts of old European buildings," but who is the agent of the destruction and transplanting (a question prompted not only by Wharton's argument, but also by her use of the passive voice)? The agency was that not of the Cloisters' buildings (which, in fact, didn't exist as such before the destruction of the buildings from which they are built) but of the architects—surely it is architects, and not buildings, who are "architectural agents." My argument that a building has no agency and cannot itself contribute to harm is not to deny that (again to quote Wharton) "nonhuman entities . . . have an effect on their environments, independent of intention." But if we are considering agency, only animate beings have it (a stipulative point on which Wharton and I disagree)—therefore buildings and other inanimate objects cannot contribute to damage by their own agency. Consider the example of a high school built in 1972 by a panel of forward-looking architects. The architects were well intentioned and good at their task, but within fifteen years it was clear that the very features of the building that seemed so promising in 1972 in fact produce effects that are deleterious. Further damage may result from what the building is like—but the damage is agented not by the building, but rather by those who designed it, built it, and crafted residential and educational policies that sent some students, but not others, to it every day. The building is not to blame. The ignorance of the architects (which is a result of the Fall, and which usefully illustrates human beings' limited capacity to rightly predict the effects of our actions, and

ought to chasten the confident predictions we make about the effects of our actions) is to blame. See Wharton, *Architectural Agents,* passim (quotations in this note are at xiv, xxi, xxiii).

5. Hornsby and Reid, *New England and the Maritime Provinces,* 163.

6. Rossetti, "The World," in *Christina Rossetti: Poems and Prose,* 44.

7. Tasso quoted in Maiorino, *The Portrait of Eccentricity,* 58.

8. Watt, *The Rise of the Novel,* 9–30; Jacobs, *Pleasures of Reading in an Age of Distraction,* 101–15, passim; and Smiley, *Thirteen Ways of Looking at the Novel,* 15.

9. Jacobs, "Narrating Ethics," 41.

10. Colson, "Mark Doty: Fire to Fire," 28.

11. Sjögren, "Access to Power Through the Family Meal," 89.

12. Renkl, "In Praise of Family Meals," 157.

13. An interesting example from Sjögren, "Access to Power Through the Family Meal," 94: "A young mother related a painful experience: she had decided to include the housekeeper's son in her group of five young children. But his manners were not the same. When he was alone with her own children it did not matter, but, in the presence of the other children, it became an obvious embarrassment, and she had to stop it."

14. Wilk, "Power at the Table": "The dinner table is often a place where parents exercise authority over children, making it a common site for struggles over the impressions made by family members in public, standards of etiquette, and moral rules" (432–33).

Eucharist

1. Roberts, *Encyclopedia of Comparative Iconography,* 183.

2. Merback, *Pilgrimage and Pogrom,* 2.

3. Rubin, "The Eucharist and the Construction of Medieval Identities," 47.

4. Ibid., 47–49, and Rubin, *Corpus Christi,* 63–82.

5. Rubin, "The Eucharist and the Construction of Medieval Identities," 47.

6. Abulafia, "Bodies in the Jewish-Christian Debate," 124–26.

7. Ibid., 129–30.

8. Ibid., 131–34.

9. Ibid., 134–35.

10. For the ongoing debates about transubstantiation, see Macy, *Treasures from the Storeroom,* 36–58; Mazza, *The Celebration of the Eucharist,* 154, 200–215, and passim; Adams, *Some Later Medieval Theories of the Eucharist,* 98–115 and passim. For the text of the council, see Tanner, *Decrees of the Ecumenical Councils,* 227–72.

11. Fourth Lateran Council, Canon 68.

12. Textual context suggests this "they" refers to both Muslims and Jews, but given the range of rule of the Latins, it probably referred in practical terms mostly to Jews. For more, see note 14 below.

13. Fourth Lateran Council, Canon 68.

14. Brian Catlos offers an illuminating discussion of the distinctions between Muslims and Jews in medieval canon law. It was at Lateran IV that "the status of subject Muslims was first addressed substantially. The context was not Islam per se, but the status of non-Christians and the preservation of the primacy and integrity of the Christian community. Thus . . . Muslims and Jews were ordered to wear distinctive (but unspecified) garments. The fear was that, unless they were clearly identifiable, Christians might accidentally have sex with them, which would open the door to apostasy. The same canon demanded they remain indoors from Good Friday to Easter Sunday, and commanded the 'secular princes' to punish them should they 'blaspheme Him who was crucified for us'" (Catlos, *Muslims of Medieval Latin Christendom*, esp. 372–76). But although paired with Jews in Lateran IV, Muslims do not appear much in the more local discussions and documents that regulated Jewish and Christian interaction, which bloom across Europe during the thirteenth century. Why? Jews and Muslims can be paired together sometimes because they fall into the category of non-Christians who might in one way or another be problems. But in every other respect, they were different. There were (comparatively) many Jews in most of the local areas in question. There were few Muslims in Latin Christendom other than in the Iberian Peninsula; thus, on the ground in towns and states hammering out practical questions, Muslims did not present the same number of practical questions as did Jews. What Christians worried about, when they worried about Jews and when they worried about Muslims, was different. Muslims posed questions about the Holy Land, and about (at least tropologically) the question of continued military threat; no one thought the Jews were about to invade Italy. Furthermore, the tenor of Christian feeling about Jews was different than it was about Muslims precisely because Christianity was derived from Judaism, Christianity and Judaism partially shared Scripture, and Jesus was a Jew. This is not to underplay Christian judgments about Muslims but rather to underscore that Christian theological concerns about Islam and Judaism, and the church's socially regulatory force as deployed toward Jews and Muslims, proceeded along different trajectories, often toward different ends, despite the intersections that surface at the Fourth Lateran Council.

15. Wakefield, *Heresy, Crusade, and Inquisition in Southern France 1100–1250*, 44 ff.; Michael, *A History of Catholic Antisemitism*, 51; Teter, *Jews and Heretics in Catholic Poland*, 181n62; Despres, "Mary of the Eucharist," 382n25.

16. Rubin calls attention to the dovetailing of Eucharistic doctrine and regulations about Jewish-Christian encounters in Lateran IV and other councils in Rubin, *Gentile Tales,* 27–31; see also Baron, *A Social and Religious History of the Jews,* 34.

17. Rubin, *Gentile Tales,* 41–43. See Abulafia, *Christian Jewish Relations,* 188.

18. The chronology of this paragraph (which is by no means a comprehensive list of host desecration violence) is drawn from Rubin, "Imagining the Jew," esp. 189–90, 205; Rubin, *Gentile Tales,* esp. 53, 68–69, 115–17; and Merback, *Pilgrimage and Pogrom,* 73–74.

19. Merback, *Pilgrimage and Pogrom,* 2.

20. Rubin, *Gentile Tales,* 44–45.

21. Merback, *Pilgrimage and Pogrom,* 3 and passim.

22. Teter, *Sinners on Trial,* 73–89, 110–41, and passim (the *kyrie* is on 89).

23. Nirenberg, *Communities of Violence,* 218; see also Newman, "The Passion of the Jews of Prague," 4–5.

24. Rubin, *Gentile Tales,* 5, 200n 13.

25. Bloom, *The Anxiety of Influence,* 14. There is potential for a form of tessera to be displayed in the Eucharistic rite's articulation to a Passover meal. (Although the Last Supper is connected to Passover in the Gospels, the connection was not drawn between *the Eucharist* and the Passover meal in the first centuries of its celebration. But relatively quickly, Christians made the connection—the habit of interpreting the Eucharist as a seder was sufficiently widespread by the fourth century that Chrysostom felt the need to homiletically correct those Christians who reasonably concluded that, since the seder was annual and the Eucharist was a Christian version of the seder, they needed to attend Mass only once a year.) In the Eucharist's articulation to a Passover meal, to what extent does the Eucharist, in its very form, represent both the appropriation and the superseding of Jewish ritual? For the argument that when Passover and Eucharist are figured as "theologically related," that relation "will model and epitomize how Judaism and Christianity are related more generally," and for a model of how the Eucharist might articulate itself to the Passover meal without claiming to supersede it, see Boulton, "Supersession or Subsession?"

26. This is why, for Christians, supersessionism must be an urgent problem—not only because of what it says about Jews (and not only because of the violence toward Jews it helps make possible), but also because of what it says about the keeper of the house: finally, supersessionism is a problem because of what it says about God and God's characteristic keeping, or not, of God's promises.

27. Wells, *God's Companions,* 8–9.

28. Williams, *Being Christian,* 46–47; Wells, *God's Companions,* 211.

29. Hauerwas and Wells, *The Blackwell Companion to Christian Ethics,* 42.

30. Hauerwas, "The Interpretation of Scripture," 263.

31. NB: my phrasing in this paragraph is, it must be admitted, a tad polemical—at least one of the most persuasive proponents of the centrality of the Eucharist, William Cavanaugh, would abjure the language of church as polis. See *Torture and Eucharist,* 269–71.

32. One of the great postliberal accounts of the Eucharist is William Cavanaugh's *Torture and Eucharist* (1998). There, Cavanaugh excavates the Pinochet regime, limning the way that state-sponsored torture works to destroy people's lifeworlds, and characterizing state-sponsored torture as "a kind of perverted liturgy" (12). Cavanaugh argues that the church in Chile created an alternative politics grounded in the practice of Eucharist. In Chile, "the actual . . . impact of the Eucharist" on the violent dictatorship of Pinochet in Chile in the 1970s and 1980s was to make possible practices of resistance, community, and presence; the Eucharist proclaimed that the state had no claim to either the bodies of Christians, or to Christians' politics (205). This is, of course, one possible account of the politics that can issue from the Eucharist. But what might we see when we create a diptych of Eucharistic politics—a diptych whose left is the Eucharist's mobilizing politics in twentieth-century Chile, and whose right is the Eucharist's mobilizing politics in medieval Franconia? In a 2014 article about the protests he participated in when living in Santiago as a young man during the early 1980s (the tail end of the Pinochet regime), Cavanaugh notes that "Street protests don't do much except put bodies in public spaces where they can be seen. That a military regime armed to the teeth would find this threatening says a lot about the way political power works. Political power is largely about configuring bodies in space in order to tell stories with them." The state, Cavanaugh says, wants to arrange bodies in space in a particular way; so, too, "the Eucharist is fundamentally an action that arranges bodies in public space." Indeed, "The Eucharist is an authoritative touchstone for configuring bodies in space and time" (Cavanaugh, "The Church in the Streets," 385, 389, 392). On the other side of the diptych, place medieval church leaders' increasing concern about Jewish bodies' nearness to the Eucharist in the streets. There, too, the Eucharist was arranging bodies in (street-)space—but with an aim toward self-protection rather than hospitality. There too, the Eucharist configured bodies to control stories – to prevent Jews' telling stories Christians fearfully imagined they might tell about Jesus, and to fund Christian stories that in turn funded violence.

33. Bader-Saye, *Israel and Church after Christendom,* 141.

34. Healy, "Practices and the New Ecclesiology," 301. I am indebted to Joseph Mangina for pointing me to Healy's article. This chapter and the next two may be seen as a historically inflected response to the concerns Healy raises—an

effort to historically instantiate his claim that the church often misperforms our practices, and to add to his criticism the suggestion that it belongs to the practices that we do so.

35. Ochs, "Morning Prayer as Redemptive Thinking," 72.

36. Ibid., 86.

37. Saliers, "Afterword: Liturgy and Ethics Revisited," 214–15. For a model of the kind of analysis of the Eucharist that Saliers calls for, see Garrigan, *The Real Peace Process,* and Garrigan, "Theology, Habermas, and Corporate Worship."

38. On questions of digestion, breaking, and the like, see Adams, *Some Later Medieval Theories of the Eucharist,* 259–75; Rubin, *Corpus Christi,* 37; Macy, "Theology of the Eucharist in the High Middle Ages," 375–88; Stone, *A History of the Doctrine of the Holy Eucharist,* 275–310. Bynum connects the host desecration choreography to yet another doctrinal debate: the question of whether "a living God resides not less in part than in whole." Bynum, *Christian Materiality,* 211–12. Many thanks to Stephanie M. Green for helping me work out and formulate this reading of the choreography of host desecration as an inversion of, and a response to, pressing theological questions about, the Eucharist.

39. Parker, *The Aesthetics of Antichrist,* 117; see also Shell, *Art and Money,* 15.

40. Rubin, "Imagining the Jew," 183–84. For another discussion of medieval Christians' recognition of "the Host's fragile vulnerability," see Merback, "Jewish Carnality, Christian Guilt, and Eucharistic Peril in the Rotterdam-Berlin Altarpiece of the Holy Sacrament," 227.

41. On eschatological Eucharists, see Griffiths, *Decreation,* 262–63; Adams, *Some Later Medieval Theories of the Eucharist,* 277–95.

42. On God as the subject of remembering, see Morrill, *Anamnesis as Dangerous Memory,* 149–51, 163.

43. Grimes, *Fugitive Saints,* 161, xi.

44. Mathews, "Sacrament and Segregation," 307.

45. Book of Common Prayer, 337.

46. It is hard for me to capture the strangeness of writing this—I am, after all, not a Gentile Christian, but a baptized Jew. So there are questions raised for me in this paragraph that I cannot answer here, or even really clearly ask, but I begin to suspect that I may know the answer before I know the question. The answer is, maybe, that just as the Gentile Christian has to allow herself to be remade, after centuries of supersession and "Gentile forgetfulness" (to use Willie Jennings's recent and forceful articulation), so too the baptized Jew must at once allow herself to be ever a baptized Jew, and, in some solidarity precisely with this sin of the church she has joined, allow herself to be remade

into a Gentile of a sort. In other words, it will not do.for the baptized Jew to
hold herself apart from the thing the Prayer of Humble Access must now, in
the face of the history this chapter reviews, come to mean.

47. Newman, "The Passion of the Jews of Prague," 1–7.

48. Merback, *Pilgrimage and Pogrom*, 72–80; Rubin, *Gentile Tales*, 65–68.

49. Rubin, "Imagining the Jew," 192–96. See also Rubin, *Gentile Tales*, 57–68.

50. Newman, "The Passion of the Jews of Prague," 24–25. See also Narin
van Court, "Critical Apertures"; and Narin van Court, "Socially Marginal,
Culturally Central."

51. Rubin quoted in Narin van Court, "Critical Apertures," 3.

52. For one account of the contest, see Bischoff, *Eucharistic Controversy*.

53. See Green, *The Gospel of Luke*, 765; Fitzmyer, *The Gospel According to
Luke*, 1409; Davies and Allison, *The Gospel According to Saint Matthew*, 464n67;
and Culpepper, *The Gospel of Luke*, 423. For interpreters who argue that Judas
did *not* receive the Eucharist, see Brown, *The Gospel According to John*, 575,
578; Schnackenburg, *The Gospel According to St. John*, 3: 30. See also the discussion of Hilary of Poitiers in Thomas Aquinas, *Summa Theologiae*, III.81.2.

54. Augustine, Sermons on the Gospel of John, 62.3.

55. Chrysostom, Homily 82 on Matthew, in Thomas Aquinas, *Catena Aurea*,
chapter 12, 248–49, 254–57. See also Thomas's extraction of Leo the Great and
Augustine. In the Middle Ages, these readings were considered sufficiently
authoritative that the rare person who argued that Judas did not receive risked
an ecclesiastical trial. Rupert of Deutz, for example, landed himself in just
such a trial in Liege in 1117, and he was spared heresy charges only because
at the "last minute," someone realized that Rupert's belief that Judas had not
received had precedent in Hilary of Poitiers. The trial, and the obscurity of
Hilary's view, suggest that while multiple interpretations of the Last Supper
were theoretically possible, the view that Judas received was normative. See
Malegam, *The Sleep of Behemoth*, 128–31.

56. For the strongest reading by a modern scholar arguing that the morsel in John is "Eucharistic," see Moloney, "A Sacramental Reading of John
13:1–38," esp. 250–54.

57. Augustine, Sermons on John, 62.3, Latin text from online database
Library of Latin Texts.

58. Heck and Cordonnier, *The Grand Medieval Bestiary*, 404.

59. Roberts, ed., *Encyclopedia of Comparative Iconography*, 182. For a bril-
liant reading of Judas's appearance in medieval artistic renderings of the
Last Supper—and, in particular, for an argument about how those images of
Judas not only participated broadly in Christian anti-Judaism but might also
have intersected with Christians' concerns about "unworthy reception"—see

Merback, "Jewish Carnality, Christian Guilt, and Eucharistic Peril in the Rotterdam-Berlin Altarpiece of the Holy Sacrament," esp. 207–15.

60. Roberts, ed., *Encyclopedia of Comparative Iconography*, 183.

61. Rubin, "Imagining the Jew," 192–93. As Rubin shows, Klosterneuberg is one of the locations in which, post facto, doubt was registered—that is, it is one of the places in which people asked, *Was there in fact a host desecration?*

Prayer

1. This is the only surviving volume, but the absence of any opening reflection on the practice of diary keeping, coupled with the pervasiveness of the practice among women in Brevard's class, strongly suggests that it was not the first volume. For more on free antebellum southern women's diary-keeping habits, see Harrison, *The Rhetoric of Rebel Women*, 14–18.

2. Brevard, in Moore, *A Plantation Mistress on the Eve of the Civil War*, 41–42.

3. There is, of course, an internal tension in Brevard's diary entry of October 19, and throughout the diary: she related that she wishes she had been born in a "Christian land" where slavery did not exist. In other words, she suggested that at some level she believed the entire system of slavery was unholy, anathema: a *real* "Christian land" would not impose this on people. In the same paragraph, she prayed to God for herself and her slaves *and* expressed misgivings about the Christian underpinnings of the entire system.

4. For example, testimony to Elizabeth Foote Washington's use of prayer in trying to compel her slaves to work survives because she wrote down her philosophy of household management for her own daughters, lest she die before she could teach them the tricks of the trade. See Winner, *A Cheerful and Comfortable Faith*, 112–15.

5. On the influence of Cary's work, see Varon, *We Mean to Be Counted*, 14.

6. Cary, *Letters on Female Character*, 64.

7. Ibid., 31.

8. Ibid., 31.

9. Winner, *A Cheerful and Comfortable Faith*, 118.

10. McCorkle Diary, Third Booklet, 1847, Record of Fifth & First Sabs, Aug./Sept., Thursday, Sept. 9.

11. Schwalm, *A Hard Fight for We*, quotation at 76, but see also 75–115. See also Wood, *Masterful Women*, 57, 169; Faust, *Mothers of Invention*, 57; Weiner, *Mistresses and Slaves*, 166–67; Harrison, *The Rhetoric of Rebel Women*, 108, 199n61; Fields, *Slavery and Freedom on the Middle Ground*, 92–105; Glymph, *Out of the House of Bondage*, 97–136, esp. 100–104.

12. Weiner, *Mistresses and Slaves,* 84.

13. The historian Thavolia Glymph notes the inherent absurdity and injustice in "white women['s] . . . 'giving' gifts like clothing (made, of course, by their purported beneficiaries of cloth purchased by their labor), and hand-me-downs (purchased, again, with profits from the labor of slaves)." Glymph, *Out of the House of Bondage,* 10.

14. Brevard, in Moore, *A Plantation Mistress on the Eve of the Civil War,* 74.

15. Glymph, *Out of the House of Bondage,* 33–35; Winner, *A Cheerful and Comfortable Faith,* 112.

16. Glymph, *Out of the House of Bondage,* esp. 45–46; Fox-Genovese, *Within the Plantation Household,* 24.

17. McCorkle quoted in Glymph, *Out of the House of Bondage,* 45.

18. Ida Henry, *Born in Oklahoma Slave Narratives (Slave Narratives from the Federal Writers' Project 1936–1938),* 13: 135. (The narratives are searchable at http://memory.loc.gov/ammem/mesnquery.html.)

19. Harriet Casey, *Missouri Slave Narratives (Slave Narratives from the Federal Writers' Project 1936–1938),* 10: 73.

20. Parris, " 'A Dutiful Obedient Wife,' " 70–71.

21. See, e.g., Cornelius, *Slave Missions and the Black Church in the Antebellum South,* 130; Carney, *Ministers and Masters,* 114–35.

22. There is very little discussion, in the historiography of antebellum and Civil War–era women, of women's using prayer as a slave-management technique. See Winner, *A Cheerful and Comfortable Faith,* 112–18, and Glymph, *Out of the House of Bondage,* 49. Harrison, *The Rhetoric of Rebel Women,* includes an extended and illuminating discussion of Civil War–era women's prayers more broadly (114–41). Her discussion focuses on women's prayers for the Confederate nation and on the questions "Could slavery as an institution be morally justified, and if so, were they meeting their personal responsibilities as slaveholders?" Harrison does not focus on the place of prayer in day-to-day household management.

23. Brevard, in Moore, *A Plantation Mistress on the Eve of the Civil War,* 40, 47.

24. "Thoughts on the Religious Instruction of Servants," *Gospel Messenger and Southern Episcopal Register,* September 1834.

25. Charles C. Jones, *A Catechism, of Scripture, Doctrine, and Practice, for Families and Sabbath Schools, Designed Also for the Oral Instruction of Colored Persons,* 6th ed., 138.

26. "Thoughts on the Religious Instruction of Servants," *Gospel Messenger and Southern Episcopal Register,* September 1834.

27. Duncan, "Benjamin Morgan Palmer," 4, 46–47, 117 (for evidence of Palmer's slave owning); Byron, "'A Catechism for Their Special Use,'" 167–68; and Palmer, *A Plain and Easy Catechism,* 47, 40.

28. Jones, "Submission, Suffering, and God," 171, 132, 68.

29. Brevard, in Moore, *A Plantation Mistress on the Eve of the Civil War,* 95.

30. Douglass, quoted in Bowman, *At the Precipice,* 246.

31. Brevard, in Moore, *A Plantation Mistress on the Eve of the Civil War,* 64.

32. Ibid., 104.

33. Diary of Susan Nye Hutchinson, January 3, 1832, quoted in Clinton, *The Plantation Mistress,* 185.

34. On slave-owning women's use of prayer after they had "failed . . . to control their tempers," see Glymph, *Out of the House of Bondage,* 49.

35. Brevard, in Moore, *A Plantation Mistress on the Eve of the Civil War,* 33. Cf. Wood, *Masterful Women,* 52.

36. Brevard, in Moore, *A Plantation Mistress on the Eve of the Civil War,* 105.

37. Glymph, *Out of the House of Bondage,* 32–62.

38. McCorkle Diary, volume 1, page 9, "2nd Sunday"; Magruder quoted in Woods, *Emotional and Sectional Conflict in the Antebellum United States,* 89.

39. McCorkle Diary, Second Sab, October 10, 1847.

40. Michael E. Woods, *Emotional and Sectional Conflict in the Antebellum United States,* 72–95.

41. Berlant and Prosser, "Life Writing and Intimate Publics," 183.

42. Berlant, *The Female Complaint,* viii.

43. Douglass, *My Bondage and My Freedom,* 106.

44. Jefferson, *Notes on the State of Virginia,* 168.

45. Brevard, in Moore, *A Plantation Mistress on the Eve of the Civil War,* 85.

46. Beasley, *Christian Ritual and the Creation of British Slave Societies,* 99.

47. Gundersen, *The Anglican Ministry in Virginia,* 111.

48. Tugwell, "Prayer, Humpty Dumpty, and Thomas Aquinas," 26.

49. For the phrase "misdirected desire" see Coakley, *God, Sexuality, and the Self,* 26, 51n, and passim.

50. Tugwell, "Prayer, Humpty Dumpty, and Thomas Aquinas," 43.

51. Book of Common Prayer, 323.

52. Stump, "Petitionary Prayer," 87, 90.

53. A naming of desire is not the only kind of statement that can carry with it an intimate offering of self, of course. Lament, which entails a disclosure of what the lamenter mourns; confession, which entails a disclosure of what the confessor regrets; thanksgiving, which entails a disclosure of what the thankful one delights in—those prayers, too, are potentially intimate offerings that might deepen friendship between the giver and the recipient.

54. In this way, erotic pursuit is an obvious partial analogy to prayer. As in prayer, in erotic pursuit one of the few things clearly visible is how unclear participants are about whether the thing they are pursuing (I want sex; I want you; I want affirmation; I want to be the kind of person who wants sex; I want to be the kind of person who offers sex) is the kind of thing they should be pursuing.

55. Berlant, *Cruel Optimism*, 1–2, 24.

56. On Brevard's marriage see John Hammond Moore, *Columbia and Richland County: A South Carolina Community, 1740–1990* (Columbia: University of South Carolina Press, 1993), 160.

57. Brevard, in Moore, *A Plantation Mistress on the Eve of the Civil War*, 77–78.

58. Brevard's eschatological vision provides a nice counterpoint to the account given in Ownby, "Patriarchy in the World Where There Is No Parting?"

59. Cassian, *The Conferences*, 300.

60. Brevard, in Moore, *A Plantation Mistress on the Eve of the Civil War*, 81.

61. Ibid., 81–82.

62. Ibid., 83.

63. Ibid., 90.

Baptism

1. Nesbit, "Melisande."

2. On the history of forced baptism, see Colish, *Faith, Fiction and Force in Medieval Baptism Debates*, 227–318.

3. For language of incorporation, see, e.g., *Dominus Iesus*, IV.17; *Unitatis Redintegratio*, II.22.

4. Historian of liturgy Susan J. White suggests that this has been true not only for American history but for most of church history: "Baptism was the premier occasion when ties of fealty and kinship were publicly displayed." White, *A History of Women in Christian Worship*, 190.

5. This is clear not only from an extension of what baptism does to the three local variables named in Galatians 3:28. It is also clear from Galatians 3:29: "And if you belong to Christ, then you are Abraham's offspring, heirs according to the promise." As Jon D. Levenson has noted, this verse upends the easy shorthand that Christianity is "universalistic," while Judaism is "particularistic." For Paul, argues Levenson, "the Church is not just a particularistic community; *it is made up exclusively of descendants of Abraham*" (emphasis in

original). Far from erasing the category of lineage, baptism turns on a transformed lineage, making the baptized "descendants of Abraham" (Levenson, *Inheriting Abraham,* 27–28). Elsewhere Paul takes up familial language in ways that suggest that family identity is overwritten but not erased in baptism. On the one hand, Paul uses familial language to speak about the relationship with God and one another that the baptized can have—suggesting that Christians' final familial identity is found in ecclesial and divine bonds, rather than nuptial and biological bonds. As E. Elizabeth Johnson has argued, Paul suggests that baptism creates a kind of adoption by God, whom the baptized can then call Father (e.g., Gal 4:6; Rom 8:23), and Christians enter a "household" of faith (Gal 6:10). Furthermore, "Christians are not merely children of God and therefore siblings of each other, they are all heirs, co-heirs with the firstborn (Rom 8:17; Gal 3:29; 4:1, 7), a remarkable use of the rule of primogeniture in a world that privileged birth order. The fictive kinship of the Christian community even takes precedence over legal and biological kinship for Paul when the church's 'peace,' rather than any religious commitment, determines whether a brother or sister agrees to be divorced from an unbelieving spouse (1 Cor 7:15)." But Paul himself maintains a sense of his "kinfolk according to the flesh"—that is, unconverted Jews—"so much so," Johnson notes, "that he would even relinquish his own connection to Christ, were it his to lose, for their sake ([Rom] 9:1–5)." Paul's language of grafting Gentiles onto the tree of the Abrahamic covenant precisely captures the both/and: God adopts (a principle that privileges ecclesial family over any earthly family), but the very thing Gentiles are being adopted into is a familial identity and covenant (and metaphor) that turns on the perduring significance of lineage. See Johnson, "Apocalyptic Family Values," 38–40; see also Hodge, *If Sons, Then Heirs,* especially her discussion of lineage on 100–106.

6. Augustine, *Confessions,* I.xi(17).

7. Augustine, *Confessions,* IX.vi(14). Jeremias also discusses the centrality of the household unit to baptism in the early church: The New Testament often speaks of the baptism of "households" (I Cor 1:16, Acts 16:15, 33, 18:8). The language suggests that a head of household (father or widow) was baptized, and with him or her, the whole household of the head. Jeremias, *Infant Baptism in the First Four Centuries,* 19–23.

8. On parents, rather than godparents, having responsibility for the child baptizand's religious formation, see Cressy, *Birth, Marriage, and Death,* 156; López, "Ecclesiastical Godparenthood in Early Modern Murcia," 81; and Hollander, "The Name of the Father," 71.

9. On the cleric's physical removal of the infant from the parents, see Muir, *Ritual in Early Modern Europe,* 23; Gillis, *A World of Their Own*

Making, 25; Robinson, *The History of Baptism,* 488; and Winner, *A Cheerful and Comfortable Faith,* 31.

10. Ferguson, *Baptism in the Early Church,* 750.

11. Jensen, "Mater Ecclesia and Fons Aeterna," 148; Berger, *Gender Differences and the Making of Liturgical History,* 81–83; and McGowan, *Ascetic Eucharists,* 99, 107–15.

12. Jensen, "Mater Ecclesia and Fons Aeterna," 153. Cf. Jensen, *Living Water,* 247–51.

13. Sonne de Torrens, "Reconsidering the Date of the Baptismal Font in San Isidoro, León, Spain," in Sonne de Torrens and Torrens, *The Visual Culture of Baptism in the Middle Ages,* 53–54, 64–65.

14. Debby, "Nel mio bel San Giovanni," in Sonne de Torrens and Torrens, *The Visual Culture of Baptism in the Middle Ages,* 21.

15. Bobbio Missal, in Whitaker, *Documents of the Baptismal Liturgy,* 266, 270.

16. By the time John's Gospel was compiled, baptism had come to be understood as a rite of *regeneration.* Jensen, "Mater Ecclesia and Fons Aeterna," 137, 139.

17. Stowe Missal, in Whitaker, *Documents of the Baptismal Liturgy,* 276, 280.

18. Syriac-Maronite rite in Whitaker, *Documents of the Baptismal Liturgy,* 99–108.

19. NB: Luke 2 conflates two rituals: the *qorban yoledet* (the mother's postpartum sacrifice) and the *pidyon haben* (the redemption of the son). There is no extra-Lukan evidence that these two events were ever actually performed together; literarily, they establish the piety of Jesus' family. For the unlikeliness that the *qorban yoledet* and the *pidyon haben* would typically have been performed together, see Ward, "The Presentation of Jesus," 21–39. See also Brown, *The Birth of the Messiah,* 447–51.

20. Karant-Nunn, *The Reformation of Ritual,* 57.

21. Beyond this reading of family and household as a small monastery or cradle of Christian formation, some Protestant communities—notably Zwinglian communities—stressed that baptism itself (in the words of liturgical historian Bryan D. Spinks) "comes as part of a family ticket!" In other words, only children of parents who were covenanted members of the church could be presented for baptism. There are twentieth-century instantiations of this view, such as Anglican theologian Gordon Kuhrt's argument that infants of nonpracticing Christian parents should not be baptized. Spinks, *Reformation and Modern Rituals and Theologies of Baptism,* 33, 153.

22. Old, *The Shaping of the Reformed Baptismal Rite in the Sixteenth Century,* 202.

23. Hollander, "In Name of the Father," 67.

24. Lynch, *Godparents and Kinship in Early Medieval Europe,* 120, 277–79. In the early church, adult baptism was the norm. When infants were baptized, Lynch explains, the rite was merely tweaked to adjust "the adult ceremony to infant realities." This was true "even when infants predominated as the baptizees." The "chief adaptation was the interposition of one adult, ordinarily a parent, to speak and act on behalf of the infant" (120). It was "the ordinary pattern . . . for a parent to act as sponsor for his or her own child at baptism," but that practice was "on the wane since at least the sixth century" (277).

25. It is still the case that parents may not serve as godparents in the Roman Catholic Church. Code of Canon Law §874.1.5: to be admitted to the role of sponsor, a person must "not be the father or the mother of the one to be baptized." The story of Protestants' general acceptance, by the nineteenth century, of parents serving as godparents/sureties/baptismal sponsors for their own children is complex. At stake for some Protestants was not only the notion of home as a cradle of religious formation but also a defense of infant baptism (contra emerging Anabaptist critiques thereof). In the face of those debates, Protestant defenses of infant baptism turn on the insistence that infant baptizands must be the children of Christian parents; ergo parents are accorded a greater role in baptismal liturgies and their role in the Christian formation of their children underlined. (See the discussion of the early-sixteenth-century rite from Strasbourg in Old, *The Shaping of the Reformed Baptismal Rite in the Sixteenth Century,* 58 and passim.) Puritans, rejecting the very framework of godparentage as "popish," argued that parents should bring children for baptism (Cressy, *Birth, Marriage, and Death,* 150); this was in keeping with Calvin's belief that the father should serve as a sponsor, enacting ritually his commitment to see to the child's religious formation. By the late seventeenth century, in many Protestant communities, parents had replaced nonparents as godparents/sureties. As Will Coster summarized, "The result was the virtual completion of a process that had begun at the Reformation of a transfer of functions to the natural parents and thus, arguably, an increased emphasis on the role of the family" (Coster, "Baptismal Names," 322). By the mid-nineteenth century, Presbyterians could say that they did not require or encourage "appearance of any other sponsors in the baptism of children than the parents, when they are living and qualified to present themselves in this character" ("Presbyterians Reject Godfathers and Godmothers in Baptism," *The Presbyterian,* June 1851). And Methodists could by 1883 say, "In the baptismal ceremony the Methodist Churches do not recognize sponsors or god-fathers, as is the custom in the Roman Catholic Church, and in the Church of England. Parents or guardians are considered

the proper persons to present their children for baptism, and to take upon them the vows for their Christian education. While parents live no persons can supersede them in these duties" (Simpson, *Cyclopedia of Methodism,* 88). By the early twentieth century it was so common in Protestant churches for parents to serve as sponsors/godparents for their own children (often along with additional godparents, who would be relatives or close friends of the family) that etiquette doyennes could write, "Parents are, *of course,* the natural sponsors" (emphasis mine). Learned, *The Etiquette of New York To-day,* 189.

26. Lynch, *Godparents and Kinship in Early Medieval Europe,* 277.

27. For different estimates of kin as godparents see Tait, "Spiritual Bonds, Social Bonds," 321; Ciappara, "Religion, Kinship, and Godparenthood as Elements of Social Cohesion in Qrendi," 184, nn119–20; Smith-Bannister, *Names and Naming Patterns in England,* 44–45.

28. Cressy, *Birth, Marriage, and Death,* 156–58; Deller, "The First Rite of Passage," 3–14; Rios, "The Politics of Kinship," 295; and Ericsson, "Godparents, Witnesses, and Social Class in Mid-Nineteenth Century Sweden," 280. See also Tait, "Spiritual Bonds, Social Bonds," 321, and White, *A History of Women in Christian Worship,* 190.

29. See Wilson, *Unmanly Men,* 193–94; Finlan, *The Family Metaphor in Jesus' Teaching,* 61–69, 74–75; Rubio, *A Christian Theology of Marriage and Family,* 59–60; Calef, "The Shape of Family and Family Values," 228–33; Good, "Jesus and the Transformation of the Family," 53–60; Martin, "Familiar Idolatry and the Christian Case Against Marriage," 17–40; and Tolbert, "Marriage and Friendship in the Christian New Testament," 41–50.

30. See, e.g., Bennett, *Water Is Thicker Than Blood;* Isasi-Díaz, "Kin-dom of God"; and Daniels, "Is Kinship Always Already Reproductive?"

31. Hall, *Conceiving Parenthood,* 6–31, 107–22, 250–90.

32. For a helpful exploration of the New Testament's not articulating "one attitude towards the family," see Greer, *Broken Lights and Mended Lives,* 96–101.

33. On the tradition of reading the genealogy in Luke as a genealogy of Mary, see Miller, "Trying to Fix the Family Trees of Jesus." (The tradition of saying that one of the genealogies is Mary's is an attempt to reconcile the two.)

34. For a powerful reading of the ways the infancy narratives show that Jesus "will indeed be in direct contact with the divine beyond gender and earthly orders," while also being "thoroughly installed in the patriline," see Kearns, *The Virgin Mary, Monotheism, and Sacrifice,* 129–62 (this note's quotation is at 151).

35. See, e.g., Vander Zee, *Christ, Baptism and the Lord's Supper,* 126; Rubio, *A Christian Theology of Marriage and Family,* 48; Rubio, "The Dual Vocation of Christian Parents," in Curran and Rubio, *Marriage,* 190; Clapp, *Families*

at the Crossroads, 80; Crossan and Watts, Who Is Jesus? 46; and Smith, "God's Passionate Vulnerability," 48–49.

36. Garafalo, "The Family of Jesus in Mark's Gospel," 269. It may be worth considering that when political radicals wish to wholly obliterate the family, they also seek to get rid of language of the family (rather than, as New Testament writers do, using it to gloss other important bonds). For example, after charting a plan to "do away with the household," Anatoly Lunacharsky, the Soviet Union's Commissar of Education from 1917 to 1929, predicted confidently that "there is no doubt that the terms 'my parents,' 'our children,' will gradually fall out of usage, being replaced by such conceptions as 'old people,' 'children,' and 'infants.' " Lunacharsky quoted in Mount, The Subversive Family, 35. It is also worth noting that people citing this passage to argue for Jesus' disruption of the family usually cite Matthew or Mark, not Luke. See Hellerman, When the Church Was a Family, 64–65; Moxnes, Putting Jesus in His Place, 58; Martin, Sex and the Single Savior, 103–24; deSilva, Honor, Patronage, Kinship, and Purity, 197; and Rubio, A Christian Theology of Marriage and Family, 38. In his redaction of the Markan passage, Luke makes certain changes that have led some scholars to argue that Luke's account, more than Matthew's and Mark's, venerates Jesus' biological family. See Brown et al., Mary in the New Testament, esp. 51–59, 168, and Fitzmyer, The Gospel According to Luke, 1059–60.

37. On the importance of Mary qua Jesus' mother in John, see Gaventa, Mary: Glimpses of the Mother of Jesus, 96–97. On Mary and the Beloved Disciple in John's crucifixion scene, see Kearns, The Virgin Mary, Monotheism, and Sacrifice, 178–80. On the intensity of the relationships between mothers and sons in the ancient Mediterranean, and on Jesus' close relationship with his mother as illustrated in the crucifixion scene, see Moxnes, Putting Jesus in His Place, 36–37. On Jesus' giving "his physical mother" a unique "spiritual role," see Brown et al., Mary in the New Testament, 213.

38. On the intimacy between Mary and Jesus being grounded not only in Mary's conformity to a family of disciples but in her actual—bodily—life as his earthly mother, and on the relation between this intimacy and the Assumption, see Levering, Mary's Bodily Assumption, 143–44.

39. Griffiths, Decreation, 220.

40. Sonne de Torrens, "Reconsidering the Date of the Baptismal Font in San Isidoro, León, Spain," in Sonne de Torrens and Torrens, The Visual Culture of Baptism in the Middle Ages, 53–54, 64–65.

41. We tend to gloss John as Jesus' "cousin," but depending on what one means by "cousin," that may be too precise. Elizabeth is called Mary's relative or kinsperson (syngenis) in Luke 1:36. Thus imagining John the Baptist as Jesus' second cousin is not specifically supported by the text—but if one

means cousin in the extended usage of any kinsperson more distant than a sibling, it is an appropriate term for Jesus' and John's relationship.

42. The ritual objects of baptism—at least as it was enacted in premodern centuries—hint at this. The white chrisom cloth in which newly baptized babies were garbed was returned to the church to be used at future baptisms, unless the baby died within a few weeks of being baptized—in which case, she was buried in her chrisom cloth. Cressy, *Birth, Marriage, and Death*, 163; Orme, *Medieval Children*, 119. For an astute revisionist account challenging the widespread view that infants were buried in their chrisoms, see Oosterwijk, "Swaddled or Shrouded?"

43. Kearns, *The Virgin Mary*, 162.

44. Balthasar, *Dare We Hope That All Men Be Saved?* 23.

45. This is so not only at the level of theory but in the history of Christians' anti-Jewish polemics, which have sometimes spoken through the idiom of baptism: Baptism represented Christianity's universality (as it was open to anyone, including women), and circumcision represented Judaism's stubborn (carnal, familial, clannish, nonspiritual) particularity (as it was not open to Gentiles or Jewish women). As Shaye Cohen explains this baptismally inflected iteration of supersessionism, "With the death and resurrection of Christ . . . the old Israel was replaced by the new Israel, the old covenant by the new covenant. Jewish particularity no longer had any reason to continue, since all of God's children were now to be brought into the universal church. Ethnic Israel, Jewish particularity, and Jewish circumcision were all supposed to come to an end. Baptism replaced circumcision, and Christianity replaced Judaism. If carnal circumcision continued to be a sign, it was a sign of Jewish obduracy and sinfulness." Cohen, *Why Aren't Jewish Women Circumcised?* 83.

46. Strauss, *The Life of Jesus, Critically Examined*, 204. On Renan and Strauss see Ellis, "Jesus and the Subversive Family," 174.

47. Heyrman, *Southern Cross*, 128.

48. Wills, *Democratic Religion*, 16.

49. Blanchard, " 'It Is Surprising That There Are Any Happy Wives,' " 38.

50. Typically the christening part of the service was short—a point underscored by observers' and participants' noting the oddity of domestic baptism ceremonies extending beyond half an hour. See, for example, "Immersed Three Times," *New York Times*, June 26, 1891.

51. Learned, *The Etiquette of New York To-day*, 191; "Nourishing Foods and Drinks for the Sick," *The Sanitarian*; Rundell, *A New System of Domestic Cookery*, 503–4; and White, *Twentieth Century Etiquette*, 317.

52. To put this more explicitly in Kristevan terms, in the Knickerbocker christening fete, a short-circuiting of the play of signifiers reduced baptismal

meaning. Helpful here is Kristeva's discussion of the signifying unit becoming more and more "material" in the reduction of the symbol to the sign. In her discussion of the proliferation of miniatures in the fifteenth century, Kristeva offers a formulation that is applicable to the reduced forms of elemental "symbols" in the baptismal rite: "The serenity of the symbol was replaced by the strained ambivalence of the *sign's* connection, which presents the elements as similar and identical, despite the fact that it first postulates them as radically different. . . . Once the relation between the signifying unit and the idea had been weakened, the signifying unity became more and more 'material' until it forgot its 'origins.' . . . This transformation reveals a law wherein the signifying unit no longer refers back to the past 'idea' behind it, but instead becomes opaque, 'materialized,' and identifies with itself. Its vertical dimension begins to lose intensity, as its possible articulations with other signifying units are accentuated." The christening party, in short, is a "pastiche" in which signs are featured as deflated symbols—per Kristeva, they "bracket and erase the transcendental basis of the symbol." When family symbols (bowl, gown) replaced church symbols (public font, new vesture), "the transcendental foundation evoked by the symbol seemed to capsize." See Kristeva, "From Symbol to Sign," 65–67. I owe the Kristeva connection and the formulation of generation replacing regeneration to Stephanie M. Green.

53. *The Good Housekeeping Hostess*, 9.

54. Insightful discussions of household baptisms at various points in church history include Beasley, *Christian Ritual and the Creation of British Slave Societies*, 66–83, and Bowes, *Private Worship, Public Values, and Religious Change in Late Antiquity*, 49–50.

55. "Christenings," *Harper's Bazaar*, December 10, 1881.

56. In the late nineteenth century, the preaching of W. S. Rainsford, an Episcopal priest and devotee of the Social Gospel, began attracting an unprecedented number of working-class men to the pews of his tony East Side parish. The robber-barons and magnates who attended and funded the church looked on with tolerant discomfort until Rainsford suggested that it would be appropriate to elect one of the newcomers to the vestry (the board of laymen who governed the parish). At this, the senior warden, J. P. Morgan, drew the line: the vestry, he said, must be "a body of gentlemen I can ask to meet in my study." This is the kind of thinking about the church that flows logically from an exclusive christening party guest list. Rainsford, *The Story of a Varied Life*, 281.

57. Learned, *The Etiquette of New York To-day*, 190.

58. Dickerman, *The House of Plant of Macon, Georgia*, 190.

59. Earle, *China Collecting in America*, 219–20.

60. "Excerpts from the Scrap Book of the Late Mrs. Stephen McCandless," 22–23.

61. Gilchrist, *Medieval Life,* 91; Cressy, *Birth, Marriage, and Death,* 149, 163; French, "The Material Culture of Childbirth," 139; Nares, *A Glossary,* 160.

62. The Metropolitan Museum of Art, *Notable Acquisitions,* 36, and Kevill-Davies, *Yesterday's Children,* 267–68.

63. *The Good Housekeeping Hostess,* 9.

64. Hahn, *The Roots of Southern Populism,* 8; Hahn, "Hunting, Fishing, and Foraging"; and Hyde, *Common as Air,* 29–44.

65. In the early church, when adult baptism was the norm, white vesture was also important to the rite. The baptizand was naked when baptized, and then clothed in white garments after exiting the font. The whiteness was taken to represent, variously, the white clothes of the saints described in Revelation; the anticipated whiteness of flesh in the resurrection; the radiance of the transfigured Christ's clothing; priestly vesture; and purity. Ambrose spoke of the angels looking down on a baptism and exclaiming, with a nod to Song of Songs 8:5, "Who is this, coming up from the desert clothed in white?" Jensen, *Living Water,* 168–70.

66. I owe the insights of this paragraph to Stephanie M. Green.

67. The readership of the *Art Interchange,* for example—the periodical from which our first description was drawn—was, according to historian Mary W. Blanchard, "generally middle- or lower middle-class." Blanchard, " 'It Is Surprising That There Are Any Happy Wives,' " 37.

68. "Christening Beatrice's Baby," *Daily Inter Ocean,* November 26, 1887.

69. "An East-Side Christening Party," *Frank Leslie's Illustrated Newspaper,* May 9, 1885; "Baby, Beer, Bullets," *Rocky Mountain News,* April 11, 1887; and "Row at a Christening," *Morning Oregonian,* October 16, 1899. As Beth Stroud has made the point, "The affluent white Protestant baptism celebration was thus partly defined by what it was not." Irene Elizabeth Stroud, S.T.M. thesis, Lutheran Theological Seminary at Philadelphia, 2010, copy in author's possession.

70. In "Beautiful Babies," Stroud has suggested a link between the display of babies' bodies at domestic christening parties, the display of babies' at church-sponsored baby shows, and eugenics. See also Stroud, "A Loftier Race." On this reading, one could argue that domestic christenings helped constitute and sustain not only social location and class but also race and genetic pristination.

71. Kilen, "Century-Old Christening Heirloom Found, Returned to Family."

72. Vande Kemp, "The Family, Religion, and Identity," in Vande Kemp, *Family Therapy,* 53.

73. Covelli-Hunt, "Lineage Maker," in Martínez, *Lines and Circles*, 29–30. Excerpts from the poem "Lineage Maker," by Robyn Covelli-Hunt, from *Lines and Circles, A Celebration of Santa Fe Families,* edited by Valerie Martínez, appear courtesy of Sunstone Press, Santa Fe, New Mexico.
74. Dilley, "Christening Gown a Family Heirloom Before Its Time."
75. Stroud, S.T.M. thesis.
76. White, *A History of Women in Christian Worship,* 190–92.
77. https://www.pinterest.com/pin/164240717633000355/, last accessed May 9, 2015.

Damaged Gifts

1. And a fourth characteristic: modishness, as a category of analysis in history, theology, and social theory for several decades now. In the estimation of one theologian, "gift" has become "almost mantric in its repetition in recent continental and North American theology." Here, "mantric" might be taken to be a polite substitute for "trite," or it might really mean that the term gift focuses our attention—in this case, away from the mantra and toward the Giver. Coakley, "Why Gift?" 224.
2. Derrida, *Given Time,* 1: 7, 12. Cf. Marion, *Being Given,* 75.
3. Marion, *Being Given,* 94–102.
4. Alcott, *Little Women,* 37–59.
5. Near the end of the biblical story of the Fall, Adam offers an account of his disobedience, and in it, he speaks of having been given two things (the Hebrew verb, like the English verb, does not carry a strong connotation of "gift"—it could just mean *handed* or *placed in my possession.* But also like the English, the Hebrew is etymologically connected to and has aural resonance with "gift"). In Adam's account, God is giver, and Eve is both giver and gift— "The woman whom thou gavest to be with me, she gave me the fruit of the tree, and I ate." Adam, it seems, might think that he is exculpating himself by noting that Eve gave him the fruit, and that God gave him Eve in the first place (and many in the tradition have half-concurred, blaming Eve with vigor and venom, if not precisely exonerating Adam). But as we have seen, gift requires reception—thus Adam's receiving the forbidden quince is just as integral to the falling fruit exchange as is Eve's offering it. That Adam doesn't recognize this simply tells us that here at the very beginning, damaged gifts get entangled with damaged accounts.
6. Eichah Rabbah 3; Pirkei D'Rabbi Eliezer, ch. 41.
7. Shabbat 88a.

8. Roberts, "In Defense of the Monarchy."

9. Davies and Allison, *The Gospel According to Saint Matthew*, 249–51.

10. See Moloney, *The Gospel of John*, 56. A second damaged reception of Jesus-as-king happens when, as John 6 tells us, after the miracle of the loaves and fishes, the people "were about to come and take him by force to make him king." (In response, Jesus withdraws to a mountain by himself.)

11. On the crucifixion as parodic enthronement of Jesus as king, see Marcus, "Crucifixion as Parodic Exaltation."

12. Marcus, *Mark 8–16*, 1075.

13. On teaching as a gift that, having given, you still possess and can give again to someone else, see Augustine, *De Doctrina* I. Cf. Griffiths, *Intellectual Appetite*, 58.

14. James, *The Golden Bowl*, 119.

15. Ibid., 292.

16. Ibid., 123–24.

17. Ibid., 475.

18. Ibid., 121.

19. On George I's bowl and on the use of Ecclesiastes in the novel's title, see Treier, *Proverbs and Ecclesiastes*, 225–26, and Wrenn, *Henry James and the Second Empire*, 137.

20. Morrison, *Jazz*, 202.

21. Ibid., 215.

22. This is Horner's translation of Jean-Luc Marion, in Horner, *Rethinking God as Gift*, 131. A slightly less forceful iteration of the same point may be found in Marion, *The Visible and the Revealed*, 90.

Appendix

1. For an astute overview, see Ted Smith, "Theories of Practice."

2. At risk of making a sweeping overgeneralization, theology is not the only field in which a scholar who studies "practice" is often studying forms and rituals the scholar likes, or at least finds interesting; in which she is usually studying something that fosters agency and aids in subject formation, and is, for the subject, liberatory (if also tensive). Perhaps it is not going too far to say that, in some scholarly communities, to designate a study as a study of "practices" is to cast a rosy glow. People study practices of resistance and of community formation—not, say, of stultification. At least, this seems the case in history and religious studies. On this point, see Lofton, "Piety, Practice, and Ritual."

3. Bourdieu, *Outline of a Theory of Practice*, 48.

4. Dykstra and Bass, "Times of Yearning, Practices of Faith," 7, and Dykstra and Bass, "Ways of Thinking About a Way of Life." 217. Contrasting Dykstra and Bass with Bourdieu is intended, of course, primarily to serve as a dramatic heuristic. There are theorists of practice much closer to, and who have much more directly influenced, Christian theologians than Bourdieu. For example, despite the differences in rhetorical register, there are clear points of overlap between the purposes to which theologians currently put practices to work, and the insight of Michel de Certeau that practices are counterhegemonic. Certeau's analysis of the means by which people "reappropriate the space organized by techniques of sociocultural production"—and it is through the study of practices that we might pursue the "urgent" task of discovering how "an entire society resists being reduced to" social disciplines—is entirely consistent with (and Certeau's map of tactics and strategies has had specific bearing on) theologians' use of practices to oppose sociopolitical and cultural powers that they see as being at odds with the norms of Christianity; and there are clearly shades of Certeau's recognition that, for example, practices can "counterbalance . . . outside the reach of panoptic power" (Certeau, *Practices of Everyday Life*, xiii–xiv, 95) and theologians' (including but not limited to Hauerwas) use of Christian practices to counter social and political arrangements of and narratives within the surrounding society. Similarly, MacIntyre's influence on Christian theological discussion has been oft-remarked. (See, e.g., Bennett, *Water Is Thicker Than Blood*, 159; Smith, "Theories of Practice," 246–48; Richter, "Religious Practices in Practical Theology," 204; and Hauerwas, "The Virtues of Alasdair MacIntyre.") To my eye, as important for theological inquiry as his famous definition of a practice (MacIntyre, *After Virtue*, 175) is MacIntyre's energetic willingness to antagonize practices one to the other. For MacIntyre, certain approaches to moral inquiry are superior to others. That point is made clear in *Three Rival Versions of Moral Enquiry*, in which, as the title suggests, the author examines three "very different and mutually antagonistic" ways of "approaching moral enquiry" (the encyclopedic, the genealogical and, MacIntyre's preferred approach, the tradition-based; MacIntyre, *Three Rival Versions of Moral Enquiry*, 3–5). In *Three Rival Versions of Moral Enquiry* and in *Whose Justice? Which Rationality?*, MacIntyre argues that some practices are in fact constituted in such a way as to fail to bring about the ends they (seemingly) seek. The "Aristotelian-Thomistic" tradition-based approach is "superior" precisely because it answers questions generated internally by the other two in ways that they themselves cannot. This leveraging of one system of enquiry against another finds a parallel in how some theologians oppose practices to one another. Finally, there are

many resonances between Christian theological reflection on practices and the work of Pierre Hadot. Hadot (who, not coincidentally, was one of the first serious readers of Wittgenstein in France [Laugier, "Pierre Hadot as a Reader of Wittgenstein"]) recast our understanding of ancient philosophy, arguing that philosophy is not a system of thought, but (again, as one of his titles makes plain) a way of life. To become a philosopher was not to think a set of thoughts or even pursue a particular pattern of reasoning ("theory is never considered an end in itself. . . . It is put in the service of practice"), but rather to embrace a set of practices (ranging from dialogue to self-control to the cultivation of disinterest). On Hadot's account, the philosophical life was existential and converting, and it aimed to "provoke a transformation of the self." Hadot, *What Is Ancient Philosophy?* 176. Practices had the capacity to remake the worldview of the practitioner, and indeed the practitioner himself—a remaking that could not happen without them. Certeau, MacIntyre, and Hadot are rarely far away from Protestant (especially postliberal) theological conversation about practices.

5. Obviously, the extent to which things like capitalism and the nation-state are Christian, not-Christian, or Christian heresies is not straightforward. For a recent discussion, see Anidjar, *Blood*, 78–154.

6. Lindbeck, *The Nature of Doctrine*, 68, 129.

7. Hauerwas's most obvious engagement with the classical theorists of practice is his building on Certeau to diagnose the church as, in Certeau's phrasing, an institution that is "easily manipulable by powers of another order" ("Weakness of Believing"), and his use of Certeau's distinction between strategies and tactics. Hauerwas's use of Certeau is much noted (see, e.g., Wells, *Transforming Fate into Destiny*, 113–15, 139–41, 171; Katongole, "Postmodern Illusions and the Challenges of African Theology," 521; and Richard Bourne, *Seek the Peace of the City*, 158, 179–81) and is not without its critics, for example, Bretherton, *Christianity and Contemporary Politics*, 190–92. See also Kerr, "*Communio Missionis*," 317–36.

8. Hauerwas, *Vision and Virtue*, 66, and Hauerwas, *After Christendom?* 101–7.

9. Hauerwas, *Vision and Virtue*, 107, 37, 108, and Hauerwas, "The Gesture of a Truthful Story," 74.

10. Hauerwas, *A Better Hope*, 17, 51. A similar impulse threads throughout the postliberal corpus. For example, consider William Cavanaugh's taking up Christian practice—specifically the Eucharist—to counter consumerism. In *Being Consumed*, Cavanaugh analyzes consumerism as a (malformed) "spiritual practice" and proposes the Eucharist as its antitype and cure: "If in consuming the Eucharist we become the body of Christ, then we are called, in

turn, to offer ourselves to be consumed by the world. The Eucharist is wholly *kenotic* in its form. To consume the Eucharist is an act of anticonsumption, for here to consume is to be consumed, to be taken up into participation into something larger than the self, yet in a way in which the identity of the self is paradoxically secured. . . . The Eucharist effects a radical decentering of the individual by incorporating the person into a larger body. In the process, the act of consumption is turned inside out, so that the consumer is consumed." Cavanaugh, *Being Consumed,* 50, 84, 95.

11. Hauerwas, "Why Gays (as a Group) Are Morally Superior to Christians (as a Group)," 521. See also Hauerwas, "Should War Be Eliminated?"; Hauerwas, "On Being a Church Capable of Addressing a World at War"; and Hauerwas, *A Better Hope,* 16–17.

12. Rogers, *Sexuality and the Christian Body,* 67–86, esp. 81–84. In a later, cowritten piece, Rogers and his coauthors use not just monasticism to prise open marriage. More explicitly than Rogers does in *Sexuality and the Christian Body,* Rogers and his coauthors also use the marriage rite itself (through a close reading of the liturgy for the Order of Marriage in the Book of Common Prayer) to show the church something about the practice of marriage, and—having shown marriage to be a doubly Christological (it signifies Christ's love of the church and it embodies Christ's love of neighbor) "training in virtue" that is intended for joy, and that finds its end, through *eros,* in *caritas*—to argue for the inclusion of same-sex couples in it. Good et al., "A Theology of Marriage Including Same-Sex Couples," especially 62–72.

13. Rogers, "Trinity, Marriage, and Homosexuality," 152–53, 156. See Rogers's use of this Butler passage vis-à-vis the Eucharist in *After the Spirit,* 130–31, and vis-à-vis ordination in "Believers and the Beloved," 529–32. I owe the insight that Rogers returns to this passage in Butler so often to Brandy Daniels. See Daniels, "Queer Theory."

14. Mount Shoop's work, and liberal feminist theology generally, is characterized by an awareness that some practices are simultaneously of the church and "in the larger culture." One such practice in Mount Shoop's book is rape. Mount Shoop analyzes extraecclesial discourses about and practices surrounding rape, but also notes that rape's norms have been constituted in part by Christian norms. To wit, Mount Shoop briefly discusses the treatment of rape in the Bible (*Let the Bones Dance,* 40), a discussion that implies that something about Scripture and/or the church's handling of Scripture has underwritten social norms around rape. Furthermore, she includes "pastors" among the many actors (from doctors to cops to family members) who fail to appropriately treat the rape victim once a rape has occurred. (*Let the Bones Dance,* 37–38, 60).

15. Mount Shoop, *Let the Bones Dance*, 3–11, 37–38, 165. See also Wendy Farley, *Wounding and Healing of Desire*, 57, 116; more broadly, 115–46; and Farley, *Gathering Those Driven Away*, 90–91.

16. Gandolfo, "Mary Kept These Things, Pondering Them in Her Heart," 164–66.

17. Miller-McLemore, *In the Midst of Chaos*, 30–32, 50–57.

18. Coakley, "Prayer as Crucible," 33. This kind of praying is a "waiting on the divine," and it can be accompanied by "a repeated phrase to ward off distractions, or be wholly silent; it may be a simple Quaker attentiveness, or take a charismatic expression (such as the use of quiet rhythmic 'tongues')." Coakley, *Powers and Submissions*, 34–35.

19. Coakley, *God, Sexuality, and the Self*, 84–86.

20. Ibid., 342–43.

21. Coakley, "Prayer as Crucible," 37.

22. "Prayer as Divine Propulsion: An Interview with Sarah Coakley," The Other Journal, https://theotherjournal.com/2012/12/20/prayer-as-divine-propulsion-an-interview-with-sarah-coakley/.

23. Coakley, *God, Sexuality, and the Self*, 16.

24. Ibid., xiii–xiv, 44, 46.

25. Ibid., 18. Here, Coakley is compatible with Hadot, although she does not discuss him much (see brief mentions at *Powers and Submissions*, xvii; *The New Asceticism*, 18, 103n1; and "Theological Scholarship as Religious Vocation," 66). Cf. *The New Asceticism*, 60, 100, 104.

26. Coakley, *God, Sexuality, and the Self*, 2–20. See also Coakley, *The New Asceticism*, 101–28.

Works Cited

Abulafia, Anna Sapir. "Bodies in the Jewish-Christian Debate." In *Framing Medieval Bodies,* ed Sarah Kay and Miri Rubin, 123–37. Manchester, UK: Manchester University Press, 1994.

———. *Christian Jewish Relations, 1000–1300: Jews in the Service of Medieval Christendom* (New York: Routledge, 2014).

Adams, Marilyn McCord. *Some Later Medieval Theories of the Eucharist: Thomas Aquinas, Gilles of Rome, Duns Scotus, and William Ockham.* New York: Oxford University Press, 2010.

Alcott, Louisa May. *Little Women: An Annotated Edition.* Ed. Daniel Shealy. Cambridge: Harvard University Press, 2013.

Anidjar, Gil. *Blood: A Critique of Christianity.* New York: Columbia University Press, 2014.

Augustine. *Augustine: Homilies on the Gospel of John, Homilies on the First Epistle of John, Soliloquies.* Nicene and Post-Nicene Fathers. Ed. Philip Schaff. Vol. 7. Peabody, MA: Hendrickson, 1999.

———. *Confessions.* Trans. Henry Chadwick. New York: Oxford University Press, 2009.

"Baby, Beer, Bullets." *Rocky Mountain News,* April 11, 1887, p. 4.

Bader-Saye, Scott. *Church and Israel After Christendom: The Politics of Election.* Eugene, OR: Wipf and Stock, 2005.

Balthasar, Hans Urs von. *Dare We Hope That All Men Be Saved? With a Short Discourse on Hell.* San Francisco: Ignatius, 1988.

Baron, Salo Wittmayer. *A Social and Religious History of the Jews.* Vol. 1. New York: Columbia University Press, 1937.

Beasley, Nicholas M. *Christian Ritual and the Creation of British Slave Societies, 1650–1780.* Athens: University of Georgia Press, 2009.

Bennett, Jana Marguerite. *Water Is Thicker Than Blood: An Augustinian Theology of Marriage and Singlehood.* New York: Oxford University Press, 2008.

Berger, Teresa. *Gender Differences and the Making of Liturgical History: Lifting a Veil on Liturgy's Past.* Burlington, VT: Ashgate, 2011.

Berlant, Lauren. *Cruel Optimism.* Durham: Duke University Press, 2011.

———. *The Female Complaint: The Unfinished Business of Sentimentality in American Culture.* Durham: Duke University Press, 2008.

Berlant, Lauren, and Jay Prosser. "Life Writing and Intimate Publics: A Conversation with Lauren Berlant." *Biography* 34, no. 1 (2011): 180–87.

Bischoff, Guntram Gerhard. "The Eucharistic Controversy Between Rupert of Deutz and His Anonymous Adversary: Studies in the Theology and Chronology of Rupert of Deutz (c. 1076–c. 1129) and His Earlier Literary Work." Th.D. diss., Princeton Theological Seminary, 1965.

Blanchard, Mary W. " 'It Is Surprising That There Are Any Happy Wives': The Art Interchange, 1878–86." *Journal of Women's History* 8, no. 3 (1996): 36–65.

Bloom, Harold. *The Anxiety of Influence: A Theory of Poetry.* 2nd ed. New York: Oxford University Press, 1997.

The Book of Common Prayer. New York: Seabury, 1979.

Bossy, J. A. "Godparenthood: The Fortunes of a Social Institution in Early Modern Christianity." In *Religion and Society in Modern Europe 1500–1800,* ed Kasper von Greyerz, 194–201.

Boulton, Matthew Myer. "Supersession or Subsession? Exodus Typology, the Christian Eucharist, and the Jewish Passover Meal." *Scottish Journal of Theology* 66, no. 1 (2013): 18–29.

Bourdieu, Pierre. *Outline of a Theory of Practice.* Cambridge: Cambridge University Press, 1977.

Bourne, Richard. *Seek the Peace of the City: Christian Political Criticism as Public, Realist, and Transformative.* Eugene, OR: Cascade, 2009.

Bowes, Kim. *Private Worship, Public Values, and Religious Change in Late Antiquity.* New York: Cambridge University Press, 2008.

Bowman, Shearer Davis. *At the Precipice: Americans North and South During the Secession Crisis.* Chapel Hill: University of North Carolina Press, 2010.

Bretherton, Luke. *Christianity and Contemporary Politics: The Conditions and Possibilities of Faithful Witness.* Malden, MA: Blackwell, 2010.

Brown, Raymond E. *The Birth of the Messiah: A Commentary on the Infancy Narratives in the Gospels of Matthew and Luke.* Anchor Yale Bible Reference Library. Updated ed. New Haven: Yale University Press, 1999.

———. *The Gospel According to John: Introduction, Translation, and Notes.* Anchor Bible Series. New York: Doubleday, 1970.

Brown, Raymond E., Karl P. Donfried, Joseph A. Fitzmyer, and John Reumann, eds. *Mary in the New Testament: Collaborative Assessment by Protestant and Roman Catholic Scholars.* Mahwah, NJ: Paulist, 1978.

Bynum, Caroline Walker. *Christian Materiality: An Essay on Religion in Late Medieval Europe.* New York: Zone, 2011.

Byron, Tammy K. " 'A Catechism for Their Special Use': Slave Catechisms in the Antebellum South." Ph.D. diss., University of Arkansas, 2008.

Calef, Susan A. "The Shape of the Family and Family Values: 'The Bible Tells Us So' or Does It?" In *Religion and the Family,* ed. Ronald A. Simkins and Gail S. Risch, 223–46. Omaha, NE: Creighton University Press, 2008.

Canon Law Society of America. *Code of Canon Law: Latin-English Edition.* New English Trans. Washington, DC: Canon Law Society of America, 2012.

Carney, Charity R. *Ministers and Masters: Methodism, Manhood, and Honor in the Old South.* Baton Rouge: Louisiana State University Press, 2011.

Cary, Virginia Randolph. *Letters on Female Character, Addressed to a Young Lady, On the Death of Her Mother.* 2nd ed., enlarged. Richmond, VA: Ariel Works, 1830.

Cassian, John. *The Conferences (A Select Library of Nicene and Post-Nicene Father of the Christian Church).* Trans. Edgar C. S. Gibson. Grand Rapids, MI: Eerdmans, 1984.

Catlos, Brian A. *Muslims of Medieval Latin Christendom, c. 1050–1614.* New York: Oxford University Press, 2014.

Cavanaugh, William T. *Being Consumed: Economics and Christian Desire.* Grand Rapids, MI: Eerdmans, 2008.

———. "The Church in the Streets: Eucharist and Politics." *Modern Theology* 30, no. 2 (2014): 384–402.

———. *Torture and Eucharist: Theology, Politics, and the Body of Christ.* Malden, MA: Blackwell, 1998.

Certeau, Michel de. *The Practice of Everyday Life.* Trans. Steven Rendall. Berkeley: University of California Press, 1984.

———. "The Weakness of Believing: From the Body to Writing, a Christian Transit." In *The Certeau Reader,* ed. Graham Ward, 214–43. Malden, MA: Blackwell, 2000.

"Christening Beatrice's Baby." *Daily Inter Ocean,* November 26, 1887, p. 10.

"Christenings." *Harper's Bazaar (1867–1912),* December 10, 1881.

Chrysostom, John. *Saint Chrysostom's Homilies on the Gospel of John and Epistle to the Hebrews.* Nicene and Post-Nicene Fathers of the Christian Church. Ed. Philip Schaff. Vol. 14. Whitefish, MT: Kessinger, 2004.

Ciappara, Frans. "Religion, Kinship, and Godparenthood as Elements of Social Cohesion in Qrendi, a Late-Eighteenth Century Maltese Parish." *Continuity and Change* 25, no. 1 (2010): 161–84.

Clapp, Rodney, R. *Families at the Crossroads: Beyond Tradition and Modern Options.* Downers Grove, IL: InterVarsity, 1993.

Clinton, Catherine. *The Plantation Mistress: Woman's World in the Old South.* New York: Pantheon, 1982.

Coakley, Sarah. *God, Sexuality, and the Self: An Essay "On the Trinity."* New York: Cambridge University Press, 2013.

———. *Powers and Submissions: Spirituality, Philosophy, and Gender.* Oxford: Blackwell, 2002.

———. "Prayer as Crucible: How My Mind Has Changed." *Christian Century* 128, no. 6 (2011): 32–40.

———. "Theological Scholarship as Religious Vocation." *Christian Higher Education* 5, no. 1 (2006): 55–68.

———. "Why Gift? Gift, Gender, and Trinitarian Relations in Milbank and Tanner." *Scottish Journal of Theology* 61, no. 2 (2008): 224–35.

Cohen, Shaye J. D. *Why Aren't Jewish Women Circumcised? Gender and Covenant in Judaism.* Berkeley: University of California Press, 2005.

Colish, Martha L. *Faith, Fiction, and Force in Medieval Baptism Debates.* Washington, DC: Catholic University of America Press, 2014.

Colson, Jonathan. "Mark Doty: Fire to Fire." *Writer's Chronicle,* August–September 2011.

A Committee of the Lay Association of Montreal. "Presbyterians Reject Godfathers and Godmothers in Baptism." In *The Presbyterian: A Missionary and Religious Record of the Presbyterian Church of Canada in Connection with the Church of the Canada.* Vol. 3. Montreal: Lovell and Gibson, 1850.

Cornelius, Janet Duitsman. *Slave Missions and the Black Church in the Antebellum South.* Columbia: University of South Carolina Press, 1999.

Coster, Will. "Baptismal Names." In *Puritans and Puritanism in Europe and America: A Comprehensive Encyclopedia,* ed. Francis J. Bremer and Tom Webster, 1: 321–22. Santa Barbara, CA: ABC-CLIO, 2006.

———. *Baptism and Spiritual Kinship in Early Modern England.* Burlington, VT: Ashgate, 2002.

Cressy, David. *Birth, Marriage, and Death: Ritual, Religion, and the Life Cycle in Tudor and Stuart England.* Oxford: Oxford University Press, 1997.

Crossan, John Dominic, and Richard G. Watts. *Who Is Jesus? Answers to Your Questions About the Historical Jesus.* Louisville, KY: Westminster John Knox Press, 1996.

Culpepper, Alan R. *The Gospel of Luke: Introduction, Commentary, and Reflections.* New Interpreter's Bible. Nashville, TN: Abingdon, 1995.

Daniels, Brandy. "Is Kinship Always Already Reproductive? An Ecclesiological, Poststructuralist Account." *Theology and Sexuality* 18, no. 3 (2012): 175–97.

———. "Queer Theory." In *Embodied Religion,* ed. Kent Brintnall, 289–308. New York: Macmillan, 2016.

Davies, W. D., and Dale C. Allison. *The Gospel According to Saint Matthew.* International Critical Commentary. Edinburgh: T and T Clark, 1997.

Debby, Nirit Ben-Aryeh. *"Nel mio bel San Giovanni, fatti per loco de' battezzatori:* Baptismal Fonts in Tuscany." In *The Visual Culture of Baptism in the Middle Ages: Essays on Medieval Fonts, Settings, and Beliefs,* ed. Harriet M. Sonne de Torrens and Miguel A. Torrens, 11–30. Burlington, VT: Ashgate, 2013.

Deller, William S. "The First Rite of Passage: Baptism in Medieval Memory." *Journal of Family History* 36, no. 1 (2011): 3–14.

Derrida, Jacques. *Given Time: I. Counterfeit Money.* Chicago: University of Chicago Press, 1992.

deSilva, David A. *Honor, Patronage, Kinship, and Purity: Unlocking New Testament Culture.* Downers Grove, IL: InterVarsity, 2000.

Despres, Denise L. "Mary of the Eucharist: Cultic Anti-Judaism in Some Fourteenth-Century English Devotional Manuscripts." In *From Witness to Witchcraft: Jews and Judaism in Medieval Christian Thought,* ed. Jeremy Cohen, 375–401. Wiesbaden, Germany: Harrassowitz Verlag, 1996.

Dickerman, George Sherwood. *The House of Plant of Macon, Georgia: With Genealogies and Historical Notes.* New Haven, CT: Tuttle, Moorehouse and Taylor, 1900.

Dilley, Rachel. 2010. "Christening Gown a Family Heirloom Before Its Time." *Columbus Dispatch,* May 1.

Dominus Iesus [Declaration on the Unicity and Salvific Universality of Jesus Christ and the Church]. Available at http://www.vatican.va.

Douglass, Frederick. *My Bondage and My Freedom.* Ed. John David Smith. New York: Penguin, 2003.

Duffy, Eamon. *The Stripping of the Altars: Traditional Religion in England, 1400–1580.* New Haven: Yale University Press, 1992.

Duncan, Christopher M. "Benjamin Morgan Palmer: Southern Presbyterian Divine." Ph.D. diss., Auburn University, 2008.

Dykstra, Craig, and Dorothy C. Bass. "A Theological Understanding of Christian Practices." In *Practicing Theology: Beliefs and Practices in Christian Life,* ed. Miroslav Volf and Dorothy C. Bass, 13–32. Grand Rapids, MI: Eerdmans, 2002.

———. "Times of Yearning, Practices of Faith." In *Practicing Our Faith: A Way of Life for a Searching People*, 2nd ed., ed. Dorothy C. Bass, 1–12. San Francisco: Jossey-Bass, 2010.

Earle, Alice Morse. *China Collecting in America*. New York: Empire State, 1924.

"An East-Side Christening Party." *Frank Leslie's Illustrated Newspaper*, May 9, 1885, p. 197.

Ellis, Ieuan. "Jesus and the Subversive Family." *Scottish Journal of Theology* 38, no. 2 (1985): 173–88.

Ericsson, Tom. "Godparents, Witnesses, and Social Class in Mid-Nineteenth Century Sweden." *History of the Family* 5, no. 3 (2000): 273–86.

"Excerpts from the Scrap Book of the Late Mrs. Stephen McCandless: The Home of Mrs. Thomas Collins, the Grandmother of Stephen C. McCandless." *Western Pennsylvania Historical Magazine* 3, no. 1 (1920): 22–23.

Farley, Wendy. *The Wounding and Healing of Desire: Weaving Heaven and Earth*. Louisville, KY: Westminster John Knox Press, 2005.

The Federal Writers' Project. *Born in Oklahoma Slave Narratives*. Slave Narratives from the Federal Writers' Project, 1936–1938. Vol. 13. Carlisle, MA: Applewood, 2006.

———. *Missouri Slave Narratives*. Slave Narratives from the Federal Writers' Project, 1936–1938. Vol. 10. Carlisle, MA: Applewood, 2006.

Ferguson, Everett. *Baptism in the Early Church: History, Theology, and Liturgy in the First Five Centuries*. Grand Rapids, MI: Eerdmans, 2009.

Fields, Barbara Jeanne. *Slavery and Freedom on the Middle Ground: Maryland During the Nineteenth Century*. New Haven: Yale University Press, 1985.

Finlan, Stephen. *The Family Metaphor in Jesus' Teaching: Gospel and Ethics*. Eugene, OR: Cascade, 2009.

Fitzmyer, Joseph A. *The Gospel According to Luke (X–XXIV)*. Anchor Bible Series. Garden City, NY: Doubleday, 1985.

Fox-Genovese, Elizabeth. *Within the Plantation Household: Black and White Women of the Old South*. Chapel Hill: University of North Carolina Press, 1988.

French, Katherine. "The Material Culture of Childbirth in Late Medieval London and Its Suburbs." *Journal of Women's History* 28 (2016): 126–48.

Gandolfo, Elizabeth O'Donnell. "Mary Kept These Things, Pondering Them in Her Heart: Breastfeeding as Contemplative Practice and Source for Theology." *Spiritus* 13 (2013): 163–86.

Garafalo, Rob. "The Family of Jesus in Mark's Gospel." *Irish Theological Quarterly* 57, no. 4 (1991): 265–76.

Garrigan, Siobhán. *The Real Peace Process: Worship, Politics, and the End of Sectarianism*. New York: Routledge, 2014.

———. "Theology, Habermas and Corporate Worship." *Irish Review* 32 (2004): 39–52.

Gaventa, Beverly Roberts. *Mary: Glimpses of the Mother of Jesus.* Columbia: University of South Carolina Press, 1995.

Genovese, Eugene D. *Roll, Jordan, Roll: The World the Slaves Made.* New York: Random House, 1974.

Genovese, Eugene D., and Elizabeth Fox-Genovese. *Fatal Self-Deception: Slaveholding Paternalism in the Old South.* New York: Cambridge University Press, 2011.

Gilchrist, Roberta. *Medieval Life: Archaeology and the Life Course.* Woodbridge, UK: Boydell, 2012.

Gillis, John R. *A World of Their Own Making: Myth, Ritual, and the Quest for Family Values.* Cambridge: Harvard University Press, 1997.

Glymph, Thavolia. *Out of the House of Bondage: The Transformation of the Plantation Household.* New York: Cambridge University Press, 2008.

Good, Deirdre. "Jesus and the Transformation of the Family." In *Fear or Freedom? Why a Warring Church Must Change,* ed. Simon Barrow, 53–60. London: Shoving Leopard, 2008.

Good, Deirdre J., Willis J. Jenkins, Cynthia B. Kitteredge, and Eugene F. Rogers. "A Theology of Marriage Including Same-Sex Couples: A View from the Liberals." *Anglican Theological Review* 93, no. 1 (2011): 51–87.

Good Housekeeping. *The Good Housekeeping Hostess: An Old-Fashioned Guide to Gracious Living.* New York: Hearst, 2003.

Green, Joel B. *The Gospel of Luke.* Grand Rapids, MI: Eerdmans, 1997.

Greer, Rowan A. *Broken Lights and Mended Lives: Theology and Common Life in the Early Church.* University Park: Pennsylvania State University Press, 1986.

Griffiths, Paul J. *Christian Flesh.* Stanford: Stanford University Press, 2018.

———. *Decreation: The Last Things of All Creatures.* Waco, TX: Baylor University Press, 2014.

———. *Intellectual Appetite: A Theological Grammar.* Washington, DC: Catholic University Press of America, 2009.

Grimes, Katie Walker. *Fugitive Slaves: Catholicism and the Politics of Slavery.* Minneapolis: Fortress, 2017.

Gundersen, Joan R. *The Anglican Ministry in Virginia, 1723–1766: A Study of Social Class.* Hamden, CT: Garland, 1989.

Haas, Louis. "Il Mio Buono Compare: Choosing Godparents and the Uses of Baptismal Kinship in Renaissance Florence." *Journal of Social History* 29, no. 2 (1995): 341–56.

Hadot, Pierre. *Philosophy as a Way of Life: Spiritual Exercises from Socrates to Foucault.* Malden, MA: Blackwell, 1995.

Hahn, Steven. "Hunting, Fishing, and Foraging: Common Rights and Class Relations in the Postbellum South." *Radical History Review* 26 (1982): 37–64.

———. *The Roots of Southern Populism: Yeoman Farmers and the Transformation of the Georgia Upcountry, 1850–1890.* New York: Oxford University Press, 1983.

Hall, Amy Laura. *Conceiving Parenthood: American Protestantism and the Spirit of Reproduction.* Grand Rapids, MI: Eerdmans, 2008.

Harrison, Kimberly. *The Rhetoric of Rebel Women: Civil War Diaries and Confederate Persuasion.* Carbondale: Southern Illinois University Press, 2013.

Harrisville, Roy A. "Jesus and the Family." *Interpretation* 23, no. 4 (1969): 425–38.

Hauerwas, Stanley. *After Christendom? How the Church Is to Behave if Freedom, Justice, and a Christian Nation Are Bad Ideas.* Nashville, TN: Abingdon, 1991.

———. *A Better Hope: Resources for a Church Confronting Capitalism, Democracy, and Postmodernity.* Grand Rapids, MI: Brazos, 2000.

———. "The Gesture of a Truthful Story." In *Critical Reflections on Stanley Hauerwas' Theology of Disability: Disabling Society, Enabling Theology,* ed. John Swinton, 71–80. Binghamton, NY: Haworth Pastoral, 2004.

———. "The Interpretation of Scripture: Why Discipleship Is Required." In Hauerwas and Berkman, *The Hauerwas Reader,* 255–66.

———. "On Being a Church Capable of Addressing a World at War: A Pacifist Response to the United Methodist Bishops' Pastoral *In Defense of Creation.*" In Hauerwas and Berkman, *The Hauerwas Reader,* 426–58.

———. "Should War Be Eliminated? A Thought Experiment." In Hauerwas and Berkman, *The Hauerwas Reader,* 392–425.

———. "The Virtues of Alasdair MacIntyre." *First Things: A Journal of Religion and Public Life* 176 (2007): 35–40.

———. *Vision and Virtue: Essays in Christian Ethical Reflection.* Notre Dame, IN: University of Notre Dame Press, 1986.

———. "Why Gays (as a Group) Are Morally Superior to Christians (as a Group)." In Hauerwas and Berkman, *The Hauerwas Reader,* 519–21.

Hauerwas, Stanley, and John Berkman, eds. *The Hauerwas Reader.* Durham: Duke University Press, 2001.

Hauerwas, Stanley, and Samuel Wells, eds. *The Blackwell Companion to Christian Ethics.* 2nd ed. Malden, MA: Blackwell, 2011.

Healy, Nicholas M. "Practices and the New Ecclesiology: Misplaced Correctness?" *International Journal of Systematic Theology* 5, no. 3 (2003): 287–308.

Heck, Christian, and Rémy Cordonnier. *The Grand Medieval Bestiary: Animals in Illustrated Manuscripts*. Trans. John Goodman, Linda Gardiner, Elizabeth Heard, Charles Penwarden, and Jane Marie Todd. New York: Abbeville, 2012.

Hellerman, Joseph H. *When the Church Was a Family: Recapturing Jesus' Vision for Authentic Christian Community*. Nashville, TN: B & H Academic, 2009.

Heyrman, Christine Leigh. *Southern Cross: The Beginnings of the Bible Belt*. Chapel Hill: University of North Carolina Press, 1997.

Hodge, Caroline Johnson. *If Sons, Then Heirs: A Study of Kinship and Ethnicity in the Letters of Paul*. New York: Oxford University Press, 2007.

Hollander, Melissa. "The Name of the Father: Baptism and the Social Construction of Fatherhood in Early Modern Edinburgh." In *Finding the Family in Medieval and Early Modern Scotland*, ed. Elizabeth Ewan and Janay Nugent, 63–72. Burlington, VT: Ashgate, 2008.

Horner, Robyn. *Rethinking God as Gift: Marion, Derrida, and the Limits of Phenomenology*. New York: Fordham University Press, 2001.

Hornsby, Stephen J., and John G. Reid, eds. *New England and the Maritime Provinces*. Montreal: McGill-Queen's University Press, 2005.

Hyde, Lewis. *Common as Air: Revolution, Art, and Ownership*. New York: Farrar, Straus and Giroux, 2010.

"Immersed Three Times." *New York Times*, June 26, 1891.

Isasi-Díaz, Ada María. "Kin-dom of God: A Mujerista Proposal." In *In Our Own Voices: Latino/a Renditions of Theology*, ed. Benjamin Valentin, 171–90. Maryknoll, NY: Orbis, 2010.

Jacobs, Alan. "Narrating Ethics." *First Things: A Journal of Religion and Public Life* 113 (2001): 39.

———. *The Pleasures of Reading in an Age of Distraction*. Oxford: Oxford University Press, 2011.

James, Henry. *The Golden Bowl*. Reissue ed. New York: Oxford University Press, 2009.

Jefferson, Thomas. *Notes on the State of Virginia*. New York: Penguin, 1999.

Jensen, Robin M. *Living Water: Images, Symbols, and Settings of Early Christian Baptism*. Leiden, the Netherlands: Brill, 2011.

———. "*Mater Ecclesia* and *Fons Aeterna*: The Church and Her Womb in Ancient Christianity." In *A Feminist Companion to Patristic Literature*, ed. Amy-Jill Levine, 137–55. New York: T & T Clark International, 2008.

Jeremias, Joachim. *Infant Baptism in the First Four Centuries*. Trans. David Cairns. London: SCM Press, 1964.

Johnson, E. Elizabeth. "Apocalyptic Family Values." *Interpretation* 56, no. 1 (2002): 34–44.

Jones, Charles C. *A Catechism, of Scripture, Doctrine, and Practice, for Families and Sabbath Schools, Designed also for the Oral Instruction of Colored Persons*. 6th ed. Savannah, GA: John M. Cooper, 1837.

Jones, Pamela Denise James. "Submission, Suffering, and God: Enslaved Christian Women's Identity in the American Antebellum Period, 1830–1865." Ph.D. diss., University of Chicago, 2010.

Jordan, Mark D., ed. *Authorizing Marriage? Canon, Tradition, and Critique in the Blessing of Same-Sex Unions*. Princeton, NJ: Princeton University Press, 2006.

Karant-Nunn, Susan. *The Reformation of Ritual: An Interpretation of Early Modern Germany*. New York: Routledge, 1997.

Katongole, Emmanuel M. "Postmodern Illusions and Challenges of African Theology: The Ecclesial Tactics of Resistance." In *An Eerdmans Reader in Contemporary Political Theology*, ed. William T. Cavanaugh, Jeffrey W. Bailey, and Craig Hovey, 503–24. Grand Rapids, MI: Eerdmans, 2012.

Kearns, Cleo McNelly. *The Virgin Mary, Monotheism, and Sacrifice*. New York: Cambridge University Press, 2008.

Kerr, Nathan. "*Communio Missionis*: Certeau, Yoder, and the Missionary Space of the Church." In *The New Yoder*, edited by Peter Dula and Chris K. Huebner, 317–35. Eugene, OR: Cascade, 2009.

Kevill-Davies, Sally. *Yesterday's Children: The Antiques and History of Childcare*. Woodbridge, UK: Antique Collectors' Club, 1992.

Kilen, Mike. "Century-Old Christening Heirloom Found, Returned to Family." *Des Moines Register*, April 26, 2009.

Kristeva, Julia. "From Symbol to Sign." In *The Kristeva Reader*, ed. Toril Moi, 62–73. Oxford: Basil Blackwell, 1986.

Learned, Ellin Craven (Mrs. Frank). *The Etiquette of New York To-day*. New York: Frederick A. Stokes, 1906.

Levenson, Jon D. *Inheriting Abraham: The Legacy of the Patriarch in Judaism, Christianity, and Islam*. Princeton: Princeton University Press, 2012.

Levering, Matthew. *Mary's Bodily Assumption*. Notre Dame, IN: University of Notre Dame Press, 2015.

Lindbeck, George A. *The Nature of Doctrine: Religion and Theology in a Post-liberal Age*. Louisville, KY: Westminster John Knox Press, 1984.

Lofton, Kathryn. "Piety, Practice, and Ritual." In *The Blackwell Companion to Religion in America*, ed. Philip Goff, 242–53. Malden, MA: Blackwell, 2010.

López, Antonio Irigoyen. "Ecclesiastical Godparenthood in Early Modern Murcia." In *Spiritual Kinship in Europe, 1500–1900*, ed. Guido Alfani and Vincent Gourdon, 74–95. New York: Palgrave Macmillan, 2012.

Lynch, Joseph H. *Godparents and Kinship in Early Medieval Europe*. Princeton: Princeton University Press, 1986.

MacIntyre, Alasdair. *After Virtue: A Study in Moral Theory*. 3rd ed. Notre Dame, IN: University of Notre Dame Press, 2007.

———. *Three Rival Versions of Moral Enquiry: Encyclopaedia, Genealogy, and Tradition*. Notre Dame, IN: University of Notre Dame Press, 1991.

Macy, Gary. *Treasures from the Storeroom: Medieval Religion and the Eucharist*. Collegeville, MN: Liturgical Press, 1999.

Maiorino, Giancarlo. *The Portrait of Eccentricity: Arcimboldo and the Mannerist Grotesque*. University Park: Pennsylvania State University Press, 1991.

Malegam, Jehangir Yezdi. *The Sleep of Behemoth: Disputing Peace and Violence in Medieval Europe, 1000–1200*. Ithaca, NY: Cornell University Press, 2013.

Marcus, Joel. "Crucifixion as Parodic Exaltation." *Journal of Biblical Literature* 125, no. 1 (2006): 73–87.

———. *Mark 8–16: A New Translation with Introduction and Commentary*. Anchor Yale Bible. New Haven: Yale University Press, 2009.

Marion, Jean-Luc. *Being Given: Toward a Phenomenology of Givenness*. Trans. Jeffrey L. Kosky. Stanford: Stanford University Press, 2002.

———. *The Visible and the Revealed*. Trans. Christina Gschwandtner. New York: Fordham University Press, 2008.

Martin, Dale B. "Familiar Idolatry and the Christian Case Against Marriage." In Jordan, *Authorizing Marriage?* 17–40.

———. *Sex and the Single Savior: Gender and Sexuality in Biblical Interpretation*. Louisville, KY: Westminster John Knox Press, 2006.

Martínez, Valerie, ed. *Lines and Circles: A Celebration of Santa Fe Families*. Santa Fe, NM: Sunstone, 2010.

Mathews, Donald G. "Sacrament and Segregation: Episcopalians in the Evangelical South." In *Religion in the Contemporary South: Changes, Continuities, and Contexts*, ed. Corrie E. Norman and Don S. Armentrout, 300–328. Knoxville: University of Tennessee Press, 2005.

Mazza, Enrico. *The Celebration of the Eucharist: The Origin of the Rite and the Development of Its Interpretation*. Collegeville, MN: Liturgical Press, 1999.

McCorkle, Lucille. Diaries. Subseries 3.1, William P. McCorkle Papers, Southern History Collection, University of North Carolina, Chapel Hill.

McGowan, Andrew. *Ascetic Eucharists: Food and Drink in Early Christian Ritual Meals*. New York: Oxford University Press, 1999.

Merback, Mitchell B. "Jewish Carnality, Christian Guilt, and Eucharistic Peril in the Rotterdam-Berlin Altarpiece of the Holy Sacrament." In *Judaism and Christian Art: Aesthetic Anxieties from the Catacombs to Colonial-*

ism, ed. Herbert L. Kessler and David Nirenberg, 203–32. Philadelphia: University of Pennsylvania Press, 2011.

———. *Pilgrimage and Pogrom: Violence, Memory, and Visual Culture at the Host-Miracle Shrines of Germany and Austria.* Chicago: University of Chicago Press, 2013.

The Metropolitan Museum of Art. *Notable Acquisitions, 1979–1980.* Foreword by Philippe de Montebello. New York: The Metropolitan Museum of Art, 1980.

Michael, Robert. *A History of Catholic Antisemitism: The Dark Side of the Church.* New York: Palgrave Macmillan, 2008.

Miller, Geoffrey. "Trying to Fix the Family Tree of Jesus." *Scripture Bulletin* 39, no. 1 (2009): 17–30.

Miller-McLemore, Bonnie J. *Also a Mother: Work and Family as Theological Dilemma.* Nashville, TN: Abingdon, 1994.

———. *Christian Theology in Practice: Discovering a Discipline.* Grand Rapids, MI: Eerdmans, 2012.

Moloney, Francis J. *The Gospel of John.* Collegeville, MN: Liturgical Press, 1998.

———. "A Sacramental Reading of John 13:1–38." *Catholic Biblical Quarterly* 53, no. 2 (1991): 237–56.

Moore, John Hammond. *Columbia and Richland County: A South Carolina Community, 1740–1990.* Columbia: University of South Carolina Press, 1993.

———, ed. *A Plantation Mistress on the Eve of the Civil War: The Diary of Keziah Goodwyn Hopkins Brevard, 1860–1861.* Columbia: University of South Carolina Press, 1993.

Morrill, Bruce T. *Anamnesis as Dangerous Memory: Political and Liturgical Theology in Dialogue.* Collegeville, MN: Liturgical Press, 2000.

Morrison, Toni. *Jazz.* New York: Knopf, 1992.

Mount, Ferdinand. *The Subversive Family: An Alternative History of Love and Marriage.* New York: Free Press, 1992.

Mount Shoop, Marcia W. *Let the Bones Dance: Embodiment and the Body of Christ.* Louisville, KY: Westminster John Knox Press, 2010.

Moxnes, Halvor. *Putting Jesus in His Place: A Radical Vision of Household and Kingdom.* Louisville, KY: Westminster John Knox Press, 2003.

Muir, Edward. *Ritual in Early Modern Europe.* 2nd ed. New York: Cambridge University Press, 2005.

Nares, Robert. *A Glossary: Or, Collection of Words, Phrases, Names, and Allusions to Customs, Proverbs, &c., which Have Been Thought to Require Illustration, in the Works of English Authors.* London: John Russell Smith, 1859.

Narin van Court, Elisa Marie. "Critical Apertures: Medieval Anti-Judaism and Middle English Narrative." Ph.D. diss., University of California, Berkeley, 1994.

———. "Socially Marginal, Culturally Central: Representing Jews in Late Medieval English Literature." *Exemplaria* 12, no. 2 (2000): 293–326.

Nesbit, E. "Melisande; or, The Long-Haired Princess: A Story for Children." *Strand Magazine: An Illustrated Monthly* 20 (1900): 108–15.

Newman, Barbara. "The Passion of the Jews of Prague: The Pogrom of 1389 and the Lessons of a Medieval Parody." *Church History* 81, no. 1 (2012): 1–26.

Nirenberg, David. *Communities of Violence: Persecution of Minorities in the Middle Ages.* Princeton: Princeton University Press, 1998.

"Nourishing Foods and Drinks for the Sick." *The Sanitarian, Devoted to the Preservation of Health, Mental, and Physical Culture* 11, no. 118 (1883): 260–61.

Ochs, Peter. "Morning Prayer as Redemptive Thinking." In *Liturgy, Time, and the Politics of Redemption,* ed. Randi Rashkover and C. C. Pecknold, 50–90. Grand Rapids, MI: Eerdmans, 2006.

Old, Hughes Oliphant. *The Shaping of the Reformed Baptismal Rite in the Sixteenth Century.* Grand Rapids, MI: Eerdmans, 1992.

Oosterwijk, Sophie. "Swaddled or Shrouded? The Interpretation of 'Chrysom' Effigies on Late Medieval Tomb Monuments." In *Weaving, Veiling, and Dressing: Textiles and Their Metaphors in the Late Middle Ages,* ed. Kathryn M. Rudy and Barbara Baert, 307–48. Turnhout, Belgium: Brepols, 2007.

Orme, Nicholas. *Medieval Children.* New Haven: Yale University Press, 2003.

Ownby, Ted. "Patriarchy in the World Where There Is No Parting? Power Relations in the Confederate Heaven." In *Southern Families at War: Loyalty and Conflict in the Civil War South,* ed. Catherine Clinton, 229–41. New York: Oxford University Press, 2000.

Palmer, Benjamin Morgan. *A Plain and Easy Catechism: Designed Chiefly for the Benefit of Coloured Persons, to Which Are Annexed Suitable Prayers and Hymns.* South Carolina: Observer Office Press, 1828.

Parker, John. *The Aesthetics of Antichrist: From Christian Drama to Christopher Marlowe.* Ithaca, NY: Cornell University Press, 2007.

Parris, Linda Eileen. " 'A Dutiful Obedient Wife': The Journal of Elizabeth Foote Washington of Virginia, 1779–1796." M.A. thesis, William and Mary University, 1984.

Rainsford, W. S. *The Story of a Varied Life: An Autobiography.* Garden City, NY: Country Life, 1922.

Renkl, Margaret. "In Praise of Family Meals." *Parenting* 14, no. 9 (2000): 156–62.

Richter, Don C. "Religious Practices in Practical Theology." In *Opening the Field of Practical Theology: An Introduction,* ed. Kathleen A. Cahalan and Gordon S. Mikoski, 203–16. Lanham, MD: Rowman and Littlefield, 2014.

Rios, Ana Maria Lugão. "The Politics of Kinship: *Compadrio* Among Slaves in Nineteenth-Century Brazil." *History of the Family* 5, no. 3 (2000): 287–98.

Roberts, Helene E., ed. *Encyclopedia of Comparative Iconography: Themes Depicted in Works of Art.* 3rd ed. Vols. 1 and 2. Chicago: Fitzroy Dearborn, 1998.

Roberts, J. J. M. "In Defense of the Monarchy: The Contribution of Israelites Kingship to Biblical Theology." In *Ancient Israelite Religion: Essays in Honor of Frank Moore Cross,* ed. Patrick D. Miller, Paul D. Hanson, and S. Dean McBride, 377–96. Minneapolis: Augsburg Fortress, 2009.

Robinson, Robert. *The History of Baptism.* Boston: Press of Lincoln and Edmands, 1817.

Rogers, Eugene F. *After the Spirit: A Constructive Pneumatology from Resources Outside the Modern West.* Grand Rapids, MI: Eerdmans, 2005.

———. "Believers and the Beloved: Some Notes on Norris's Christology." *Anglican Theological Review* 90, no. 3 (2008): 527–32.

———. *Sexuality and the Christian Body: Their Way into the Triune God.* Malden, MA: Blackwell, 1999.

———. "Trinity, Marriage, and Homosexuality." In Jordan, *Authorizing Marriage?* 151–64.

Rossetti, Christina. *Christina Rossetti: Poems and Prose.* Oxford: Oxford University Press, 2008.

"Row at a Christening." *Morning Oregonian,* October 16, 1899, p. 6.

Rubin, Miri. *Corpus Christi: The Eucharist in Late Medieval Culture.* New York: Cambridge University Press, 1991.

———. "The Eucharist and the Construction of Medieval Identities." In *Culture and History, 1350–1600: Essays on English Communities, Identities, and Writing,* ed. David Aers, 43–64. Detroit: Wayne State University Press, 1992.

———. *Gentile Tales: The Narrative Assault on Late Medieval Jews.* New Haven: Yale University Press, 1999.

———. "Imagining the Jew: The Late Medieval Eucharistic Discourse." In *In and Out of the Ghetto: Jewish-Gentile Relations in Late Medieval and Early Modern Germany,* ed. R. Po-chia Hsia and Hartmut Lehmann, 177–208. New York: Press Syndicate of the University of Cambridge, 1995.

Rubio, Julie Hanlon. *A Christian Theology of Marriage and Family.* Mahwah, NJ: Paulist, 2003.

———. "The Dual Vocation of Christian Parents." In *Marriage,* ed Charles E. Curran and Julie Hanlon Rubio, 178–210. Mahwah, NJ: Paulist, 2009.

Rundell, Maria Eliza Ketelby. *A New System of Domestic Cookery.* London: S. Hamilton, 1813.

Saliers, Don E. "Afterword: Liturgy and Ethics Revisited." In *Liturgy and the Moral Self: Humanity at Full Stretch Before God,* ed. E. Byron Anderson and Bruce T. Morrill, 209–24. Collegeville, MN: Liturgical Press, 1998.

Schnackenburg, Rudolf. *The Gospel According to St. John.* Trans. D. Smith and G. A. Kon. Vol. 3. New York: Crossroad, 1982.

Schwalm, Leslie A. *A Hard Fight for We: Women's Transition from Slavery to Freedom in South Carolina.* Urbana: University of Illinois Press, 1997.

Shell, Marc. *Art and Money.* Chicago: University of Chicago Press, 1995.

Simpson, Matthew, ed. *Cyclopedia of Methodism: Embracing Sketches of Its Rise, Progress, and Present Condition with Biographical Notices and Numerous Illustrations.* 5th rev. ed. Philadelphia: Louis H. Everts, 1883.

Sjögren, Annick. "Access to Power Through the Family Meal: A Study of the Parisian Bourgeoisie of Today." *Etnofoor* 4, no. 1 (1991): 89–102.

Smiley, Jane. *Thirteen Ways of Looking at the Novel.* New York: Knopf, 2005.

Smith, Martin L. "God's Passionate Vulnerability." *Sojourners* 41, no. 6 (2012): 48–49.

Smith, Ted A. "Theories of Practice." In *The Wiley Blackwell Companion to Practical Theology,* ed. Bonnie J. Miller-McLemore, 244–54. Malden, MA: Blackwell, 2012.

Smith-Bannister, Scott. *Names and Naming Patterns in England, 1538–1700.* New York: Oxford University Press, 1997.

Spierling, Karen E. *Infant Baptism in Reformation Geneva: The Shaping of a Community, 1536–1564.* Louisville, KY: Westminster John Knox Press, 2009.

Spinks, Bryan D. *Reformation and Modern Rituals and Theologies of Baptism: From Luther to Contemporary Practices.* Burlington, VT: Ashgate, 2006.

Strauss, David Friedrich. *The Life of Jesus, Critically Examined.* Trans. George Eliot. Vol. II. London: George Woodfall and Son, 1846.

Stroud, Irene Elizabeth. "Beautiful Babies: Eugenic Display of the White Infant Body, 1854–1922." *Bulletin for the Study of Religion* 43, no. 2 (2014): 23–26.

———. "A Loftier Race: American Liberal Protestants and Eugenics, 1877–1929." Ph.D. diss., Princeton University, 2018.

———. S.T.M. thesis, Lutheran Theological Seminary at Philadelphia, 2010.

Stump, Eleonore. "Petitionary Prayer." *American Philosophical Quarterly* 16, no. 2 (1979): 81–91.

Tait, Clodagh. "Spiritual Bonds, Social Bonds: Baptism and Godparenthood in Ireland, 1530–1690." *Cultural and Social History* 2, no. 3 (2005): 301–27.

Tanner, Norman, ed. *Decrees of the Ecumenical Councils.* Vol. 1. Washington, DC: Georgetown University Press, 1990.

Teter, Magda. *Jews and Heretics in Catholic Poland: A Beleaguered Church in the Post-Reformation Era.* New York: Cambridge University Press, 2006.

———. *Sinners on Trial: Jews and Sacrilege After the Reformation.* Cambridge: Harvard University Press, 2011.

Thomas Aquinas. *Catena Aurea: Commentary on the Four Gospels: St. John.* Vol. 4. Ed. Paul A. Boer. Trans. John Henry Newman. N.p.: Veritatis Splendor, 2012.

"Thoughts on the Religious Instruction of Servants." *Gospel Messenger and Southern Episcopal Register (1826–1834),* 1834, 257–68.

Tolbert, Mary Ann. "Marriage and Friendship in the Christian New Testament: Ancient Resources for Contemporary Same-Sex Unions." In Jordan, *Authorizing Marriage?* 41–51.

Torrens, Harriet M. Sonne de. "Reconsidering the Date of the Baptismal Font in San Isidoro, León, Spain." In *The Visual Culture of Baptism in the Middle Ages: Essays on Medieval Fonts, Settings and Beliefs,* ed. Harriet M. Sonne de Torrens and Miguel A. Torrens, 49–76. Burlington, VT: Ashgate, 2013.

Treier, Daniel J. *Proverbs and Ecclesiastes.* Brazos Theological Commentary on the Bible. Ada, MI: Brazos, 2011.

Tugwell, Simon. "Prayer, Humpty Dumpty, and Thomas Aquinas." In *Language, Meaning and God: Essays in Honor of Herbert McCabe OP,* ed. Brian Davies, 24–50. Eugene, OR: Wipf and Stock, 2010.

Unitatis Redintegratio [Decree on Ecumenism]. Available at *http://www.vatican.va.*

Vande Kemp, Hendrika. "The Family, Religion, and Identity: A Reformed Perspective." In *Family Therapy: Christian Perspectives,* ed. Hendrika Vande Kemp, 39–75. Grand Rapids, MI: Baker, 1991.

Vander Zee, Leonard J. *Christ, Baptism, and the Lord's Supper: Recovering the Sacraments for Evangelical Worship.* Downers Grove, IL: InterVarsity, 2004.

Varon, Elizabeth R. *We Mean to Be Counted: White Women and Politics in Antebellum Virginia.* Chapel Hill: University of North Carolina Press, 1998.

Wakefield, Walter L. *Heresy, Crusade, and Inquisition in Southern France, 1100–1250.* Berkeley: University of California Press, 1974.

Ward, Seth. "The Presentation of Jesus: Jewish Perspectives on Luke 2:22–24." *Shofar: An Interdisciplinary Journal of Jewish Studies* 21, no. 2 (2003): 21–39.

Watt, Ian. *The Rise of the Novel: Studies in Defoe, Richardson, and Fielding.* London: Random House, 1957.

Weiner, Marli F. *Mistresses and Slaves: Plantation Women in South Carolina, 1830–80.* Urbana: University of Illinois Press, 1998.

Wells, Samuel. *God's Companions: Reimagining Christian Ethics.* Malden, MA: Blackwell, 2006.

———. *Transforming Fate into Destiny: The Theological Ethics of Stanley Hauerwas.* Eugene, OR: Cascade, 1998.

Wharton, Annabel Jane. *Architectural Agents: The Delusional, Abusive, Addictive Lives of Buildings.* Minneapolis: University of Minnesota Press, 2015.

Whitaker, E. C. *Documents of the Baptismal Liturgy.* Rev. and expanded ed. Collegeville, MN: Liturgical, 2003.

White, Annie Randall. *Twentieth Century Etiquette: An Up-To-Date Book for Polite Society.* Chicago: Monarch, 1901.

White, Susan J. *A History of Women in Christian Worship.* Cleveland: Pilgrim, 2003.

Wilk, Richard. "Power at the Table: Food Fights and Happy Meals." *Cultural Studies, Critical Methodologies* 10, no. 6 (2010): 428–36.

Williams, Rowan. *Being Christian: Baptism, Bible, Eucharist, and Prayer.* Grand Rapids, MI: Eerdmans, 2014.

Wills, Gregory A. *Democratic Religion: Freedom, Authority, and Church Discipline in the Baptist South, 1785–1900.* New York: Oxford University Press, 1997.

Wilson, Brittany E. *Unmanly Men: Refigurations of Manhood in Luke–Acts.* New York: Oxford University Press, 2015.

Winner, Lauren F. *A Cheerful and Comfortable Faith: Anglican Religious Practice in the Elite Households of Eighteenth-Century Virginia.* New Haven: Yale University Press, 2010.

Wood, Kirsten E. *Masterful Women: Slaveholding Women from the American Revolution Through the Civil War.* Chapel Hill: University of North Carolina Press, 2004.

Woods, Michael E. *Emotional and Sectional Conflict in the Antebellum United States.* New York: Cambridge University Press, 2014.

Wrenn, Angus. *Henry James and the Second Empire.* Oxford: Legenda, 2009.

Acknowledgments

While I was writing *The Dangers of Christian Practice*, the generosity of friends, colleagues, and students regularly astounded me. I am deeply grateful to each of the many people who gave me conversation, time, insight, criticism, skill, ideas, knowledge, and love (gratitude that, of course, does not imply their agreement with my arguments or readings)—I am more grateful, really, than I know how to say: Carole Baker, Jennifer Banks, Molly Bosscher, Kate Bowler, Luke Bretherton, Jamie Brummitt, Chuck Campbell, Jay Carter, Stephen Chapman, Brandy Daniels, Diane Decker, Liz Degaynor, Susan Eastman, Siobhán Garrigan, Thavolia Glymph, Heather Gold, Stephanie M. Green, Eric Gregory, Paul Griffiths, Esther Hamori, Joelle Hathaway, Stanley Hauerwas, Peter Hawkins, Dan Heaton, Alisha Hines, Alan Jacobs, Willie Jennings, Sarah Jobe, Martin Kavka, Adrienne Koch, Katie Lofton, Paul MacDonald, Kevin Madigan, Joseph Mangina, Carol Mann, Joel Marcus, Rhody Mastin, Chuck Matthews, Laurie Jean Medford, David Myers, Stephanie Paulsell, Thea Portier-Young, Gerry Postema, Steve Prothero, Randi Rashkover, Michael Reinke, Jana Riess, Gene Rogers, Lester Ruth, Warren Smith, Beth Stroud, Mark Valeri, Isaac Villegas, Greg Williams, and Brittany Wilson.

I began work on the baptism chapter of this book as a fellow at Yale University's Institute of Sacred Music, and I presented work on baptismal bowls at a conference sponsored by the Museum of Early Southern Decorative Arts. For those institutions' support, I am very grateful.

Thank you, thank you, thank you.

Index